Llewellyn's
2006
Magical Almanac

Featuring

Elizabeth Barrette, Nancy Bennett, Stephanie Rose Bird,
Nina Lee Braden, Boudica, Neil Campbell, Mavesper Cy Ceridwen,
Dallas Jennifer Cobb, Ellen Dugan, Denise Dumars, Ember, Emely
Flak, Linda Foubister, Lily Gardner, Karen Glasgow-Follett, Granny
Green Witch, Magenta Griffith, Elizabeth Hazel, Eileen Holland,
James Kambos, Kristin Madden, Muse, Sharynne NicMhacha,
Olivia O'Meir, Diana Rajchel, Laurel Reufner, Sheri Richerson,
Michelle Santos, Sedwyn, Cerridwen Iris Shea, Sorita,
Lynne Sturtevant, Tammy Sullivan, Twilight Bard,
Gail Wood, and S. Y. Zenith

Llewellyn's 2006 Magical Almanac

ISBN 0-7387-0150-5. Copyright © 2005 by Llewellyn. All rights reserved. Printed in the United States. Llewellyn is a registered trademark of Llewellyn Worldwide, Ltd.

Editor/Designer: Michael Fallon

Cover Illustration: © Eric Hotz

Calendar Pages Design: Andrea Neff and Michael Fallon

Calendar Pages Illustrations: © Kerigwen

Interior Illustrations © Helen Michaels, pages: 17, 21, 46, 58, 77, 80, 85, 124, 135, 160, 229, 250, 252, 285, 299, 307, 310, 311, 318, 320, 339, 345, 357, 381, 383; © Wendy Froshay and Debi Blount, pages: 29, 31, 52, 55, 61, 65, 86, 89, 90, 120, 127, 150, 236, 238, 246, 273, 290, 292, 326, 328, 343, 350, 353, 355, 361, 363

Clip Art Illustrations: Dover Publications

Special thanks to Amber Wolfe for the use of daily color and incense correspondences. For more detailed information, please see *Personal Alchemy* by Amber Wolfe.

You can order Llewellyn annuals and books from *New Worlds*, Llewellyn's magazine catalog. To request a free copy of the catalog, call toll-free 1-877-NEWWRLD, or visit our website at http://www.llewellyn.com.

Astrological calculations are performed by the Kepler 6 astrology software program, specially created for Llewellyn Publications and used with the kind permission of Cosmic Patterns Software, Inc., www.AstroSoftware.com.

Llewellyn Worldwide
Dept. 0-7387-0150-5
P.O. Box 64383
St. Paul, MN 55164-0838

About the Authors

ELIZABETH BARRETTE serves as the managing editor of *PanGaia* and assistant editor of *SageWoman*. She has been involved with the Pagan community for fifteen-plus years, and in 2003 earned ordination as a priestess through Sanctuary of the Silver Moon. Her writing fields include speculative fiction and gender studies. She lives in central Illinois and enjoys herbal landscaping and gardening. Visit her website at: http://www.worthlink.net/~ysabet/index.html.

NANCY BENNETT'S work has appeared in *Silver Wheel,* several We'Moon publications, and several Llewellyn annuals. She lives on Vancouver Island with her family, where she strives to balance a writing life with a love of nature and a historical sewing habit.

STEPHANIE ROSE BIRD is an artist, writer, herbalist, healer, mother, and companion. She studied Australian Aboriginal art and ritual as a Fulbright Senior Scholar and is a faculty member in the painting and drawing department at the school of the Art Institute of Chicago. Her column "Ase! from the Crossroads" is featured in *Sage-Woman,* and she is author of the Llewellyn book *Sticks, Stones, Roots & Bones: Hoodoo, Mojo & Conjuring.*

NINA LEE BRADEN lives, works, and worships in Tennessee. She is the proud mother of two grown daughters. Tarot, astrology, and ritual are important parts of her life.

BOUDICA is reviews editor and co-owner of *The Wiccan/Pagan Times* and owner of *The Zodiac Bistro,* both online publications. She teaches for the CroneSpeak organization, both on and off the Internet and as guest speaker at many festivals and gatherings. A former New Yorker, she now resides with her husband in Ohio.

NEIL CAMPBELL lives on the rural west coast of Scotland. From a young age, he has practiced the western magical arts and studied vedic and tantric teachings. Neil still enjoys a healthy interest in

the western mystery traditions, though he is most devoted to tantric shaivism and his guru-shishya lineage.

MAVESPER CY CERIDWEN lives in Brasilia, the capital of Brazil. She has been involved in the craft for about twelve years and is one of the founders of the Brazilian Dianic Wicca Tradition. She is also president of Abrawicca, the Brazilian Association of Wicca, and runs conferences and workshops in all Brazil to teach about Wicca. She has written a guide to the rituals of Brazilian indigenous goddesses and a work of comparative mythology.

DALLAS JENNIFER COBB lives an enchanted life in a waterfront village and writes about what she loves most: mothering, gardening, magic, and alternative economics. She is forever scheming novel ways to pay the bills when she is not running country roads or wandering the beach. Her essays have appeared in *Three Ring Circus* and *Far from Home,* recent anthologies from Seal Press. This year her video documentary "Disparate Places" was produced on TV Ontario's Planet Parent. She is a regular contributor to Llewellyn's almanacs.

ELLEN DUGAN, also known as the "Garden Witch," is a psychic-clairvoyant and practicing Witch of more than eighteen years. A regular contributor to the almanacs, Ellen is a master gardener, teaching classes on gardening and flower folklore at a local community college. She is the author of the Llewellyn books *Garden Witchery: Magick from the Ground Up* and *Elements of Witchcraft: Natural Magick for Teens.* With her husband, she raises three teenagers and tends to an enchanted garden in Missouri.

DENISE DUMARS is the cofounder of the Iseum of Isis Paedusis, an Isian open circle that presents programming on the major sabbats in the South Bay area of Los Angeles. She is currently working on a novel and a metaphysical book. She writes regularly for Llewellyn's annuals.

EMBER is a freelance writer and poet who follows a path of earth-centered spirituality. Her work has been published in *newWitch*

and *PanGaia* magazines and in several Llewellyn annuals. She lives in the midwest with her husband of ten years and two feline companions.

EMELY FLAK has been a practicing solitary Witch for eleven years. She is a freelance writer based in Daylesford, Australia, who is also employed as a learning and development professional. Much of her work is dedicated to embracing the ancient wisdom of Wicca for the personal empowerment of women in the competitive work environment.

LINDA FOURBISTER is a student of mythology. She has contributed articles to various e-zines and magazines, focusing on mythological interpretations of seasonal and cultural change. She is also author of *Goddess in the Grass: Serpentine Mythology and the Great Goddess* (EcceNova Editions, 2003).

LILY GARDNER has studied folklore and mythology since she learned to read. In addition to her contributions to the Llewellyn annuals, her short stories are beginning to show up in literary journals. Lily lives in Portland, Oregon and is a member of the Power of Three coven.

KAREN GLASGOW-FOLLETT has been teaching meditation since 1979 and practicing witchcraft since 1972. Karen is an initiated Georgian and currently practices as a solitary. Karen lives in the midwest with her husband and two young-adult sons. When not writing, Karen teaches various classes related to psychic development, meditation, and energy.

GRANNY GREEN WITCH teaches earth exploration. She has taught Pagan-based earth crafts at festivals in Florida and Georgia and welcomes all invitations to share her knowledge of earth crafts with the Pagan community. When she isn't crafting or writing, her time is spent with the loves of her life: her husband and son.

MAGENTA GRIFFITH has been a Witch more than twenty-five years, a high priestess for thirteen years, and a founding member of the

coven Prodea. She leads rituals and workshops in the Midwest and is currently librarian for the New Alexandria Library, a Pagan magical resource center (http://www.magusbooks.com/newalexandria).

ELIZABETH HAZEL is a mystic astrologer and tarotist interested in the ancient history of divination. A member of the International Tarot Society and the American Tarot Association, she enjoys attending tarot conferences.

EILEEN HOLLAND is a Wiccan priestess and a solitary eclectic Witch. She is the author of *The Wicca Handbook* (Weiser, 2000), *Spells for the Solitary Witch* (Weiser, 2004), and coauthor with Cerelia of *A Witch's Book of Answers* (Weiser, 2003). She is also the webmaster of Open Sesame (www.open-sesame.com) and a regular contributor to Llewellyn's annuals.

JAMES KAMBOS is a writer and painter who has had a lifelong interest in folk magic. He has written numerous articles concerning the folk magic traditions of Greece, the Near East, and the Appalachian region of the United States. He writes and paints at his home in the beautiful Appalachian hills of southern Ohio.

KRISTIN MADDEN is a homeschooling mom and author of several books on shamanism, paganism, and parenting. She is dean of Ardantane's School of Shamanic Studies and a tutor in the Order of Bards, Ovates, and Druids. In her spare time, Kristin rehabilitates wild birds. Visit her online at http://www.kristinmadden.com.

MUSE lives in Colorado Springs, Colorado and has always had a fascination with the unseen world. She is an avid traveler, aspiring writer, grad student, and professional in the field of eCommerce. She holds a degree in European History, and still finds time to do yoga and read the latest Harry Potter book.

SHARYNNE NICMHACHA, a Celtic priestess and Witch, is a direct descendant of Clan MacLeod—long recorded in oral tradition to have connections to the sidhe, or fairy folk. She has studied Old

Irish, Scottish Gaelic, and Celtic mythology through Harvard University, where she has published a number of research papers. She teaches workshops, sings, and plays bodran, woodwinds, and stringed instruments with the group Devandaurae (and previously with the Moors). Sharynne has recently published her first book.

OLIVIA O'MEIR has written for *The Beltane Papers, newWitch,* and Llewellyn's *Magical Almanac,* and is currently working on her first book. She is a feminist Dianic Witch, priestess of the Goddess, and ordained reverend. Olivia is also a professional tarot counselor and runs Diana's Den, a Dianic group in the Philadelphia area. She is a member of many women's spirituality and goddess-focused groups on and off-line. Visit her at www.geocities.com/medusa_athene.

DIANA RAJCHEL is a third-degree Wiccan priestess with a bent for intelligent cartoons and good food. She lives in Minneapolis, surrounded by her friends and Pagan family. Someday she hopes to learn the name of the local city spirit.

LAUREL REUFNER'S mother can verify that she grew up a "wild child" in farming country. She's been Pagan for nearly twenty years now, and she enjoys writing about topics that grab her attention. Laurel has always lived in Southeastern Ohio and currently calls Athens County home, where she lives with her wonderful husband and two wild children. Her website is www.spiritrealm.com/laurelreufner.

SHERI RICHERSON has more than twenty years of experience in newspaper, magazine, and creative writing. She is also a lifetime member of the International Thespian Society, and a longtime member of the Garden Writers Association of America and the American Horticultural Society. Her favorite pastimes are riding horses and motorcycles, visiting arboretums, traveling, and working in her garden. She specializes in herb gardening and cultivating tropical, subtropical, and other exotic plants.

SEDWYN is an explorer of Celtic history, myth, and magic, and an initiate of the Hearth of Brigid Lyceum. She is an artist who works

in photography and pastels, and who occasionally exhibits at a local gallery. Sedwyn enjoys leading workshops, rituals, and drumming circles.

CERRIDWEN IRIS SHEA is a tarot-reading, horse-playing ice-hockey–addicted, Broadway-dresser kitchen witch. She contributes regularly to the Llewellyn annuals, writes the tarot column "In the Cards" for *Fayth* magazine, and pens the occult horror serial *Angel Hunt* for www.keepitcoming.net. Her website is www.cerridwens-cottage.com.

SORITA has been Wiccan for more than a decade, and is high priestess for a number groups she runs with her high priest and partner, David Rankine, in the London area. She is a fulltime writer, contributing to a number of magazines on a regular basis. She also leads regular workshops on witchcraft, astral projection, psychic development, and healing. When she is not working, she loves traveling around to the forgotten sacred sites of Wales and Cornwall. To find out more, visit her online at www.avalonia.co.uk.

LYNNE STURTEVANT is a freelance writer specializing in folklore, mythology, fairy tales, and the paranormal. She has been a solitary practitioner following an eclectic path since 1970. She holds a bachelor's degree in philosophy and is a regular contributor to Llewellyn's annuals. Her work has also appeared in *Fate* magazine.

TAMMY SULLIVAN is a fulltime writer and solitary Witch who works from her home in the foothills of the Great Smoky Mountains. She is the author of *Pagan Anger Magic,* soon to be released by Citadel Press. Her work has appeared in Llewellyn's annuals and *Circle* magazine.

TWILIGHT BARD has walked the Wiccan path for thirteen years and loves the act of creating through words and images. She is a freelance writer of fiction and nonfiction, and also enjoys drawing, painting, photography, and scrapbooking. She is married to her Pagan soul mate, and homeschools their three children, trying to foster in them a lust for learning.

S. Y. ZENITH is three-quarters Chinese, one tad Irish, and a full life-long solitary eclectic Pagan. She has lived and traveled extensively in Asia to such countries as India, Nepal, Thailand, Malaysia, Singapore, Borneo, and Japan over two decades. She is now based in Australia where her time is divided between writing, experimenting with alternative remedies, and teaching the use of gems, holy beads, and religious objects from India and the Himalayas. She is also a member of the Australian Society of Authors.

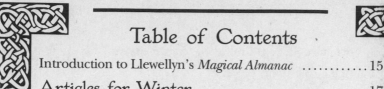
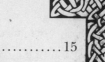

Table of Contents

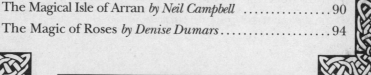

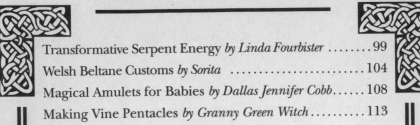

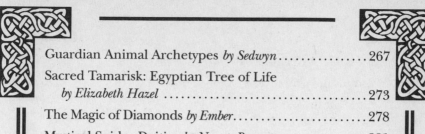

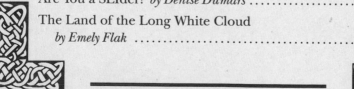

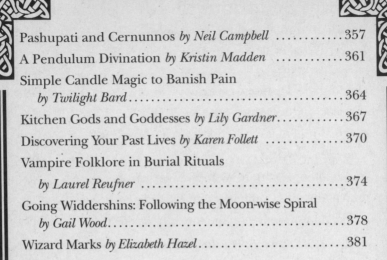

Introduction to Llewellyn's Magical Almanac

The *Magical Almanac* turns sweet sixteen this year, one step further into full adult maturity. The offerings in this edition reflect a sweetly mature sense of the magic and wonder of the universe and its inhabitants.

In this edition, our authors look at some of the most sweetly magical of topics in the universe—shooting stars, diamonds, rainbows, colored rain, guardian animals, stepping stones, wishing herbs, mantras and yantras, streetlights, roses, and sacred trees. We bring to these pages some of the most innovative and original thinkers and writers on these subjects.

This focus on the old ways—on the lore of men and women around the world who knew and understood the power of their ancestors—is important today, as we work to renew a world overwhelmed by problems: terrorism, water shortages, environmental degradation, internecine battles, and simple discourtesy. While we don't want to assign blame or cast any other aspersions, this state of affairs is not surprising considering so many of us—each one of us—is out of touch with the old ways. Many of us spend too much of our lives rushing about in a technological bubble—striving to make money, being everywhere but here, living life in fast-forward. We forget, at times, to stop, take a deep breath, and act our age.

Still, the news is not all bad. People are still fighting to make us all more aware of the magical, beautiful things in the world. Pagan and Wiccan communities, for instance, are thriving across the country and throughout the world. In this edition of the *Magical Almanac,* writers from as far away as Australia, Canada, Brazil, and England—as well as across the whole of the United States—contribute to an expanding volume of knowledge, lore, and magical ritual.

In the 2006 edition of the *Magical Almanac,* we pay tribute and homage to the sweetness of a maturing understanding of the magic, beauty, and balance of our ancestors—and to the magic of all the ages. This may sound a bit corny and idealistic, but those who say so likely have never put what has been written in this almanac over the past sixteen years to good use. They probably forget, too, how magical a time the age of sixteen was!

Magic is an ancient tool whose time has come back around to help us restore balance in our lives. More and more people are using magic, celebrating the elements, praying to the Goddess and the various incarnations of the divine, and studying the myths and legends, lore and tales of the past. In the end, one person at a time, using ancient wisdom, we can make a new world.

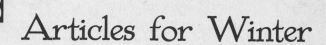

Articles for Winter

Gods and Monsters
of the Winter Solstice

by Lily Gardner

Because Santa Claus has presided over the Yule festival for the last two hundred years, many of us are unaware of the other mysterious beings that visit during the dark days of the solstice season. Benevolent goddesses, formidable gods, and malevolent monsters emerge from the shadows to bless or wreak havoc on us.

Holda

Holda, "the gracious one," reigns over the skies from her crystal palace. When it snows, Holda is shaking her feather bed. Every day she spins at her wheel—the closer to the solstice, the slower the wheel turns. By Yule, her wheel grinds to a halt.

At Yuletide Holda descends from her palace to visit mankind. A tall, golden-haired beauty, she fertilizes the fields as she drives through the countryside. When people are of service to her, she rewards them with gold. Out of respect towards her, no wheels should turn during this period.

From this custom comes the saying: "From Yule Day to New Year's Day, neither wheel nor windlass must go round." In the old days, this meant women got a break from spinning; but they still had to keep a neat house, because sloppy workmanship angered the benevolent goddess.

Berchta

Holda's dark twin is Berchta, a gray-haired snaggle-toothed hag. Berchta, although not evil, is most definitely on the cranky side. She demands that the wisdom and skills of her and her sister goddesses be practiced with diligence and appreciation by mankind. Her feast day is January 5. It is a very good idea

18

to eat her feast foods of fish and oat-cakes on this day, so as not to anger her.

La Befana and Baboushka

Berchta is not the only Yuletide hag. La Befana, the Italian crone goddess, rides around the world on her broom leaving candies and gifts to well-behaved children. One way to entice her into your household is to place a rag doll in her likeness by your front door or window.

Baboushka is the Russian counterpart of La Befana.

The Callieach, Louhi, and Skadi

Though no Yule or Christmas customs are associated with these crone goddesses, the Callieach, Louhi, and Skadi deserve mention—and perhaps a ritual in their honor—at this time. The Callieach, known as the old hag of winter, may be the crone aspect of Bridget. She begins her reign on Samhain. With a giant hammer she strikes the earth. Cracks of frost appear where she's struck until the earth is covered with ice. Louhi, the Finnish "witch goddess," kidnapped the Sun and Moon and held them captive inside a mountain. This was the world's first Winter Solstice. She was eventually forced to return the celestial bodies and to allow light to be restored. From Scandinavia, we have Skadi, a giantess who married into the Norse pantheon. She invented skis and snowshoes. Pray to Skadi when you find yourself in a dangerous winter landscape.

The Forest God

The mysterious Forest God, with his cloven feet and stag horns, has been known variously for the past four-thousand years as Cernunnos, Enkidu, Priapus, Pan, and the Green Man. Ancient man believed he maintained the balance and order of the seasons. People observed his decline from autumn to winter. He would die then come back to life in the same way as plants.

A ritual of death and renewal is enacted at Yule to dramatize this belief. During the Middle Ages, mummers went from house to house at Yule to pantomime a rough version of this ritual. A burlesque group of figures evolved from the mummer plays. The Forest God took on various shapes: Beelzebub, Johnny Jack, or

 the Fool, depending on the nature god's standing in the culture.

Although these figures were rough and hairy with horns and blackened faces, they were intended not only to frighten their audience but to make them laugh as well. His consort, known as the Bessy, was a bearded man dressed in women's clothing. This figure was a man-woman probably because the hermaphrodite archetype is a powerful fertility symbol. The couple performed a mock-copulation, after which the Fool was mock-killed.

Wodan

In Norse mythology, Wodan acts as the god of the dead and of darkness. Leading the Wild Host, a hunting party of ghosts and hell-hounds, he rides the winter winds. Woe to anyone wandering outdoors at night when the Wild Host is abroad. If you are out on a stormy night and hear the barking of hounds and the gallop of a thousand hooves, you must throw yourself face down in a ditch. If you're lucky, the Wild Host will take no notice of you; if you're not, you may be made to ride with the ghosts to the end of time.

Kallikantzaroi

In Greece, the Kallikantzaroi awake when the world turns to darkness. These malevolent figures are half-human, half-animal, sporting tusks, red eyes, and long red curling tongues. Black and hairy, they represent the dark time of the year. Entering through the cellar or down the chimney, they eat all your food, drink your liquor, and break everything they can find. Householders can protect themselves by locking their homes and keeping a stout fire burning in the hearth from Yule until Twelfth Night.

Tomtes

The Swedish tomtes are a gentler race. Under four feet in height, with long white beards and little red caps, the tomtes tidy the house. All they ask for their labor is to be left a nice rice pudding on Yule. If the householder is too stingy to provide the tomte his treat, he simply departs and leaves the business of running a household to the owners.

Manes and Lares

by Elizabeth Hazel

The Manes and Lares are ghost-like entities worshiped by the ancient Romans. Natives of the Italian peninsula honored the dead long before the founding of Rome. The worship originated in the spiritual life of the Etruscans, the tribe that inhabited the area now known as Tuscany.

The powers, duties, and associations of Manes and Lares evolved over time, as the Romans integrated Greek concepts of the underworld into their own beliefs. Ancient documents show that by the time of the

Caesars, ancestor worship was elaborate and sophisticated, and regularly commemorated in annual festivals.

The Beliefs of the Greeks

The ancient Greeks had complex rituals for contacting the dead. In Homer's *Odyssey*, written circa 700 BC, there is a detailed description of Odysseus making sacrifices in order to speak with the dead prophet Teiresias. The text describes a hero digging a pit and pouring in a drink offering for All Souls—first with honey and milk, then with fine wine, and the third time with water. He then sprinkles barley over the liquid and prays to the "empty shells of the dead." Then the souls of the dead who had passed away come up from Erebus. Odysseus does not let the dead come near until he asks his question of Teiresias. Teiresias repays Odysseus for his offering by foretelling the hero's future.

The extent of Greek influence on later Roman beliefs becomes clear in Virgil's *Aeneid*. Written during the time of Augustus, the Latin poet offers a strikingly similar ritual. In it, Andromache pours a drink offering to Hector's ashes in a ritual of sacrifice. She calls "on Hector's spirit at his cenotaph of green turf, where she had reverently set up two altars as a place for her mourning."

The Manes

Manes are a kind of ghostly demon that reside in the underworld. These non-carnate spirits preside over burial grounds and monuments of the dead. They were invoked by the augers of the temple during prayers over sacrificial animals. The number three was sacred to the Manes, so invocations were repeated three times.

The etymology of the word Manes may derive from Mania, the mother of the Manes. Alternately, the root source could be *manis,* an old Latin term that means "good" or "propitious." Late Latin sources refer to them as *di manes,* the "good gods." They were honored as underworld entities that protected the dead. Grave stone were inscribed with the initials "DM," or *Dis Manibus,* meaning that the ashes or corpse buried beneath the stone had been dedicated to the Manes and should not be disturbed. The Manes had a feast day in their honor called Parentalia, when gifts were left at their sacred sites.

The Lares

Lares, by contrast, were family ghosts, the disembodied spirits of ancestors revered by the preservation of tokens and relics. They were inferior to the Manes, but perhaps more greatly loved for their powers of preserving the home and family. The first two Lares were said to be the sons of Lara fathered by Mercury, the god who leads dead souls to the underworld. As with their father Mercury, the scope of the Lares expanded over time.

Lares Familiares presided over the home. Lares Urbani presided over cities; Lares Rustici over the countryside; Lares Compitales over crossroads; Lares Marini over the sea; Lares Viales over roads; and Lares Patellarii over sacred places.

The worship of Lares began as a result of people burying deceased family members (or their cremated remains) in the house or on family property. It was believed that the spirit continued to hover around the house to protect the inhabitants.

The word Lares most likely derives from the Etruscan word *lars,* which means "conductor" or "leader." Statutes of Lares were very primitive and cast in bronze. Sometimes they were small heads or monkey-like images, each wrapped or dressed in dog skin. As family members died, their dedicated statues were placed in a special niche behind the front door as a protection totem. Lares statues were sometimes supplemented with small sculptures of barking dogs, who exemplified the traits of care and vigilance.

Incense was burned at the family altar for ancestors, and a sow was sacrificed on significant days—to memorialize an ancestor's birth or death date or mark a special triumph. The official Lares festival was in May. At this time, the family niche and its statues were decorated with garlands of flowers and fruit. Wealthier families had a mold cast from the face of the corpse before cremation. Masks fashioned from the plaster cast were worn during the Lares festival. Masks and other ancestral tokens were also carried in funeral processions.

A large display of ancestral relics demonstrated the importance and wealth of the family. Aristocratic families had fabulously carved cabinets with dozens of drawers for storing family masks and tokens. Of course, poor families were unable to preserve such family mementos. They were not accorded large, conspicuous, public processions when a member was buried. A poor person's Lares might consist of several crude bronze statuettes that represented all of their ancestors.

Commemorating the Dead

It is clear that the Romans believed in ghostly spirits and communication with the dead. The Manes protected the dead, and the Lares protected the living. These ghostly guardians were offered prayers, incense, food, wine, flowers, and sacrificial animals in regular remembrance ceremonies.

Worship of the Manes and Lares was both public and private. In the film *Gladiator,* the hero Maximus is shown praying to two small bronze statues. These are his family Lares, and his private worship is accurate to what we know of Lares worship. His servant Cicero restores these statues to him later in the film, confirming the reverent esteem Maximus has for these precious tokens.

Roman funeral customs continue to this day in contemporary death rites. Flowers are offered, and a formal procession or cortege conveys the body to the burial ground, with members of the immediate family following directly behind the hearse. We return to grave sites on special days to leave flowers at headstones. We celebrate a national Memorial Day at the end of May.

In contemporary Pagan worship, the souls of the dead are honored on Samhain, the festival of All Souls. The concepts of the afterlife haven't changed much since the days of Homer—disembodied souls still reside in a realm of the dead (the underworld, the summerland, or other), and specific ancestors or relatives may sometimes visit, communicate with, advise, and protect the living.

The concepts of heaven, hell, and the reincarnation or transmigration of souls may seem to blur the issue, but research indicates that burial ceremonies—and the tendency to regard dead ancestors as helpful entities—remain remarkably intact after thousands of years of cultural development.

Imbolc Blessing Powder
by Eileen Holland

Whether you call her Brigid, Brigit, Bricta, Bride (pronounced "breed"), or by another of the many variations of her name, this Celtic goddess of fire, water, smithcraft, and the hearth is the presiding deity of Imbolc. The many blessings that she bestows include healing, fertility, protection, warmth, wisdom, sustenance, inspiration, and creativity. Imbolc is a wonderful time to call upon her for blessings.

Brigid is known for, among other things, her kindness to animals. This recipe makes a powder that not only calls forth her blessings, but also provides winter food for birds and other small animals.

Powder Recipe

To make it you will need:

- 3 parts powdered milk
- 2 parts birdseed
- 2 parts oatmeal
- 2 parts bread crumbs
- 1 part salt (sea salt is best)
- 1 part silver glitter
- 1 white candle
- 1 container, such as a glass jar

  White or brightly colored ribbon

  Celtic music, corn dolly, Brigid cross, large
  sea shell (all optional)

Make the powder a day or two before Imbolc. Assemble the ingredients. Play Celtic music, if you have it, and create sacred space. Light the candle, and focus on all the bright blessings that you want in the incoming season.

Combine the ingredients in the container. Use your projective hand (or an athame held in that hand), and stir deosil to mix thoroughly. As you do this, say:

> *By the lady of the forge,*
> *Imbolc blessings are called forth.*
> *By the lady of the hearth,*
> *This powder is blessed through Witches' art.*
> *By the high one, blessed be.*
> *By the bright one, blessed be.*
> *By Bride the beautiful, blessed be.*

Tie the ribbons around the container in any manner that pleases you. Place the container beside the candle, being careful to keep the ribbons away from the flame. If you have a corn dolly or a Brigid cross, place it near the container.

Monitor the candle until it burns down. Meditate on Imbolc and the welcome changes you want the turning of the season to bring. Touch or hold the container as you do this, charging the powder with the power of your intent.

Discard the candle once it flickers out. Put the container with its ribbons in a safe place until Imbolc, such as on your altar or a sunny window sill (along with the corn dolly or Brigid's cross, if you are using either of those). If you have a fireplace, place the container on the mantle or beside the hearth.

Take the container outside on Imbolc morning and sprinkle the powder around your home to attract blessings to yourself and your household. Start in the east. Focus on your intent, working with an attitude of positive expectancy. Whistling is a traditional way to invoke Brigid, so whistling cheerfully as you toss the powder adds to its magic. Alternatively, you could use this invocation:

> *Bright arrow, banish fallow.*
> *Bright arrow, banish fallow.*
> *Bride of the white hills,*
> *Tend our fires, cure our ills.*
>
> *Lady of the hearth,*
> *Keep our house, keep our health,*

Keep us safe all year.
Bright arrow, banish fallow.
Bright arrow, banish fallow.

Sprinkle the powder with your right hand, wherever you can and in whatever way you feel is best. If the weather is terrible, you can simply toss it from a doorway or window. Some of the powder can also be placed in a large sea shell and left as an offering on an outdoor altar.

The ribbons may either be discarded afterward or retained as a charm.

The Magic of Synchronicity
by Emely Flak

Whenever a friend calls you just as you have thought of him or her, you might well ask: Is it coincidence, luck, or just meant to be? Or when a car pulls out of a parking space just at the time when you need it, you might well think yourself blessed by the universe.

This strange feeling, when something occurs just as you want it to, is what Swiss psychoanalyst Carl Jung called "synchronicity," meaning a "meaningful coincidence." According to Jung, there is no such thing as a coincidence without meaning or connection.

Still, in the speed and turmoil of our contemporary lifestyles and technology-driven world, we are quick to dismiss many experiences as mere coincidences. We rarely stop to reflect, remember our dreams, or try to establish connections between events.

Carl Jung and Spirituality

As part of his theory on synchronicity, Jung proposed the idea that we have archetypal images in our minds. An archetype is a mental model or image that links us to the human spirit and to our intuitive wisdom.

Jung argued that as humans we are all linked to a "collective unconscious." The collective unconscious is the place where myths and legends are stored. It's where the archetypes of gods and goddesses reside in our mental archive, connecting us.

A synchronistic event, therefore, activates an archetype that is embedded in our collective memory. This means that meaningful coincidences are connected to a higher universal force.

Synchronicity and Magical Intent

Synchronicity is aligned with a magical way of life. It's the thread that links many seemingly irrelevant pieces of experience. It gives you a new sense of awareness as it helps you notice events and people around you. By keeping a personal journal or a dream journal, you can connect events you have experienced or witnessed. Dreams are an example of synchronicity at work—as dreams release both subconscious thought and collective knowledge. Your dreams are rich in symbols, revealing messages and clues to the collective truth.

Alternative spirituality is aligned with synchronicity through an awareness of interconnectedness and magical intent. Discuss this with others, and you will hear many stories of how someone wanted or needed something, sent out a message through magical intent or visualization, and watched a series of alleged "chance" encounters help them materialize their wish. No doubt this has already happened to you. The right person, book, or cycle of events arrives to offer you a solution to a problem at just the opportune time.

Tuning into synchronicity is first about trusting your intuition. You can probably recall a time when you have dismissed an isolated incident as coincidence, only to discover later that it was more than chance. After a while, you will learn to see when a series of events form a meaningful pattern.

Once you have faith in your intuitive mind, you will strongly connect your own emotions and awareness to the world around you. Synchronicity affirms the link between your thoughts and the subsequent results. Your awareness adds a new dimension. This is like being able to see color while others are still watching life in black and white.

How Synchronicity Empowers You

An awareness of interconnected events is empowering, because the messages are individually designed as inner guidance for you. This explains why you might notice a book in a store that you specifically need to read, while numerous other customers walk past it without a second glance. An experience like this takes place exactly when you weren't looking for anything in particular. What may at first have appeared random is, in fact, a series of events that led you to exactly what you needed at the time.

Open your mind to the forces of the universe and to the concept of synchronicity. We learn most of our life lessons outside a traditional classroom—in events, relationships, or conflicts that come at a time when we are ready for personal growth. Events that appear to be coincidences are often lessons and unique messages for you.

When you face a difficult situation, consider it a lesson instead of a drawback. Any perceived failure teaches us something. If you miss the learning experience, the lesson will be repeated and you will fail again. Have you ever wondered why some people attract the same type of unsuitable or incompatible partner more than once? You will probably find that they have not learned a lesson that has been repeated to them many times.

Belief in synchronicity makes you tolerant when things are not going as smoothly or as quickly as you expected. By being accepting of such challenges, you minimize stress and take a calmer approach to dealing with it. Consider synchronous events to be part of a higher plan with unique messages and lessons that are designed for you.

The Paradox

There lies a paradox within the theory of synchronicity. If you regard the concept too seriously, you may risk taking a passive view of life with an unhealthy dependence on the notion of pre-determined destiny. Synchronicity isn't designed to mean that fate is absolute, or that there is no need to take responsibility for your own actions. Try not to interpret every word and event obsessively. Synchronicity is a balance of trusting your inner guidance while you pay attention to external messages.

The Art of Interpretation

Awareness of synchronicity becomes an art of individual interpretation. With practice, you will see meaningful coincidences as gateways to the collective unconscious and to your conscious mind. Follow these tips to enhance your magical life with synchronicity:

> Make a mental note of events and occurrences, and of whom you bump into unexpectedly, even if you think it's a coincidence.

> Ask yourself why something has happened. How is it a meaningful coincidence? How is it connected to your conscious thoughts? How is it related to your subconscious thoughts—that is, spontaneous thoughts that have come during meditation or dreaming?

> To what extent have you created any of these events through magical intent?

> If you cannot connect one event to another, ask yourself what lesson or message the universe is sending you? Why do you need this lesson? If you are receiving the same or similar messages, take note of the underlying lesson that begs to be understood.

Your Unique Messenger

Events in the world around us are abundant with surprising symbolism that many people fail to notice. From a series of seemingly random events, the meaningless becomes meaningful and patterns of connection emerge.

Some messages will be obvious in hindsight—after you have had opportunity to reflect and assess the situation. In time, as you take note of these meaningful coincidences, you will become more adept at identifying themes quickly. The magic lies here: The more you believe in synchronicity, the more you recognize it and benefit from meaningful events.

Synchronicity is based on the belief that nothing happens by chance. As you increase your awareness of events and explore their relevance to your thoughts and the collective unconscious, you will see a connection between events that you may have once dismissed or missed all together.

It helps you trust the universe and listen to the magical messages it has for you.

Classic Poetry for Pagans

by Magenta Griffith

Do you find it hard to write good invocations? How about taking a page, literally, from some classic poetry?

Most eighteenth- and nineteenth-century poets studied the writings of Pagan Greece and Rome. During the early nineteenth century, a school of English poets called the Romantics glorified virtues we might call Pagan. Here are some examples of such poetry to use as inspiration.

Hymn To Apollo
by John Keats

God of the golden bow,
And of the golden lyre,
And of the golden hair,
And of the golden fire,
Charioteer
Of the patient year,
Where—where slept thine ire,
When like a blank idiot I put on thy wreath,
Thy laurel, thy glory,
The light of thy story,
Or was I a worm—too low crawling for death?
O Delphic Apollo!

Prosperine is a variant spelling of Persephone, who was kidnapped by Hades and taken to the underworld. Her mother, Demeter, was so upset that she neglected to make the crops grow.

from The Garden of Prosperine
by Algernon Charles Swinburne

Here, where the world is quiet,
Here, where all trouble seems

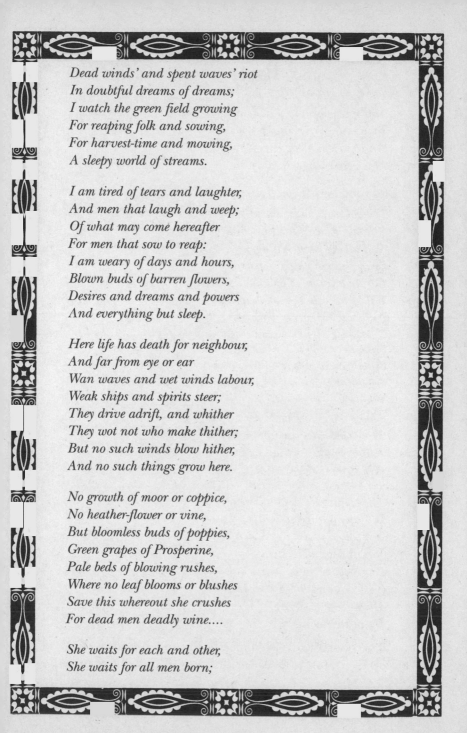

Dead winds' and spent waves' riot
In doubtful dreams of dreams;
I watch the green field growing
For reaping folk and sowing,
For harvest-time and mowing,
A sleepy world of streams.

I am tired of tears and laughter,
And men that laugh and weep;
Of what may come hereafter
For men that sow to reap:
I am weary of days and hours,
Blown buds of barren flowers,
Desires and dreams and powers
And everything but sleep.

Here life has death for neighbour,
And far from eye or ear
Wan waves and wet winds labour,
Weak ships and spirits steer;
They drive adrift, and whither
They wot not who make thither;
But no such winds blow hither,
And no such things grow here.

No growth of moor or coppice,
No heather-flower or vine,
But bloomless buds of poppies,
Green grapes of Prosperine,
Pale beds of blowing rushes,
Where no leaf blooms or blushes
Save this whereout she crushes
For dead men deadly wine....

She waits for each and other,
She waits for all men born;

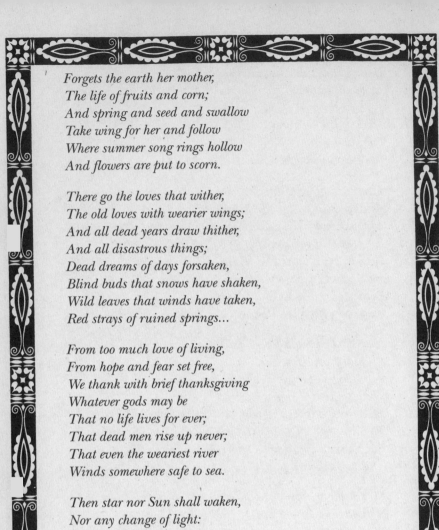

Forgets the earth her mother,
The life of fruits and corn;
And spring and seed and swallow
Take wing for her and follow
Where summer song rings hollow
And flowers are put to scorn.

There go the loves that wither,
The old loves with wearier wings;
And all dead years draw thither,
And all disastrous things;
Dead dreams of days forsaken,
Blind buds that snows have shaken,
Wild leaves that winds have taken,
Red strays of ruined springs...

From too much love of living,
From hope and fear set free,
We thank with brief thanksgiving
Whatever gods may be
That no life lives for ever;
That dead men rise up never;
That even the weariest river
Winds somewhere safe to sea.

Then star nor Sun shall waken,
Nor any change of light:
Nor sound of waters shaken,
Nor any sound or sight:
Nor wintry leaves nor vernal,
Nor days nor things diurnal;
Only the sleep eternal
In an eternal night.

The poem below isn't specifically an invocation, but I've always liked it. If you read it carefully, it's all about how the

poet wishes he could be a Pagan; he thinks he would enjoy life more if he were.

The World Is Too Much with Us
by William Wordsworth

The world is too much with us; late and soon,
Getting and spending, we lay waste our powers;
Little we see in Nature that is ours;
We have given our hearts away, a sordid boon!
This Sea that bares her bosom to the Moon,
The winds that will be howling at all hours,
And are up-gathered now like sleeping flowers,
For this, for everything, we are out of tune;
It moves us not.—Great God! I'd rather be
A Pagan suckled in a creed outworn,—
So might I, standing on this pleasant lea,
Have glimpses that would make me less forlorn;
Have sight of Proteus rising from the sea;
Or hear old Triton blow his wreathed horn.

The poem below is a wonderful verse to Bacchus. In fact, there were many good poems to Bacchus back then.

Alexander's Feast, or the Power of Music, part 3
by John Dryden

The praise of Bacchus then the sweet musician sung,
Of Bacchus ever fair and ever young:
The jolly god in triumph comes;
Sound the trumpets; beat the drums;
Flush'd with a purple grace
He shews his honest face:

Now give the hautboys breath; he comes, he comes.
Bacchus, ever fair and young
Drinking joys did first ordain;
Bacchus' blessings are a treasure,

Drinking is the soldier's pleasure;
Rich the treasure,
Sweet the pleasure,
Sweet is pleasure after pain.

Speaking of Bacchus, the American national anthem, "The Star Spangled Banner" by Francis Scott Key, took the tune of an older song called "To Anacreon in Heaven." This drinking song was first published in England around 1780. The poem took its name from Anacreon, a Greek poet (c. 582-485 BC), whose surviving poetry is devoted to the goddess of love and the god of wine.

from **To Anacreon in Heaven**
Anonymous

To Anacreon in heaven where he sat in full glee,
A few sons of harmony sent a petition,
That he their inspirer and patron would be,
When this answer arrived from the jolly old Grecian:
Voice, fiddle and flute, no longer be mute,
I'll lend you my name and inspire you to boot!
And besides I'll instruct you like me to entwine
The myrtle of Venus and Bacchus's vine.

The news through Olympus immediately flew,
When old Thunder pretended to give himself airs,
If these mortals are suffered their scheme to pursue,
The devil a goddess will stay above stairs,
Hark! already they cry, in transports of joy,
A fig for Parnassus, to Rowley's we'll fly,
And there my good fellows, we'll learn to entwine
The myrtle of Venus and Bacchus's vine...

Using Mantra

by S. Y. Zenith

Mantras are sacred Sanskrit invocations containing mystical syllables. They have been used by Indian sages, seers, saints, *nagababas* (incarnates of Lord Shiva), *sadhus* (ascetics), yogis, and various types of holy men and women of India and the Himalayas since ancient times. These holy words of power have been passed down the generations from guru to disciple and from parents to children.

As a result of the potency of mantras, they have survived for millennia. Mantras continue to be used today by the layman and advanced practitioner alike. This use is not limited to selected background, nationality, race, caste, color, or religion. Mantras can be used by anyone wishing to gain blessings from deities of the Hindu pantheon. Such blessings may be for protection, good health, peace of mind, comfort in times of trauma, success in endeavors, prosperity, love, academic or career achievements, difficult circumstances, exorcism, purification, relaxation, and spiritual evolution, among other uses.

The single-minded focus on a mantra reinforces and propels meditation from verbal levels through mental and telepathic states of pure thought energy. Sanskrit is revered as one of the languages of the divine, serving the purpose of transiting one from the daily humdrum and from karmic bondages to a transcendental state. Due to their affinity to the fifty primeval sounds, Sanskrit mantras are powerful sound energies when practiced with devotion.

Mantra is an ancient science that takes innumerable volumes and possibly even many zillions of lifetimes to explore or properly explain. There are various types of mantras—such as saguna, beeja, japa, gayatri mantra, gayatris of different deities, and abstract mantras.

This brief article is merely the tiniest tip of the iceberg and attempts to explain the basics of the most generally used mantras.

Saguna or Deity Mantra

Spiritual aspirants wishing to attain "god-realization" commonly use deity mantras known as *saguna,* which encapsulate the essence of a particular deity and assist in the process of conceptualization just as do visual symbols, pictures, and statues.

Being a sound-body of consciousness, the saguna mantra is the deity itself, manifesting in a tangible bit a sound. When attempting saguna, it is important to focus on the syllables and keep a disciplined rhythm. The vibrations of saguna mantras provide guidance and arouse the devotee to the relevant inner equilibrium required to give form to the deity being petitioned. Examples of common saguna mantras for general meditation and chanting are:

Mantra for Lord Ganesha as remover of obstacles and granter of success: *Om Sri Maha-Ganapataye Namah*

For Shiva as cosmic dancer and part of the Hindu trinity of Brahma and Vishnu: *Om Namah Shivaya*

For Narayana, one of Lord Vishnu's names as preserver of the universe: *Om Namo Narayana*

For Rama, an incarnation of Vishnu who upheld righteousness and virtue: *Om Sri Ramaya Namah*

For Mother Durga, protector and benefactor: *Om Sri Durgaye Namah*

For Saraswati, goddess of learning, the arts, music, knowledge, and wisdom: *Om Aim Saraswatiye Namah*

For Lakshmi, goddess of abundance and wealth, both spiritual and material: *Om Sri Maha Lakshmiye Namah*

Abstract Mantras

Om is the highest mantra of the cosmos. It is abstract and guides the aspirant to merge with nature or the "shakti of existence" that underlies and permeates all. It is said that all mantras are encompassed by Om from which the universe manifests, where all worlds rest, and into which they dissolve. Also spelled "Aum," this mantra encapsulates the threefold experience of humankind as follows: "a" represents the physical plane, "u" represents the mental plane, and "m" represents the deep sleep state and all that is beyond intellect or science.

Due to its complete universality, Om can be used as a mantra for those who are isolated or unable to find a genuine guru. By the same token, the formless abstract Om can be difficult for the new aspirant to fully grasp unless he or she possesses unwavering focus. As with all spiritual practices where practice makes perfect, the intoning of Om and other abstract mantras gradually transforms the psyche and atoms within the physical body, infusing it with positive vibrations. In some cases, practice may result in arousing dormant mental, physical, and spiritual abilities. Other abstract mantras are:

> *Sohum* (I am that I am)—When an aspirant manages to identify with Sohum, he or she becomes "existence" itself, which is formless but yet full of form. It is without qualities and has no past, present, or future. In this regard, the aspirant is set free of bondage, limitation, or restriction.

> *Aham Brahma Asmi* (I am Brahman)—A timeless vedantic formula, this abstract mantra enables one to assert the self as being "one with God," thus defusing all physical and mental confinements.

> *Tat Twam Asi* (That thou art)—*Tat* means the eternal Brahman. "Thou" here is the aspirant who is one and the same with Brahman, the absolute substratum of creation.

Beeja or Seed Mantras

Beeja mantras are known as "seed letters" or "sounds" derived from the traditional fifty primeval sounds. Beeja is also spelled as *bija* or *beej*. Although generally consisting of one single letter at times compounded and seemingly meaningless in sound, each beeja mantra contains in-depth mystical meaning. Each of the universal five elements of ether, air, fire, water, and earth has its own beeja syllable as does every deity of the Hindu pantheon.

Examples of Beeja mantras are:

Dum—For goddess Durga

Aim—For goddess Saraswati

Gum—For Lord Ganesha

Kleem—For Kamadeva, the lord of desire, as well as for Lord Krishna

Kreem—For MahaKali

Shreem—For goddess MahaLakshmi

Basic Mantra Meditation

There are various methods for inducing meditative states when reciting and counting mantra rounds. The most common is the use of a *japa mala*, a "Hindu rosary" consisting of 108 + one beads. The traditional Hindu rosary has a knot tied in between each bead. They are strung in orange, white, or red thread with a variety of beads—such as rudraksha, tulasi or holy basil sacred to Vishnu, lotus-seed sacred to Lakshmi, clear quartz crystal for all forms of goddess worship, coral for Ganesha and Hanuman, and rosewood and white sandalwood for various purposes. A rosary is conducive to rhythmic modes and continuous repetition during mantra practice. Usually a mantra is chanted 108 times, hence the 108 beads on a rosary for most Hindus and Buddhists. The additional 109th bead is called *meru* or *sumeru*. It is where the power of mantras is stored.

Before commencing meditation with mantras, prepare the sacred space with flowers, incense, a votive candle or ghee lamp, and other materials of significance. When ready, sit in a comfortable position. With eyes closed, inhale and exhale gently and evenly to regulate breath. Disperse all thoughts and problems from the mind, visualize the deity of choice in the third eye, and say a prayer for guidance and protection. If learning a mantra from a tape or CD, set the stereo on low volume and chant along with it. With practice, one will gradually pick up distinct sounds, be able to pronounce them properly, and reach a stage when no mistakes are made.

Book Pendant Amulets

by Laurel Reufner

Imagine a little book that makes a nifty amulet for almost any purpose you can imagine. You can wear it around your neck like a pendant, hang it from a window or rearview mirror, or even tuck it into a purse or wallet. This project produces such a book no bigger than one-half by just over one inches.

While the book is designed for use as a pendant that hangs from beaded cords, it would be a simple matter to omit the jump rings so you can tuck it into your wallet or purse.

These little books make great magical amulets, providing page space for spell words or drawings. You can construct the book during ritual, making all of its creation a magical experience, or perform a ritual later to draw and write in the book.

The materials you need include: a sheet of paper, eight-and-a-half by eleven inches; a small piece of mat board or other sturdy cardboard; decorative paper for the covers; a contrasting sheet of paper for the spine (optional); jump rings, or wire and pliers to make them; eighth-inch-wide ribbon, twenty to twenty-four inches long.

The tools you need include: a craft knife; a metal ruler; an awl or needle tool for piercing holes; PVA adhesive or other white glue; a brush to apply glue; a small binder clip.

To make the pages, cut a strip of paper that is one inch wide by eleven inches long. Fold the paper in half lengthwise so the dimensions are now five-and-a-half inches by one inch. Fold it in half three more times. Rearrange the folds so you have a series of pleats forming a little accordion that measures about one inch by about one-half inch. (For those familiar with origami, this gives you a series of alternating valley and mountain folds.)

Measure and cut a piece of paper one by one-half inch. Fold it in half to find the middle. Look carefully at your page block. When you glue the pages down to the cover, you want to make sure that the first and last folds of paper are towards the spine of the book, rather than toward the front. Coat the decorative paper with glue, and using the fold line to help center it, press the paper down onto the page block, making sure the first fold is towards the inside, or spine, of the book. Carefully slide the binder clip onto the back of the page block to hold everything in place and set aside to dry.

Cut two pieces of mat board. The first should be one and one-eighth inches by one-half inch. The other should be one inch by one-half inch. The taller of the two pieces will be the back cover of your book. The extra eighth-inch provides room to attach the jump rings without interfering with the book pages. Now is a good time to mark which side of the boards will be the inside of the covers and which will be on the outside, as well as top and bottom. Make any marks on the insides of the boards, as these surfaces will be the last to be covered.

On the cover boards, measure up one-quarter inch from the bottom and in one-quarter inch from the back edge. Mark off a line about one-eighth inch long and cut a slit on the mark. Carefully widen the slit until it is about one-eighth inch by one-thirty-second of an inch. It's fine if this little notch in the board isn't exactly even or square, as the cover paper will hide its roughness. Align the front cover with the back cover so that the back and bottom sides match up. Use a pencil to mark through the opening in the front cover onto the back cover. Using the pencil marks as a guide, make a similar notch in the back cover. These will give you openings to thread your ribbon through.

Cut two pieces of the decorative paper about one-and-a-half inches square. Place glue on the outside of the front cover, center over one of the pieces of paper and press down, being careful to get out any wrinkles or air bubbles. Before wrapping the edges of the paper around to the inside of the boards, carefully cut the corners off on a diagonal, leaving a one-eighth inch edge of paper behind. This will make the corners lie neatly when glued down. Repeat with the back cover and then set aside to dry. Once the boards are dry, carefully use the craft knife to cut through the paper on the covers and open up the holes for the ribbon.

Getting the ribbon ties in place and gluing the whole thing together requires a little patience. You want to thread the ribbon through the holes in the cover boards from the inside to the outside. Make sure you have the boards facing the right directions and use the dull edge of the craft knife to help ease the ribbon through their threading holes. Pull the ends of the ribbon snug, wrapping the ribbon around the spine of the page block. Carefully glue the inside surface of the board, align it with the back and bottom edges of the page block, and press into place. Snug up any excess ribbon on the other side and repeat the gluing process on the back cover as well. Carefully ease a binder clip onto the back of your book and set it aside to dry completely. To protect the pages from becoming stuck together while the glue is drying, slip small pieces of wax paper in between the inside covers and the page block.

There you have it: a beautiful little book. Finish the project up by suspending it from decorative thread or chain. Hemp jewelry twine is a good choice for thread, as it is sturdy and comes in a variety of colors. Make sure it's color fast if you wish to wear it.

Add some beads here and there, holding them in place by knotting the thread. Your new accessory is sure to be an attention getter; no one need be any the wiser about its magical use.

If you found this project interesting and want to explore further projects, I'd recommend the following resources as good starting places. Gabrielle Fox's *The Essential Guide to Making Handmade Books* (Northlight Books, 2000) is the book that first got me hooked on bookmaking. Her directions and photos are fabulous. Alisa Golden's *Creating Handmade Books* (Sterling Publishing, 1998) is a great alternative if you are a beginner. Her directions aren't quite as clear, but they can still be followed pretty easily. Linda Fry Kenzle's *Pages: Innovative Bookmaking Techniques* (Krause Publications, 1997) would make a great follow-up book to either of the first two. And finally, Shereen LaPlanz's *Cover to Cover: Creative Techniques for Making Beautiful Books* (Lark Books, 1995) contains techniques different from the other books.

The Spell Drawer

by Cerridwen Iris Shea

Spells are the focus and manifestation of magic. The more used to integrating magic into everyday life one becomes, the less one needs the props called for in many spells. Since the magic comes from within, it's completely possible to cast spells without tools or props.

However, tools and props help with focus and visualization. In spells that call for letting the physical components sit as the spell manifests, seeing those items on a regular basis helps convince your mind and your will to cause manifestation. Sometimes you can leave your items out in a safe, undisturbed place as the spell manifests. Other times, there is no such place—sometimes you need a contained space in order to do your work. That's when a spell drawer comes in handy.

A spell drawer can be made from any drawer in a dresser or desk that belongs to you. It needs to be sacred space that will remain undisturbed as your spells collect energy. It also serves as a mini-altar—you can pull it out whenever you wish to work.

Preparation

Once you choose a drawer, remove it from the dresser or desk. Make sure it is clean, both physically and spiritually. Clean it with whatever sort of cleanser won't hurt the drawer, then pass it through an incense like sage or

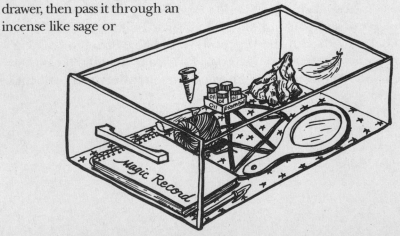

rosemary to cleanse any negativity. Consecrate the drawer according to your tradition.

Choose a shelf paper or other type of liner for the bottom of the drawer and fasten it in firmly. Luxurious fabric can work if it's stain resistant. Otherwise, you can change the fabric as necessary. If you use semi-permanent adhesive, you can also change the lining of your drawer seasonally or for each sabbat.

Figure out the compass orientation of the drawer—which side is north, south, east, west. At the top of each direction, fasten a small symbol of each direction inside the drawer. If the drawer is particularly small, you can fasten the symbols to the sides of the drawer, leaving the bottom free for work.

For north, consider using a stone or crystal, or a clear vial of earth or sand. You can't burn incense inside a drawer, but a feather or a sachet can represent the east/air. Obviously, you can't use candles inside a drawer. Find a different representation for fire, such as a salamander figurine, a picture of a campfire, or a cauldron. Likewise, an open container of water can get messy. Instead, consider using a shell or a securely closed vial to represent water. If you perform magic with animal totems, consider a small animal charm to represent each of the four directions. The center can be left clear, or you can draw a pentacle in it.

If it's safe, use candles and an incense burner on the top of the dresser when you perform spell work. If you need to use candles just for your work and then put them away, do so. Refrain from storing libations in the drawer, as bread crumbs and the like can bring in vermin.

Using Your Drawer

Once the drawer and its contents are consecrated, you can use it for daily devotionals and meditations. You can use it to hold spells you've cast, such as a gris-gris bag created for a specific purpose, a charged crystal, or a written spell or wish list.

The use of a spell drawer combines two facets of spell casting that sometimes seem contradictory. The first part is the idea that you should work a spell and then forget about it. This means that you release the magic so that it can manifest and don't obsess on it. If you hold it too close and don't let it go out and do its work, you prevent manifestation. On the other hand, the second part of the spell-working is visualizing. The point of visualization is to open yourself up to options. The purpose of doing a spell and visualizing an outcome is to change your perception of the world around you and open you to opportunities you might otherwise miss. By being aware of what you want and need in your life, you are more open to fresh choices that help get you there.

A spell drawer helps you achieve both of these goals: You have a space to hide away props that you can forget about after manifesting a spell or you can take them out to help your visualizations at any moment.

Maintenance

Don't neglect your drawer. As with any sacred space, it needs to be maintained, fed, and respected. Make sure the drawer stays neat and clean. Dust it out, change objects as necessary. When a spell is done and you dispose of the central workings in the drawer, smudge it to bring it back to the neutral sacred space necessary for your next working.

The more work you do with the drawer, the more energy accumulates there. Consider placing a guardian on the top of the dresser—such as a small statue of a gargoyle, dragon, or even a stuffed animal that makes you feel safe. Cleanse and consecrate this being and ask it to protect your spell drawer. Remember to thank your guardian whenever you pass it or see it.

You can also use an invisibility spell or protection spell on the drawer. If you live in an open situation where you don't have to hide what you do, you can let the drawer's magic shine.

In these days of constrained space, using a spell drawer is a way to create practical, contained sacred space that will grow with you along your spiritual path.

Dream Interpretation

by Kristin Madden

For many people, native and otherwise, dreaming holds the keys to power and health. Dreams often tell us far more about an illness than physical symptoms, and they provide us with deep insights. As a result, traditional shamans tend to be interested in the dreams of those they are called to work with, not only current dreams but dreams going back months or even years. For healers, dreams not only give clues to cause and cure, but they also serve as warnings. Premonitions of injury, illness, and death come through dreams.

During dreaming, the rational, analytical mind is shut down. This allows us to experience direct connection with the spirit world. Anything is possible during dreaming. Dreams can be so symbolic that we are left wondering what they mean.

The need to interpret dreams has fostered a market of books, websites, and classes. Many of these are quite good, but some are far too rigid to be of value. The truth is that while much of the symbolism we receive during dreams and journeys may be interpreted according to common or cultural beliefs and myths, often it is one's personal symbolism that comes through. Therefore, it is often best to develop your own ways of knowing. There are three very useful methods that will help you do just that.

An association web is a wonderfully simple tool to get quick insights into various aspects of a dream.

To use this, simply write down one word to use as your root word. This may be the one image, color, or event that stands out most from your dream. Then free associate and draw lines out from the root word. These secondary words may also give rise to lines of their own, creating a web of words that you associate with this image. Webs often give us insight into areas of the dream that hold the most emotional charge or need further exploration.

To delve deeper into the dream and its meanings, record everything that happened in as much detail as possible. Be very specific about how you felt, what you were wearing, what colors you saw, and any associated smells, sounds, and colors. Include beings or objects that you experienced, the time of day or night, the location, and any activity that occurred. Notice that I use the term "experienced" rather than "saw" or "heard." Sometimes other senses are awakened during dreaming, allowing us to experience or know of a presence without seeing or hearing it.

Use the association web or this deeper record to go into meditation and find greater insight into the meanings of the dream. Pay attention to aspects that evoke various emotions or memories for you. Interpret each scene, then a series of scenes, and eventually the entire dream as a whole. Gradually interpreting from the pieces up to the whole dream has proven very effective. Practicing this method with everyday dreams only increases your ability to interpret your own symbolism.

Finally, developing a dialogue with your dream can be a powerful tool for interpretation. Just as you

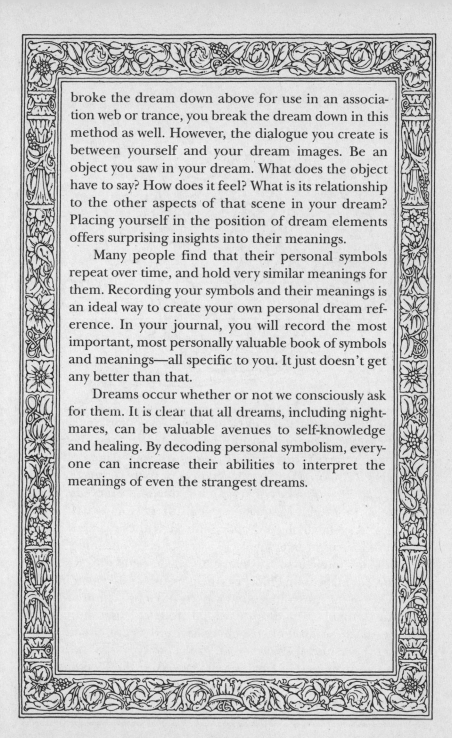

broke the dream down above for use in an association web or trance, you break the dream down in this method as well. However, the dialogue you create is between yourself and your dream images. Be an object you saw in your dream. What does the object have to say? How does it feel? What is its relationship to the other aspects of that scene in your dream? Placing yourself in the position of dream elements offers surprising insights into their meanings.

Many people find that their personal symbols repeat over time, and hold very similar meanings for them. Recording your symbols and their meanings is an ideal way to create your own personal dream reference. In your journal, you will record the most important, most personally valuable book of symbols and meanings—all specific to you. It just doesn't get any better than that.

Dreams occur whether or not we consciously ask for them. It is clear that all dreams, including nightmares, can be valuable avenues to self-knowledge and healing. By decoding personal symbolism, everyone can increase their abilities to interpret the meanings of even the strangest dreams.

The Gods of the Picts

by Sharynne NicMhacha

The Picts were an ancient Celtic people who lived in Scotland before the advent of written history. At that time, their land was often referred to as Pictland, and the whole island of Britain was called Albion. From what we know of their language (from place names and names of kings), it is much like an older form of Welsh (a P-Celtic language, which differs from Q-Celtic languages like Old Irish or Gaelic, although these come from a common ancestor language). Words like *aber*—meaning "river-mouth" and found in the city name Aberdeen—and *pit*—"a portion of land," as in the town Pitlochry—help us know where they lived.

One of the most interesting aspects of Pictish culture was the unique symbols carved onto symbol stones or used in jewelry. Many of these symbols—such as stylized representations of horses, boars, deer, snakes, fish, eagles, wolves—are beautiful. These animals were probably very sacred to the Picts (as they were to other Celtic peoples), and may have served as markers of a particular tribe's territory. They are also likely to have had sacred energies or symbolism, and may have also been associated with gods or goddesses of the tribe or area.

Gods and goddesses associated with these sacred animals are found in other Celtic areas, and it may be that deities like these also formed part of ancient Pictish religion. Here is a list of some of Celtic deities from Ireland, Britain, and Gaul who were associated with the sacred animals venerated by the Picts:

Horse: Rhiannon (Wales); Epona (Britain); Macha (Ireland)

Boar: Arduinna (Gaul); hunter gods

Salmon: Finn mac Cumhaill/Gwynn ap Nudd (Ireland, Wales); Mabon (Wales)

Deer: Cernunnos (Britain, Gaul); Callirius (Britain)

Bull: Tarvos Trigaranus (Gaul); Donn (Ireland)

Snake: Bridget (Scotland); Sirona (Gaul)

Dolphin: Dylan Eil Ton (Wales); Coventina (Britain)

Eagle: Llew Llaw Gyffes (Wales); various sky gods (Britain, Gaul)

Wolf: Mórrigan (Ireland); various hunter/battle deities (Britain, Gaul)

The Celts, wherever they were found, had a deep respect for nature. Gods and goddesses were sometimes associated with culture, and connected with attributes like wisdom, healing, power, skill, fertility, or protection. Other deities were associated with the landscape. Water was especially sacred. In most cases, bodies of water were associated with goddesses or female spirits. For example, in Ireland, the rivers Boyne and Shannon were associated with the goddesses Boand and Sinann. In Britain, the Severn was connected with the goddess Sabrina. The Arthurian Lady of the Lake is a manifestation of this ancient Celtic concept.

The same concept seems to have been in place in ancient Scotland, for we know the ancient names of many rivers (and thus, the goddesses who were worshiped in those places). Many of these goddess names refer to an attribute of the river that was in turn a manifestation of the power and personality of the goddess who inhabited the sacred waters. Here are some of the river goddesses of ancient Pictland:

Berba (in Aberbervie): The Boiling or Tempestuous One

Boderia (in Aberbothri): The Noiseless or Silent One

Brutaca (in Arbroath): The Warm or Boiling One

Buadhnat (in Arbuthnott): The Virtuous or Healing One

Devona (in Aberdeen): Divine Goddess

Dubrona (in Aberdour): Flowing One

Gelidia (in Abergeldie): White or Pure One

Labara (in Aberlour): The Loud One

Lemonaca (in Aberlemno): River of the Elm Trees

Luathnat (in Aberluthnot): Little Swift One

Nectona (in Abernethy): Pure One

There are several rivers in Scotland whose names reflect a local goddess or female spirit's habitation. These include the River Don and the River Dee in Aberdeenshire. Their names come from earlier Celtic words meaning "divine goddess." The mouth of the river seems to have been particularly sacred. River names meaning "divine goddess" are found in other parts of Britain, as well as in Ireland and on the continent.

Another widespread group of goddess/river names seem to have existed since earliest times. These are rivers whose name come from the root word *danu–*, which is an Old Indo-European word for "river." These rivers include the Danube, the Dnieper, the Dniester, and many rivers whose names are now spelled Don in Britain and elsewhere. This may or may not be the same root that formed the name of the Irish goddess Danu.

Finally, there are a group of river names from Pictland whose meaning is so obscure that the goddesses or spirits honored in these names is lost. However, these sacred river spirits were recognized and venerated by the Picts once they came to live in these lands. These include the Nairn, the Earn, the Spey, the Findhorn, the Tay, and the Deveron. Perhaps by journeying to contact the spirit of these ancient waters, we can gain more knowledge about the divine gods and goddesses who inhabited the landscape of ancient Pictland.

Mars, The God of Transition

by James Kambos

He was the son of Jupiter and Juno. He was the lover of Venus. Among the deities of the ancient Romans, Mars was most powerful and complex. He was a god of change, sometimes violent, and a god of protection and transition. For all his power, however, information on his following is scarce. The legends surrounding Mars are taken mostly from the ancient Greek god of war, Ares.

Typically, Mars is depicted as the blood-thirsty god of war and aggression. Soldiers invoked his power before going into battle. Like many deities, Mars has a dual nature, and his traits are more varied than you may think.

Before he was a god of war, Mars was an earth god. He ruled agriculture, fruitfulness, and plenty. During early spring, ancient farmers would walk their fields with high priests, who asked for his blessings to ensure good crops and a bountiful harvest. This ancient ritual continued for thousands of years and manifested in a Christianized form throughout colonial-era New England.

Exactly when and why Mars was transformed into a god of war is unknown. Perhaps, since he was seen as a protector of the land itself, his role may have been expanded into that of the warrior god aspect.

Depicting Mars as merely a god of aggression denies his multi-faceted nature. He is actually both healer and destroyer. Once the battleground where he was honored returned to a time of peace, he regenerated the land so it would once again yield life-sustaining crops. When the volatile side of his nature could be channeled into a positive force, Mars was a powerful protector.

Mars also took on the roles of paternal nurturer and passionate lover. His awesome powers include strength, vitality, and new beginnings. It is only fitting that the first month of the Roman calendar, March, was named in his honor. March is still a time of new beginnings. Spring begins, and the earth awakens from winter's grip. During Mars' month of March, plows return to the fields and turn the sacred soil, starting the planting cycle anew. This is appropriate, since Mars was one of the original agricultural gods.

Ways to Honor Mars

As a warrior god figure, Mars is frequently viewed only in his negative aspect. However, there are also many positive qualities associated with Mars that the modern magical practitioner may call upon.

One of the best times to ask for his aid is when you have the need to cast a spell for protection. Perform your spell on a Tuesday—his day. Decorate your magical space with candles in colors ranging from orange to deepest reds. Scents you may use might include cinnamon, ginger, pine, and honeysuckle. Photos or figures of wolves and chickens may also be placed on your altar. These animals are sacred to Mars. Wolves are associated with him because they represent the qualities of transition and shapeshifting. Chickens, being symbols of fertility, call upon Mars's early role as a god of abundance.

Perform the protection spell of your choice as usual. Mention Mars by name and use the aids mentioned above. Never ask Mars to assist in any form of revenge magic, or you may receive a violent backlash. His blessings should only be used for protection and to repel negativity.

Being a male deity, Mars may also be asked to assist in spells concerning male sexuality, virility, and the male mysteries. Men might feel comfortable invoking Mars concerning romantic situations.

Athletes can also ask Mars to help in strength conditioning and endurance.

The most favored time of year for a Mars ritual, if possible, would be a windy March day. Embrace his energy by facing the direction from which the wind is blowing. Announce your magical intent, letting the March wind carry your wishes to him. The winds of March are the voice of Mars, as is the crack of thawing ice on the pond and the rush of water tumbling over rocks in the brook.

Listen to him, and respect his power, which lives in all nature. Breathe deeply after speaking your charm. Breathe until you smell the moist earth. This is his scent.

To thank Mars and end your magical ritual dedicated to him, drink a cup of spicy herbal tea. Ginger or masala chai tea would be good choices. Then leave an offering, such as a piece of gingerbread or a spice cookie, in a field or garden.

Walk away, knowing he has heard you.

Clearing Out the Cobwebs
by Twilight Bard

Do you feel your thoughts are more disorganized than your closet? Have you had trouble recalling information or focusing on a problem? When excess stress comes our way, our mental clarity can be reduced. This meditation will help.

When you are ready to start, dim the lights and sit or lie in a comfortable position. Envision yourself standing in a large, pleasant elevator, like those you find in luxury hotels. The doors are closed, and you are the only one inside. The carpeting is plush, and the walls are a soothing color. It is very comfortable inside.

There is a bench piled with thick, velvety pillows. You sink into the soft cushions, instantly comfortable and relaxed. Looking up, you notice that you can just reach the elevator control. It consists of a single lever, which is currently in the down position. You reach out and flick it up.

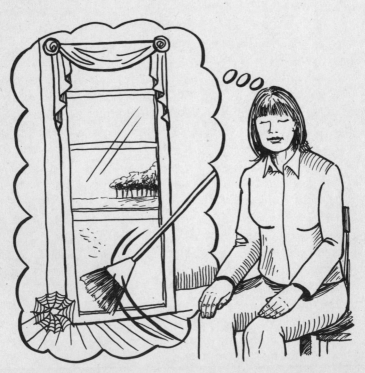

The elevator gently begins to lift off the ground. Above the door, you notice a screen. On the screen appears a red number one. The elevator continues to rise, and you grow more and more at ease. Your breathing becomes slow and rhythmic. The number changes to an orange two. You continue to rise, and a warm, heavy feeling starts in your feet, relaxing you completely. The number changes again, this time to a yellow three. The warm feeling is making its way up to your hips, your buttocks, and lower back. The number changes to four, and it is green. The elevator continues to rise, as does the warm feeling of relaxation—into your abdomen, waist, and up your spine one vertebra at a time.

The number is now a blue five. The warmth circles around to your chest; your breathing becomes easy and light. The elevator feels like a womb, and you seem to be floating within it. As an indigo six appears, the feeling extends down your shoulders, through your arms, into your hands and fingers. The number becomes a violet seven, and the feeling makes its way into your neck, head, face, all the way up to your scalp. You are completely relaxed now. The numbers disappear, and the elevator stops. You stand up and wait in front of the doors, which slide open to reveal a room like an office. This represents your mental state.

Look around. You may notice it is unkempt in certain areas. Perhaps the whole place is a mess. Maybe there are messy open drawers, stacks of papers, and files all around. Perhaps there are cluttered shelves or a cluttered desk. The air may be swirling with dust particles, and cobwebs may be hanging in the corners.

If the place is very messy, don't despair. Know that you can begin to fix it. Visualize yourself picking up things off the floor and the desk. Note that all the papers and files are labeled. Some might be ideas, some may be fantasies, some memories, and some emotions. Begin to sort them into piles. You already notice an improvement. Next, go through your shelves, drawers, or boxes. Make sure everything belongs. If anything seems to be in the wrong place or doesn't fit right, remove it and put it in its appropriate pile or throw it out.

When you have organized your drawers and shelves, begin restocking them with the piles you have made. File everything in the proper place, under the proper category, so that it will be easy to find when you need it.

Browse through your dream files. Are there any that are particularly disturbing? Have a look at them now and see what bothers you about them. Are they trying to tell you something or just playing on your fears? Write a post-it note to yourself and tack it on the folder, saying that the next time this dream resurfaces, you will make sense out of it and be able to either file it away or throw it out.

You may wish to begin putting anything you feel is useless or outdated in a large garbage bag. There may be bad feelings—regrets, doubts, grudges you have held for far too long. There may be some old ideas you no longer need. It is time to rid yourself of them. Find a big trash chute and dump them.

You notice a broom in the corner. Take the broom and begin to sweep. Notice any swirls of negative energy that might be coming up. Some of that energy might be lurking in the corners in the form of cobwebs or on the floor as dust. Sweep it all up. Then, open a door or window and sweep it out into the universe, back to where it originated.

When you feel satisfied with the work you have done, get back on the elevator. The doors will automatically close behind you. Have a seat, flick the lever down, and feel the elevator descend.

The violet seven will appear above the door again. You begin to become aware of your physical body, of the blood pumping through your veins, of the air on your face. As the number turns to an indigo six, you notice your back against the chair. As it goes to a blue five, you begin to wiggle your fingers and toes. The elevator continues to descend, bringing you back to the waking world.

When you see the green four, you begin to gently stretch and move your arms and legs. At the yellow three, you begin to notice the little sounds around you. As it turns to an orange two, inhale deeply and gently stretch your back and neck.

When the red one comes, and the doors open, step off the elevator. Open your eyes. You should be feeling refreshed and alert, you mind clear and uncluttered. Know that you can go back any time you wish; just close your eyes and step inside.

Mayan Calendars

by Laurel Reufner

Imagine standing inside the Caracol at Chichen Itza during sunset at equinox. As moments pass, you can see the Sun's light inch its way down the tunnel-like window to your right, illuminating the room with its warmth. The Maya were avid sky watchers, seeking to record and predict the patterns of the heavens above them. They knew the length not only of the solar year, but had also measured the lunar month to within twenty-three seconds of modern measurements. Considering the tools they had to work with, usually a pair of crossed sticks as a sighting aid, this is an impressive accomplishment.

It should also be noted that the Maya had a fairly sophisticated grasp of mathematics and writing. They were one of the first civilizations to utilize the number zero, a numerical value that seems obvious to us today but was a major breakthrough at the time. They also used a base 20, or vigesimal, system of counting, rather than our base 10 system. Their writing system was a combination of hieroglyphs representing ideas and things as well as phonetic sounds. Many of their writings and mathematical calculations recorded astronomical and calendrical information for their sophisticated almanacs that listed equinoxes, solar and lunar eclipses, and other astronomical phenomena.

The everyday calendar of the common Maya was a solar calendar, called the *Haab'*. Containing 360 days, the Haab' was eighteen months (*uinal*) composed of twenty days (*kin*) each. The months were called *Pohp, Wo, Sip, Sotz', Tzek, Xul, Yaxk'in, Mol, Ch'en, Yax, Sak, Keh, Mak, K'ank'in, Muwan, Pax, K'ayab'*, and *Kumk'u.*

We assume the Haab' was agricultural because like months were grouped together. The water months were followed by the earth-named months. Next were months associated with the growing of the maize crops. The cycle ended with months named for the dry season. To finish out the time necessary for a full year (*tun*), the Maya added on a five day period at the end of the year known as *Uayeb*, or "the sleep."

Uayeb was a dangerous time to the Maya. Barriers between the middleworld and underworld were broken, allowing malevolent deities to spread death, disease, famine, and any other misery to our world. To protect themselves and propitiate the gods, the Maya carried out elaborate rituals involving the entire city and lasting the full five days of Uayeb.

In addition to the Haab' calendrical cycle, the Maya also used a sacred calendar known as the sacred almanac or the *Tzolk'in*. There were the twenty named days: *Imix, Ik', Ak'b'al, K'an, Chikchan, Kimi, Manik', Lamat, Muluk, Ok, Chuwen, Eb', B'en, Ix, Men, Kib', Kab'an, Etz'nab', Kawak,* and *Ahaw.* These were aired with thirteen numbers. The cycle started with 1 Imix, then 2 Ik' and so on. Upon reaching 13 B'en, it started again with 1 Ix, 2 Men and continued cycling through until it eventually ended on 13 Ahaw.

The Tzolk'in didn't have a year designation, like the Haab's tun, although it took 260 days to complete a full cycle and reach 13 Ahaw. No one is sure how the Maya devised such a system, or even why 260 is such an important number. It has been speculated that there are connections to the lunar month. Normal gestation takes approximately ten lunar months, or 260 days before birth occurs. We know that midwives used the sacred almanac to predict delivery dates for their patients. Thirteen days is also the approximate time it takes to go from New Moon to Full Moon and vice versa. With so many Mayan writings destroyed and so many of the carvings suffering from erosion, we'll probably never know how the Maya developed the sacred almanac.

The sacred almanac was used to predict auspicious and inauspicious days for persons and the community at large. The Maya had a long-standing belief that if something bad happened on a given day, when that day repeated so would the event. Furthermore, every day had its own patron deity and each number had a set of associations. Days for engaging in warfare were especially carefully chosen. Midwives, priests, and diviners carefully considered the naming day of a person.

Combining both the Haab' and sacred almanac, the Maya created a cycle that takes fifty-two years to complete. Each day within this time frame had its own unique date. It was a good system for recording the passage of time, but didn't allow for differentiation between each fifty-two year period. Eventually the Maya developed what we know as the Long Count, allowing them to pinpoint a single date in time. A hieroglyph begins the date, followed by decreasingly smaller measures of time. Usually the dating would begin with the recording of the *bak'tun*, which placed the day within a 144,000-day time period and the *k'atun*, or twenty-year cycle.

All of these systems helped the Maya organize their lives. Cycles were important to the Maya, allowing them to organize their surroundings into a sense of harmony. Their lives were composed of intricately interlocking cycles of life and death, where predictions of the future helped them better prepare. Their rulers and priests could determine appropriate rituals to propitiate the gods and hopefully lessen any suffering.

Mayan accomplishments in calendrical events and astronomy were amazing. They accurately predicted movements of the Sun and Moon, as well as their attendant eclipses, along with the movements of the inner planets, constellations, and even particular stars in the heavens. That so much of Mayan knowledge was lost in the meeting of Old and New Worlds is a historical and archaeological tragedy.

The Lokapalas:
Circle Guardian Dieties

by Neil Campbell

Within India's Vedic tradition, guardians protect the four cardinal directions. These figures appear in the *Rig Veda*, the world's oldest religious text. During the Vedic period, invoking the four cardinal guardians became a ritualized practice. Eventually the practice of invoking eight or more Lokapalas, also known as the Ashta-Dikpalas, became established. The name *Lokapalas* is Sanskrit and derived from two words, *loka* meaning "world" and *pala* meaning "protectors." The original four Lokapalas spread far through the east, especially with the movement of Buddhism. Variations are found in Tibet, China, Japan, and Korea.

In Western ceremonial traditions the four cardinal directions (or quarters) are generally associated with the watchtowers, while in earth-based practices, they are usually allied with the elemental lords or deities specific to a tradition. Many of these share similarities with the Lokapalas. The quarters of a magic circle in both ceremonial and earth-based practices are typically associated with the elements of air in the east, fire in the south, water in the west, and earth in the north. The same is also found with the Lokapalas.

Each of the Lokapalas is an independent deity. Many of them have been venerated individually since the era of the *Rig Veda*. In their role as protectors, the Lokapalas are invoked along with an individual animal vehicle or a guardian elephant. The guardian elephants are called the *Dig-Gajas*, meaning "elephants of space."

In Indian tradition, elephants represent strength, intelligence, royalty, and the fertility of the land. To encourage rain, stables full of elephants were kept to be paraded during state and religious occasions. It was believed that the elephants would attract clouds and rainfall, promising a healthy crop.

Starting in the East and following the circle in a clockwise direction, the Lokapalas are:

East—Indra, king of the gods. Indra is the god of rain, thunder, and lightning. The warrior king of the gods, he is robust. He dresses in royal splendor with yellow silk garments and has a bold face and tawny beard. His magical weapon is the *vajra*, the glowing thunderbolt. Indra is the chief god of the *Rig Veda Samhita*, within which most prayers are addressed to him. He is also father to Arjuna, the prince who converses with Krishna in the *Bhagavad Gita*. His elephant is Airavata.

Southeast—Agni, god of fire. Agni is the conveyor of sacrifice. Next to Indra, Agni receives the most attention in the *Rig Veda*. Descriptions of his appearance can vary. One is of a young man with a bright red complexion and golden hair. Another describes him dressed in black, with a mouth full of sharp golden teeth and seven flickering tongues, hair aflame, and fiery red eyes. Agni's weapon is a blazing spear. He is a messenger between humanity and the gods. Agni also consumes the bodies of the dead in the funeral pyre and takes them to the Yama's *pitriloka*, the land of the ancestors. Agni is also considered to be the fire in the belly, the digestive flame. Agni's elephant is Pundarika.

South—Yama, lord of death. The south is associated with death in Indian traditions because of the position of the hot daytime Sun. Yama, lord of death, is seen as a large being of green, dressed in a dark, red-hooded garment. He has luminous eyes and a moustache, below which fangs protrude. Sometimes he wears a crown. His weaponry varies from a body-length staff, mace, sceptre, or noose. Two fierce dogs, each with four eyes and flaring nostrils, guard the road to his residence. Texts tell how Yama was the first man to die before taking up the position of lord of the dead. Some texts call him the child or charioteer of the Sun. The elephant of Yama is Vamana.

Southwest—Surya, the Sun god. Surya has a body of fired copper, from which shine forth seven rays of brilliant light. He rides a golden chariot across the sky. Above his red-tinted eyes is a head of yellow hair, upon which sits a tall crown. In the crown are twelve shining jewels and crystals and three red eagle feathers. Surya is clad in gold. His right hand is made of gold. This is a replacement for the original hand he lost in a sacrifice. Even the Sun lord's tongue is of gold, symbolic of his illuminating mantras. Surya worship has been carried over into modern mainstream yoga in *Surya Namaskara*, or "salutations to the sun." Kamuda is the elephant of Surya.

West—Varuna, god of waters. Varuna is the god of oceans, pools, and heavenly waters. His body is white in color, symbolic of his pure and divine nature. Over his white body he wears a polished golden suit of armor, from which hangs a robe made from a celestial material. Varuna's weapon is a long noose made from a serpent. He rides the Makcara, a crocodile-like sea beast. He is said to have a palace deep in the ocean constructed of crystal. Ajana is the name of Varuna's elephant.

Northwest—Vayu, god of the air. The lord of air and wind, Vayu has a lean young figure, symbolic of his swiftness.

He holds a bow with a set of arrows slung over his shoulder. Vayu can be restless and turbulent at times. He pervades all places, purifying them as he goes with sweet fragrances followed by blissful music. He is depicted riding an antelope. Vayu's child is Hanuman, the god of devotion and loyal servant to Rama. Vayu's elephant is Puspadanta.

North—Kubera, lord of the earth. Kubera is king of the Yaksas and lord of treasures. Yaksas main associations are with vegetation, treasure, magic, and the inner earth. These are sometimes called the Punyajanas, or the "good people." Kubera is described as small and squat with a ruddy appearance, thick beard, and large gold earrings. Several lavish necklaces hang around his neck, complementing the heavily ornamented crown upon his head. His belly is round and broad like a cauldron. From his portly waist hang two bags, one of mongoose skin holding jewels, the other of embroidered silk holding silver and gold coins and a set of dice. He grasps a fly whisk made of a yak's tail with a shining silver handle. His weapon is a swinging mace. Sarvabhauma is his elephant.

Northeast—Soma, god of the Moon. Soma's position in the circle is opposite Surya, the Sun god. Soma is of youthful appearance with a tawny colored body. His inner layer of clothing is bright golden-hued. His outer garments are long flowing robes the color of milk and water. He has been described in the *Rig Veda* as having two crescent horns similar to a cow's. He holds a chalice full of the revered sacred mead of the gods, which is also known as Soma. Supratika is the Moon lord's elephant.

The Lokapalas protect the outer space so that the practitioner may successfully and safely explore inner space. It has been said that all lies within, and it is within ourselves that we must eventually turn to find our divine nature. May you travel that inner road and be met with spiritual success.

The Folklore of Bread

by Magenta Griffith

The Hungarians have a saying that "bread is older than Man." Bread is almost certainly one of the first foods that we humans learned to make, as opposed to finding it from a tree or out of the ground. Consequently the history of bread and bread-making is full of legends and folklore.

As long as 12,000 years ago, people learned to grind grains between two flat stones to make a coarse flour. They mixed it with water, and made flat breads that they baked on stones near the fire.

Modern yeast breads, meanwhile, date back to ancient Egypt. The warm climate was a perfect place for wild yeasts to grow. Legend has it that a slave in a royal Egyptian household set aside some dough and forgot about it. When he found it some time later, it had doubled in size. Trying to hide the mistake, he punched down the dough and baked it. The result was a lighter bread than anyone had ever tasted.

Wheat, the most common grain in Egypt at that time, made excellent bread. Osiris was worshiped in Egypt as the god of grain. Bread was used instead of money; the workers who built the pyramids were paid in bread. Archaeologists digging in Egyptian ruins have found grinding stones and baking chambers, as well as 4,000-year-old drawings of bakeries.

Archeological findings in Egypt have revealed murals showing the process of baking bread, as well as loaves of bread buried with the dead to nourish them during their journey to the afterlife. The Metropolitan Museum of Art in New York has a loaf of bread found in an Egyptian tomb thought to be over 3,500 years old. In early Egyptian times, a prayer for the deceased began with a wish of 1,000 loaves of bread for his or her spirit.

The ancient Greeks had over fifty kinds of bread. Public bakeries and ovens were built by the government for everyone's use. These were popular places to socialize while your bread was baking.

The ancient Romans developed the *quern*—a circular stone wheel that turned on another fixed stone. This was the basis of all milling until the nineteenth century. Stoneground flour is produced using this method. The finest grade of flour was sifted through silk sheets. In Rome, February 17 was celebrated as the Fornacalia—dedicated to Fornax, the Roman goddess of furnaces, ovens, and bread.

Early Saxon farmers made a special loaf out of the first of the wheat harvest. Often they formed the loaves into special shapes and offered them to the local gods. The loaf was sometimes shaped like a person, the spirit of the grain, or a fertility goddess. The loaf was buried in the field or burned in a fire. The tradition of making loaves in human shapes survives in the gingerbread men we bake at the winter holidays, among other traditions.

Challah is a traditional Jewish egg bread. Challah means "dough offering" in Hebrew. This custom goes back to the Temple in Jerusalem in 280 BC, when a portion of dough from the Sabbath loaf was given to the temple priests. The act of "challah" is to burn a small part of the dough as an offering before the remaining dough is baked.

Challah is served on Friday nights for the Sabbath dinner and also on holidays. The Friday night challah is generally braided, but challah for Rosh Hashanah, the Jewish New Year, is always round and smooth, to symbolize the continuity of the year. On Rosh Hashanah, it is customary to dip a piece of challah in honey to symbolize the sweetness of the new year. A blessing is said, then the bread is broken, never sliced, at the beginning of the meal. Each person breaks off a piece and passes the challah around the table.

Bread Lore

There are many superstitions surrounding bread. If a crumb drops out of your mouth, death will come to the house in a week. If a loaf is cut at both ends, the devil will fly over your house. There are people who believe that bread can prevent illness. At one time it was thought to cure whooping cough. In much of Europe, a common custom is to place bread briefly in a newborn's mouth to ensure the baby's health and happiness. Bread was tucked into a bride's shoe to bring fertility. Giving bread has always been a sign of friendship, particularly when given to a sick or bereaved person.

Bread is vital in many cultures, and their languages reflect this. For example, in Arabic, the words for "bread" and "life" are related. The Russian word for hospitality translates into "bread and salt." In Russia, it is customary to give a round, freshly baked loaf of bread to a guest along with a small wooden bowl of salt when greeting them.

To this day, Scots still eat large, round Beltane bannocks on May Day, but they no longer roll them down hillsides as did the early Celts to celebrate spring. It is a part of Irish tradition on All Hallow's Eve to bake a wedding ring in the *barm brack*. Barm brack is a spicy, round yeast bread dotted with currants and baked in a cast-iron pot suspended over a fire. The belief is that whoever finds the ring will become engaged before the year is out.

December 13, the shortest day and longest night according to the old Julian calendar, is widely celebrated in Sweden, Italy, and other countries as a feast day in honor of St. Lucy or Santa Lucia. She was a fourth-century Sicilian who became a Christian and devoted her life to serving the poor. She was eventually tortured and killed in an unsuccessful attempt to get her to renounce her faith.

On this day in Sweden, the oldest daughter in the family dresses in a white robe and wears a crown of candles. She brings her family breakfast in bed, consisting of coffee and special saffron-flavored Lucy breads. These breads may be shaped in many traditional ways, including a crown, a cross, a simple "S" figure, or a wreath. The lighted crown and saffron-colored dough is also said to symbolize the Sun that will soon return.

In Ukraine, bread is an integral part of wedding ceremonies. Seven bridesmaids grind flour from wheat grown in seven different fields; those flours are sifted together and made into bread dough. This good luck loaf is shaped by the bridesmaids themselves and ornamented with rosettes, doves, and hearts.

Pan de los Muertos (literally "bread of the dead") is baked to commemorate the departed members of one's family on All Souls' Day, November 2. Mexican bakers fashion the bread into any number of shapes such as dolls, crosses, flowers, or plain loaves. They may also write the name of the deceased on top with sugar icing. At funerals in Wales, a loaf of bread represents the sins of the dead person. Eating the bread frees the spirit and keeps it from haunting people.

From the oldest times up to today, bread has been an important part of our life and lore.

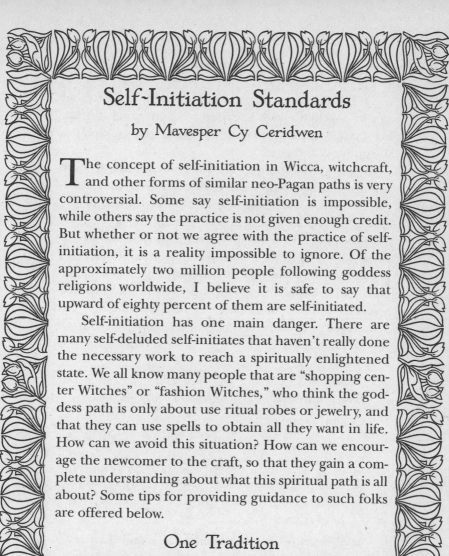

Self-Initiation Standards

by Mavesper Cy Ceridwen

The concept of self-initiation in Wicca, witchcraft, and other forms of similar neo-Pagan paths is very controversial. Some say self-initiation is impossible, while others say the practice is not given enough credit. But whether or not we agree with the practice of self-initiation, it is a reality impossible to ignore. Of the approximately two million people following goddess religions worldwide, I believe it is safe to say that upward of eighty percent of them are self-initiated.

Self-initiation has one main danger. There are many self-deluded self-initiates that haven't really done the necessary work to reach a spiritually enlightened state. We all know many people that are "shopping center Witches" or "fashion Witches," who think the goddess path is only about use ritual robes or jewelry, and that they can use spells to obtain all they want in life. How can we avoid this situation? How can we encourage the newcomer to the craft, so that they gain a complete understanding about what this spiritual path is all about? Some tips for providing guidance to such folks are offered below.

One Tradition

It is of course easiest for a newcomer to be initiated in a regular coven, in one established tradition. Still, there are many more people interested in following a path than there are covens to receive then. So, the solitary practitioner needs information about what a Witch is and what is necessary to learn to become a Pagan.

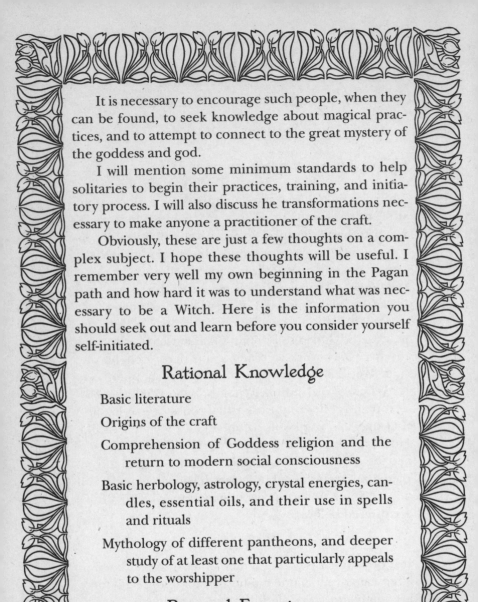

It is necessary to encourage such people, when they can be found, to seek knowledge about magical practices, and to attempt to connect to the great mystery of the goddess and god.

I will mention some minimum standards to help solitaries to begin their practices, training, and initiatory process. I will also discuss he transformations necessary to make anyone a practitioner of the craft.

Obviously, these are just a few thoughts on a complex subject. I hope these thoughts will be useful. I remember very well my own beginning in the Pagan path and how hard it was to understand what was necessary to be a Witch. Here is the information you should seek out and learn before you consider yourself self-initiated.

Rational Knowledge

Basic literature

Origins of the craft

Comprehension of Goddess religion and the return to modern social consciousness

Basic herbology, astrology, crystal energies, candles, essential oils, and their use in spells and rituals

Mythology of different pantheons, and deeper study of at least one that particularly appeals to the worshipper

Personal Experience

Understanding of all sabbats and esbats and associated practices

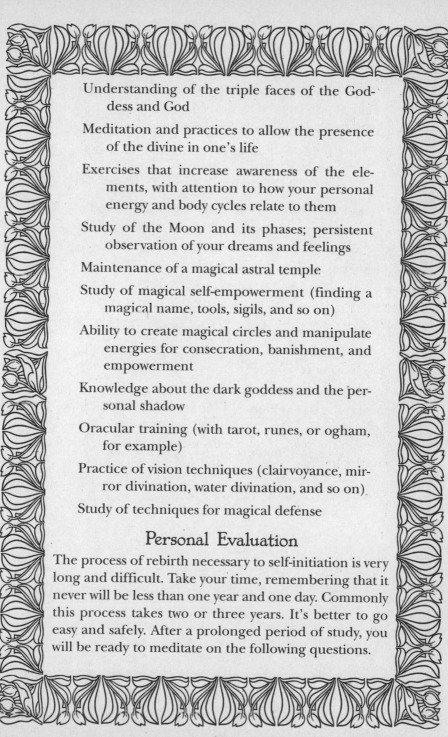

Understanding of the triple faces of the Goddess and God

Meditation and practices to allow the presence of the divine in one's life

Exercises that increase awareness of the elements, with attention to how your personal energy and body cycles relate to them

Study of the Moon and its phases; persistent observation of your dreams and feelings

Maintenance of a magical astral temple

Study of magical self-empowerment (finding a magical name, tools, sigils, and so on)

Ability to create magical circles and manipulate energies for consecration, banishment, and empowerment

Knowledge about the dark goddess and the personal shadow

Oracular training (with tarot, runes, or ogham, for example)

Practice of vision techniques (clairvoyance, mirror divination, water divination, and so on)

Study of techniques for magical defense

Personal Evaluation

The process of rebirth necessary to self-initiation is very long and difficult. Take your time, remembering that it never will be less than one year and one day. Commonly this process takes two or three years. It's better to go easy and safely. After a prolonged period of study, you will be ready to meditate on the following questions.

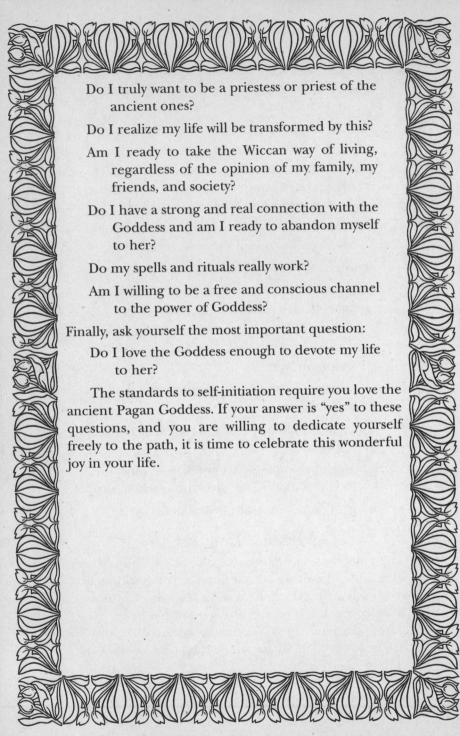

Do I truly want to be a priestess or priest of the ancient ones?

Do I realize my life will be transformed by this?

Am I ready to take the Wiccan way of living, regardless of the opinion of my family, my friends, and society?

Do I have a strong and real connection with the Goddess and am I ready to abandon myself to her?

Do my spells and rituals really work?

Am I willing to be a free and conscious channel to the power of Goddess?

Finally, ask yourself the most important question:

Do I love the Goddess enough to devote my life to her?

The standards to self-initiation require you love the ancient Pagan Goddess. If your answer is "yes" to these questions, and you are willing to dedicate yourself freely to the path, it is time to celebrate this wonderful joy in your life.

Pagan Rosaries and Prayer Beads

by Olivia O'Meir

Rosaries and prayers are a new addition to Pagan and Wiccan practices, but their history goes back thousands of years. When we think of rosaries, we think of the Dominican object associated with Roman Catholicism. However, prayer beads called *baijanti mala* were used in India by the Hindus as early as 185 BC.

It is believed that Buddha himself used prayer beads. From this Buddhist tradition, the use of prayer beads spread to Tibet, China, Japan, and then to Persia and the Middle East. It is possible that Catholicism may have learned about the rosary during the Crusades or the Muslim invasion of Spain. In the 1800s, Sister Maria Jaricott brought the rosary into Christianity.

Many prayer beads and rosaries relate to flowers and gardens in some way. In fact, the word "rosary" comes from the Latin *rosarium*, meaning "rose garden." In Tibet and India, prayer beads are called *mala*, meaning "garden" or "garland of flowers." Hindus also use the word *japamala* for prayer beads. Japamala means "rose chaplet," because the beads were first made with rose

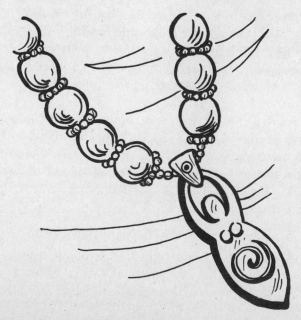

petals. In Christianity, the rosary is considered to represent the Virgin Mary's rose garden.

While most rosaries and prayer beads have similarities, they are very different in terms of bead count, arrangement, and bead materials. Beads have been made from herbs and flowers, like sandalwood and rose. Rocks and semiprecious stones also make beautiful beads. In addition, fingers and knots were used to count prayers. For example, in the Greek Orthodox Church, a knotted rosary known as a *kombologion* is used.

Creating and using prayer beads is a solitary and personal practice. To be meaningful, the prayers need to resonate in one's soul, and the bead's shape and color must be attractive to the user's eyes. You can make many prayer beads, each with a different purpose. Or you can make one main set of prayer beads to use for all your prayers and meditations.

Your Prayer Bead Purpose

In planning a set of prayer beads, many things must be considered. The first is the purpose of the beads. What do you want to achieve when you use them? You can use prayer beads to connect to the divine, meditate, cast spells, or facilitate ritual. Prayer beads are most well-known for being a tool to honor and worship a deity. Prayer beads can be used as a meditative tool. You can concentrate on a thought or idea while moving your hands over the beads. Using the prayer beads to cast spells provides a nice twist to your magical working. This type of spell work is similar to knot magic. You can perform an entire ritual using the prayer beads alone.

After you have your purpose in mind, the next thing to do is break down your goal. For example, the first set of prayer beads I made was aimed at connecting to the Goddess. I broke down meaningful aspects of this goal into key words and phrases. This helped me to choose the beads I wanted to use and what prayers I needed to write.

Prayer Bead Supplies

Once you've determined your purpose, it's time to search for supplies. The supplies depend on what type of prayer beads you are making and your beading skill and experience. Thankfully, there are many guides online and in print to help you make the beads. Remember, there is no limit to what kinds of beads you can use. I suggest using any beads that are beautiful and appeal to you. Some options include gemstones, sandalwood or rose beads, dried seeds, and other natural elements such as acorns or frankincense tears. All rosaries have an amulet of some type—a crucifix or religious icon, a tassel, a special bead, a relic, a pentacle, or a goddess figure.

For my prayer beads, I found a pretty goddess pendant at a local New Age shop. I was shopping at a crafts store and found a container of round black and hematite glass beads, which instantly attracted me for use as counting beads. Counting beads are used to keep track of the number of prayers recited. I also found some black and iridescent round disks to use to represent the Moon. I found round silver spacer beads and silver findings. I chose silver because it resonates with the Goddess.

The Purpose of Your Prayer Beads

After you collect your supplies, sit down to plan your prayer bead rosary. (This can also be done before you buy supplies.) I decided to make a short, bracelet-sized set of beads that I could carry around with me for use anytime and anywhere. Some people may prefer to make necklaces so their prayer beads can be worn around the neck.

Now, think about what concepts and numbers are the most meaningful to you. Take a few minutes to jot down some ideas. When making my beads, I knew I wanted to work in some Moon and goddess symbolism. I also wanted to work in some sabbat symbolism. In deciding the amount of counting beads to use, I chose the number thirteen, to represent the number of Moons per year. I placed each of the sabbat beads after its Moon month.

After putting together the beads, it's time to create some prayers suited to the rosary's purpose. Generally, it's best to use short and sweet prayers, poems, or sayings that are personally meaningful. The prayers can be something you write yourself or borrow from an inspiring author or poet.

To use the prayer beads, begin by choosing the bead you wish to start from. I use a larger center bead. For the starting prayer,

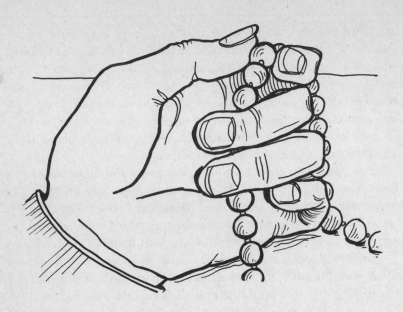

state the intention of your beads. I have used the following: "I honor the great Goddess of 10,000 names and faces. I am her and she is me. Blessed be!"

Then, I move to the Moon beads: "I honor the cycles of the Moon and myself. I am the light. I am the darkness. I am the balance. Blessed be!"

For the counting beads, I want to use something easy to remember, so I repeat the first prayer. For the sabbat beads, I use the names of the goddesses that I feel close to or want to know better.

After going around the loop, I return to the large bead and repeat the prayer one last time with feeling, ending with "So mote it be!"

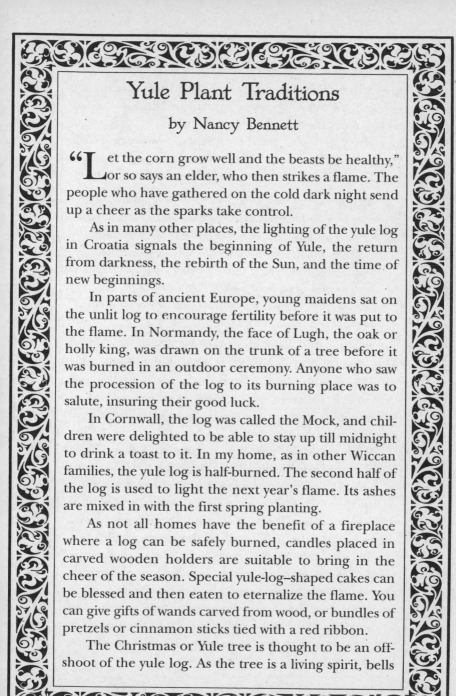

Yule Plant Traditions

by Nancy Bennett

"Let the corn grow well and the beasts be healthy," or so says an elder, who then strikes a flame. The people who have gathered on the cold dark night send up a cheer as the sparks take control.

As in many other places, the lighting of the yule log in Croatia signals the beginning of Yule, the return from darkness, the rebirth of the Sun, and the time of new beginnings.

In parts of ancient Europe, young maidens sat on the unlit log to encourage fertility before it was put to the flame. In Normandy, the face of Lugh, the oak or holly king, was drawn on the trunk of a tree before it was burned in an outdoor ceremony. Anyone who saw the procession of the log to its burning place was to salute, insuring their good luck.

In Cornwall, the log was called the Mock, and children were delighted to be able to stay up till midnight to drink a toast to it. In my home, as in other Wiccan families, the yule log is half-burned. The second half of the log is used to light the next year's flame. Its ashes are mixed in with the first spring planting.

As not all homes have the benefit of a fireplace where a log can be safely burned, candles placed in carved wooden holders are suitable to bring in the cheer of the season. Special yule-log–shaped cakes can be blessed and then eaten to eternalize the flame. You can give gifts of wands carved from wood, or bundles of pretzels or cinnamon sticks tied with a red ribbon.

The Christmas or Yule tree is thought to be an offshoot of the yule log. As the tree is a living spirit, bells are hung on it for reverence. Food and treats are offered to "feed" the tree spirit, and moon-shaped sickle decorations and stars adorn it.

The yule log is not the only plant associated with the midwinter season. Mistletoe holds a sacred place, as Pliny the Elder observed in Roman times:

> *After preparing for a sacrifice and a feast under the oak, they hail the mistletoe as a cure-all and bring two white bulls there, whose horns have never been bound before. A priest dressed in a white robe climbs the oak and with a golden sickle cuts the mistletoe, which is caught in a white cloak. Then they sacrifice the victims, begging the god, who gave them the mistletoe as a gift, to make it propitious for them..."*

The mistletoe was the plant of peace in ancient Scandinavia. If two enemies met by chance beneath it in a forest, they would lay down their weapons and leave each other in peace. Mistletoe was sacred to lovers, and when one stole a kiss from under it, it gave magical peace to the couple.

With mistletoe came a set of rituals. For each kiss a berry should be plucked. When none are left, the magic is gone. If the plant was not burned on the twelfth night, those who kissed beneath it would not wed in the year to come. It was also hung above a baby's cradle to keep fairies from stealing the newborn child.

Though mistletoe is sacred to Yule, care must be taken. The plant is poisonous, especially to young children and pets. Never ingest the berries, even though in olden days they were thought to bring dreams of immortality. If you have concerns about the health of your family, you may want to invest in a fake mistletoe bough.

Holly or ivy—which one enters your home first? And does it matter? In olden times the Holly King and the Ivy Queen would have a ritual chase at Yule—he with his wand of holly and she with her wreath of ivy. Depending on which one crossed the threshold first, either men or women would rule the household for the coming year.

In the ritual chase, the dance comes to a climax when the Ivy Queen allows the Holly King to catch her. She drops her wreath over his wand, symbolizing a coarse kind of fertility for the year. Consider this as a wonderful addition to your Yule party!

The holly's berries are linked to the Goddess. White is for the Moon and red is for her blood. Holly was also sacred to the god Saturn in Roman times, and was associated with time and agriculture. Ivy is feminine, associated with the Greek myth of Cissos, a girl who danced herself to death in reverence to Dionysus. She was granted immortality in the form of a vine that forever twined and grew.

Other plants you may want to consider adding to your Yule include rosemary (scattered on the floor for luck), evergreen boughs (a symbol of life, protection and prosperity), and wreaths or dollies made from wheat (another symbol of life and growth for the coming new year). An incense made of bayberry, cedar, pine, and rosemary is also recommended for any Yule-time rituals.

Fire and light—what Yule would be without them? Make sure you have many candles burning now, using colors of red, gold, green, and silver. Setting up separate altars in each direction helps infuse the mood of the day. In the coldest and darkest time of the year, our ancestors knew how to raise their spirits and remind themselves of the warm times ahead. If you do not have a fireplace, consider these options. If you have a yard and you live in a warm climate, plan a Yule barbeque. Light up the coals and serve some mulled wine.

Take time at Yule to examine your Pagan roots. Salute a log as it is heralded through the forest on a dark and frosty Yule eve. Weave a crown of ivy and make peace beneath the mistletoe.

And don't forget to "let the corn grow well and the beasts be healthy."

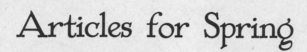

Articles for Spring

The Many-Cultured Snake Goddess

by Mavesper Cy Ceridwen

The snake form is one of the ancient faces of the Goddess. Snakes fascinated our ancestors, who believed the animal was magic. Serpents live in water and underground, and our ancestors believed snakes could fly, so the animal was associated with three of the four elements.

Many cultures worship sacred serpents as symbols of life. Many myths connect snakes to waters and tides. The serpent is also connected with menstrual blood and the female mysteries. It symbolizes sacred sex for religious purposes. In fact, many priestesses in ancient times worshiped snakes as representing the Goddess herself.

It is no coincidence the snake is the animal that symbolizes the Devil in Christian tales. This was calculated to represent the end of the old Great Mother and the power of her priestesses. Today, it is very important for Pagans to reclaim the power of the serpent. Pagans should rewelcome the power of the snake and all this represents: pleasure, freedom, peace, healing, sacred sex, joy, and the celebration of life.

To help us reclaim snake power, I will talk about thirteen snake goddesses from different pantheons around the world. This will help us to see and realize the many forms of the snake in goddess worship.

Tiamat is a primordial Babylonian snake goddess. She is the creator of the world and comes from the waters. She is the lady of dragons and snakes, representing the inner self and the deepest forms of our soul. She is terrible, but at the same time brings healing and love.

Lilith is a dark maiden. Her power and wisdom come from her serpent form, which represents rebirth, regeneration, and eternity. She was hated by many patriarchal nations, but she is beloved in Sumeria. She is capable of bringing us back to sacred sexual pleasure. She is also a source of wisdom, liberty, and protection.

Python is a Greek goddess, sometimes called Delphyne. She is a ancient daughter of the earth, a great snake that knows all from the present, past, and future. Even after the Delphic oracle was usurped by Apollo, Python was still allowed to receive the oracle. We can worship her as a goddess to bring us visions.

Uadzit is the snake goddess of lower Egypt and the Nile delta. She is partner to the goddess Nekhbet (from higher Egypt) in representing the unification of the country. We may reclaim her power to reunite parts of our self. She is a giant snake shaped like the Nile itself and has great fertility power.

Dictynna is the snake goddess of Crete, representing the warrior. The serpent is the symbol of female power and the capacity to be reborn. We can connect to her to reach the strongest power of ourselves.

Hecate is a great mother, also called "the big snake." She is older than the Greek pantheon and originally a triple goddess of Thracia. She is the transformer, capable of opening the initiation door as queen of magic. She is the matron of all Witches and can teach us the best paths to follow.

Nu-Kwa is a Chinese serpent and dragon goddess. She is the ruler of the world who made human beings from mud. To protect her creation, she then created the pillars of the world and the sky and marked the cardinal points with blue stones. She is powerful enough to bring order to our life.

Snake Woman is a sacred goddess to Native American tribes. She is a healer who helps us shed our skins and banish habits, thoughts, or feelings that are no longer healthy or useful to us.

Aida-Wedo is a goddess from the Voodoo traditions of Haiti. She is the rainbow snake who creates a bridge between earth and sky and can make our dreams come true. Her blessings are abundance and harmony.

Ix-Chel is a Mayan snake goddess of the Moon, water, childbirth, and weaving. Her symbol is the dragonfly. She wears a serpent skirt that regenerates. Invoke her when you wish to became pregnant or to be creative.

Cobra Grande (or "big snake") is an indigenous Brazilian goddess that made the world as we know it. Once upon a time, the world was different and Cobra Grande did not like it. She swallowed everything and then regurgitated things as they are nowadays. Her body is the Amazon River itself. She is a good goddess to ask for empowerment and to help make things go differently.

Gefjon, a Scandinavian giant snake goddess, represents the virgin and the generous earth. She is an old form of Freya that is especially considered a protectress.

Brighid is a celtic goddess connected with serpent wisdom. In her myth, serpents are symbols of physical healing and connecting with waters. Brighid can heal our inner child by giving us spiritual improvement.

Snake goddesses are very rich in power, knowledge, protection, and healing. Make your personal way to these goddesses, and remember always that the serpent is sacred to Witches. It is a good idea to have some contact occasionally with real snakes. As Pagans, we have to reclaim the sacred snake within.

The Magical Isle of Arran

by Neil Campbell

On the west coast of Scotland, the Isle of Arran rises from the misty waters of the Firth of Clyde. With its green, fertile lowlands, rocky peaks, and rich coastline, Arran epitomizes the character and beauty of Scotland. Believed to be the paradise of the Celts, and also the fabled Avalon, Arran has a unique and magical heritage.

The deity most associated with Arran is Manannan, a Celtic sea god. Manannan, also known as Manannan Mac Lir and Manawydden, is the protector of the Isle of Arran and ferryman to the "land of promise," as the island was known in Celtic times. Manannan is also described as a shape-shifting magician, sometimes turning into a seabird. Draped in a cloak that can change color and is pinned with a silver brooch, and wearing a golden helmet adorned with two magic jewels that are as bright as the sun, Manannan's appearance is striking. Along with impenetrable armor, Manannan is said to have special weapons: two spears called Yellow Shaft and Red Javelin, and three magical swords called Great Fury, Little Fury, and the Retaliator.

As lord of the sea, Manannan possesses a boat called the Wave Sweeper that is steered not by rudder but by the will of its passenger. Celtic tales also speak of Manannan riding out from Arran on a chariot pulled by his magnificent steed, Anobarr, "the Splendid Mane." It was written that his magical horse travels over both water and land quicker than the spring wind.

On the Isle of Arran, Manannan has a sacred apple grove where the magical silver apple branch is found. He also has a palace on Arran called "Emhain of the Apple Trees," where he sits upon a conch shell throne. Once every thirty-three years, Manannan holds a great feast in his palace that grants immortality to those who attend. The Feast of Age, as it is known, fed the Tuatha De Danaan and granted them eternal life.

In addition to being the Celtic paradise, Arran is believed to be the fabled Avalon of Arthurian myth. The earliest written accounts of Avalon come from the twelfth-century clergyman Geoffrey of Monmouth in his *Historia Regum Brittaniae* and *Vita Merlini*. In the latter text, Arthur is ferried to the island by Manannan. Some tales say that Arthur died on Avalon; others suggest Arthur lies waiting to lead the people once again. On Goatfell, the island's 2,867-foot-high peak, a silhouetted outline called the Sleeping Warrior perpetuates the idea of Arthur enjoying a period of magical rejuvenation on the island.

Said to be skilled in the magical arts, Manannan carries with him a crane-skin pouch. In it, he keeps an assortment of objects pertinent to his craft, such as the Cup of Truth. In his palace he keeps his greatest magical tool, a cauldron of magnificent regenerative power. Such "cauldrons of plenty," as they are known in Celtic tales, are thought to be the inspiration behind the Holy Grail. Many people believe that the actual Holy Grail was brought by the Knights Templar to rest on the opposite side of Scotland, beneath Rosslyn Chapel in Fife. One of Arran's many stone circles is also connected to a cauldron myth. A double stone circle on the island is known as the Suidhe Choir

Fhionn or "Fingal's Cauldron Seat." In the outer circle there stands a stone with a hole through it, where, legend says, the giant Fingal tied up his hound Bran. In the inner circle, Fingal, sometimes known as Finn or Fionn, sat cooking using a great cauldron. The mythological figure of Fingal is also associated with a large cave on Arran.

Fingal's Cave was the setting for one of Scotland's most memorable tales. In 1307 AD, Scotland was under oppressive English rule and the Pope in Rome had excommunicated the entire nation of Scotland. Robert the Bruce, the rightful king of Scotland and a close associate of William Wallace (the figure depicted in the film Braveheart), had sought refuge on Arran. Robert, with his small band of followers, was fighting against the tyranny of the English King Edward. Battle-weary and dejected, he met an old clairvoyant woman who told him that he would lead Scotland to freedom. She then ordered her two sons to join his liberating band of warriors. He nevertheless remained unconvinced and pessimistic.

Then, while hiding out in Fingal's Cave, he watched a small spider trying to spin a web. Each attempt ended in failure but the spider persevered. This display of determination and fortitude shown by the *wee beastie* left a deep and enduring impression on him, from which ensued several more years of freedom fighting. On Midsummer's day in 1314, although heavily out numbered, Robert the Bruce, together with his small band of followers and some of the Knights Templar, led his homeland to freedom at the battle of Bannockburn.

In Arran's Lamlash village bay is the Holy Isle, a smaller island that was inhabited 1,500 years ago by the Irish Saint Molaise. At the tender age of fourteen, the young saint began his formal training and embarked on a monastic life. Towards the end of the sixth century he used a cave on the Holy Isle as a refuge for prayer and meditation. Near the cave is St. Molaise's well, which is claimed to have healing power. Within the cave, Pictish symbols suggest that the cave was used even before the saint's time. Historically important Viking runes are also inscribed on the cave walls, a reminder of the four hundred year period during which Arran was ruled by the Vikings.

During that period, the Viking's social and religious customs blended with that of the islanders. Evidence of this can be found in some of the island's place names, burial mounds, and runic inscriptions. Indeed, the most notable of the Viking rulers was called Magnus Barelegs (so-called because he wore a Scottish kilt). The Viking runes in the cave tell of Viking King Haakon's fighting forces. It appears the runes were inscribed hours before the Vikings were defeated by the Scots in the Battle of Largs.

The Vikings, along with the Picts and the Celts, have undoubtedly left their mark on Arran. The summit of the Holy Isle was still used for Beltane fires up until the nineteenth century, a testimony to the depth of the Celtic traditions.

The history of Arran took another turn when in 1992 the Holy Isle was purchased by the Samy Ling Buddhist Center. This Tibetan Buddhist monk community lives on the Holy Isle, thus reestablishing the island as a place of prayer and meditation.

Today on Arran, in addition to the Buddhist presence there are echoes of a Pagan Celtic past. Two new indigenous species of Rowan tree were recently found on the island. Rowan, long considered a favorite of the fairy folk, remains the wood of choice for magical tools today. The tree has a long-standing association with Arran: one of the island's villages, Lochranza, means "Loch of the Rowan Tree."

During sabbats and esbats, modern Celtic Pagans can be found at the standing stones and sacred sites performing their rites and rituals in worshipping the ancient mighty ones. Some of them may even tell you that the magic has returned to Arran, but I would argue that it never really left. Like Manannan, the magic has only altered its form.

Arran is, and always has been, a magical isle.

The Magic of Roses

by Denise Dumars

Who doesn't love roses? They are, after all, the very symbol of romance and love.

First cultivated by the Chinese, roses made their way across Asia where they not only were prized for their beauty in Persia, but figured significantly in that culture's cuisine, just as they do to this day. From there, they traveled to Egypt, then to Europe, where they were cultivated widely. Today, the Bulgarian rose fields are the premier world source of perfume-grade rose oil.

Roses are native to the northern hemisphere. It is believed that there were no roses in Australia, New Zealand, or other southern hemisphere countries not physically connected to the northern hemisphere until immigrants from the British Isles brought them to those lands.

Rose Lore

Folk customs give different meanings to different colors of roses. When I was a child, the custom was to wear a rose on Mother's Day. If your mother was living, you wore a red rose; if she had passed on, you wore a white one. Perhaps this custom had its origins in China, the original cultivator of roses, in which the color white is worn at funerals.

Giving roses also had symbolic meaning. Red roses indicated passionate love, ardor, and lust. They were appropriate for Valentine's Day, or any day when love was expressed between two people. A new suitor, however, would do better to send pink roses, as red ones might be assuming too much at the beginning of a relationship.

Pink roses are great for friends' birthdays and other celebrations, as pink is the color of friendship. Some people love white roses and find themselves spiritually connected to them, seeing white roses as a symbol of piety. The followers of the orisha Obatala, for example, favor white roses. White roses also symbolize peace.

Many people are also fond of yellow roses. They have perhaps the most expressive scent of all the roses. Hybridization for color, size, and shape has all but eliminated scent from other hybrid roses, but now rose fanciers are beginning to breed roses specifically for their scent.

Roses can decorate the altars of many deities. For example, red roses are suitable for Aphrodite, Venus, Eros, Bacchus, Hathor, Parvati, Lakshmi, and Erzulie. White roses are appropriate for Sarisvati, Shiva, Obatala, Hella, and Osiris. Pink roses are suitable for Isis, Cupid, and Rhiannon. Yellow roses are appropriate for Oshun, Brigid, and Al-Lat. Blue roses (which are actually lavender, as no true blue rose exists in nature) are suitable for Yemaya, Nuit, and Mari.

The rose was associated with the Goddess, so when Europe became Christianized, church leaders originally banned roses. They chose the lily as the symbol of Mary, but as the many rose windows in churches testify, the rose became more favored as a symbol of Mary.

The blossom of the rose has been used as a symbol in literature and art to represent the heart, the triple goddess, the mandala, and peace. In Apuleius' story "The Golden Ass," the hero, who has been turned into a donkey, sees a vision of Isis and eats some roses, thereby turning himself back into a man.

Rose Treatments

Alchemists call the red rose "masculine," and the white rose "feminine," and they use the two to symbolize the male-female duality in their rituals. In Bach flower remedies, Rock Rose is used to alleviate states of hysteria and to prevent nightmares. Wild Rose is used to treat those who have resigned themselves to their circumstances and have lost the desire to try and improve their condition.

The aromatherapist Robert Tisserand uses rose aromatherapy oil to treat many ailments, including liver and gallbladder problems, impotency (when it has no physical cause), emotional problems, and skin disorders. Anyone who has used rosewater and glycerin hand lotion can testify to its ability to soften skin and improve skin texture.

Virtually any book of magic will include love magic utilizing roses, so below you will find a few other magical ways to use this precious flower and its attar, or essential oil. Rose oil is very expensive, but highly diluted—and thus more affordable. Rose attar or oil is available in a carrier oil such as jojoba. For aromatherapy uses, use real rose products, not synthetics. For some magical uses, the synthetics are all right, but the genuine item is always preferred.

Rose Nightmare Dispelling

If you are plagued by nightmares, or have restless sleep or general trouble sleeping, try this "rose remedy." Smudge the bedroom with rose incense or use a diffuser with diluted rose oil in it a few hours before you go to bed. Just before bedtime, place vases of fresh roses (the more aromatic the better) around your bedroom. Say the following words before retiring:

Nightmares begone,
Restful sleep come to me.
Roses beautiful, roses true,
Guard my rest,
Bring me peace.

Keep the roses in the room until they start to wilt, then remove them promptly. Do this spell at least once a month or whenever nightmares return.

Rose Sadness Dispelling

Buy a small amount of natural rose oil. Use a few drops in a diffuser to scent your home. At a Middle Eastern store or a well-stocked supermarket, buy pomegranate juice and rose water. While the rose oil is heating up and starting to scent the room, mix together in a blender a cup of pomegranate juice, a teaspoon (or more to taste) of rosewater, and a few ice cubes. Blend the mixture until smooth; you may also add blueberries or raspberries to taste if you wish.

Sip this smoothie slowly, feeling a connection with the ancients who knew the magic of roses and pomegranates. Inhale the rose aroma.

Sit down in a comfortable place. Close your eyes, take a few deep breaths, and visualize your sadness dropping from your shoulders like a worn-out cloak. Feel free and renewed. Then continue to sip the smoothie, being mindful of its taste. Feel it soothing and calming you internally.

Repeat as necessary, adding Bach flower essences Rock Rose and Rescue Remedy if you wish.

Rose Peace at Home Spell

If loved ones or roommates are squabbling at home, buy a bouquet of white roses. Put them in a vase in a prominent part of the home where everyone will see them, such as the kitchen table. When you are home alone, stand before the roses and say:

White roses of peace,
Bless my living space
And all of those within.
Let us understand each other's needs,
And live serenely with each other.
Peace be with this house,
And strife be gone.

If you wish you can also burn a peaceful home candle that you have anointed with a little rose oil.

Rose Self-Esteem Spell

Buy a body lotion that contains rosewater or rose oil. Stand before the mirror as you use the lotion to massage your hands, arms, throat, and shoulders. You can also use it on the face, but in some people this may cause the skin to break out.

If you wish, place a statue of a patron goddess, such as Isis, Mary, or Venus, before the mirror as well. As you use the lotion, repeat the simple phrase: "I am beautiful, and I am loved."

Repeat this phrase several times until you feel you really mean it. Use this lotion and a rose-based perfume any time you wish to go out and feel extra-appealing. Do this simple ritual often to improve your self-esteem.

Transformative Serpent Energy

by Linda Fourbister

O rder dissolves into chaos, which is then attacked and subdued to return to order. This is the eternal cycle of transformation. For me, the concept of transformation triggers the image of the serpent. Since prehistoric times, this image has signaled change, whether it is seasonal renewal or a major shift from one era to the next. Understanding the serpentine image of transformation can help us prepare for the changes in our lives, the ebb and flow of chaos and order.

From Change of Season to Change of Era

As long ago as the Ice Age, people linked the serpent to seasonal renewal, to the fertility that emerges from winter's dark. An Ice Age baton shows two snakes, two seals, a salmon, and a flower—all images of spring. The baton was carved by the last of the hunter-gathers, the Magdalenian people of prehistoric Europe (17,000–11,000 BC). In Ice Age Europe, early spring (mid-April to May) was the time that the local grass snakes emerged from hibernation to mate. As I looked into such images, I found that the association of snakes with seasonal renewal continued for centuries.

In Celtic mythology, the goddess, Brigit, took the form of a snake emerging from her mound on Imbolc, around February 1, the first day of the Celtic spring. In the 1880s, an aphorism that was recorded in the Scottish highlands stated that the queen would emerge from the mound on St. Bride's Day, and

that if no one molested her, she would harm no one. In Lithuania, the people celebrated the "Day of Serpents" on January 25 as the beginning of spring renewal. They prepared food for the snakes and invited them into their homes. The early Lithuanians showed reverence to Saule, their Sun goddess, by taking care of her sacred green snake. She would be generous to families who treated her snake with kindness, but treated as sacrilege the killing of a snake.

In Norse cosmology, the world serpent, Jormungand, lived at the bottom of the ocean, where it grew so long that it encircled the world, biting its own tail. The Norse believed in cycles of creation, with the end of the world occurring at Ragnarok. At this time, Jormungand will rise out of the sea and kill the god Thor. The earth will sink into the sea, then rise again in a new cycle of creation. Maya myth also predicts this end-of-the world-cycle.

A change from one era to the next may be signaled by a hero killing a snake. One of the earliest myths in the world comes from ancient Mesopotamia. The Babylonian epic of creation, the *Enuma Elish*, recounts the tale of how the hero, Marduk, slew the Mother Goddess, Tiamat. Tiamat was known as the serpent goddess of the watery abyss and personified the sea. Marduk killed Tiamat by driving an evil wind into her

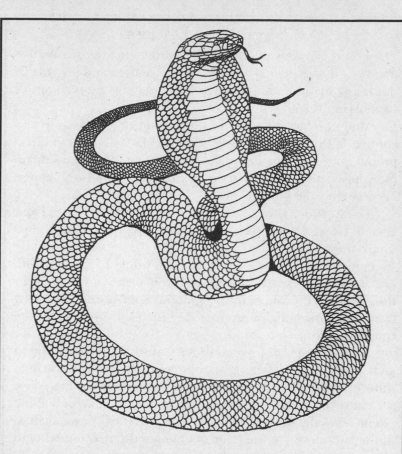

mouth, then splitting her body like a shellfish, creating the sky and the earth from the two parts.

Originally, Tiamat was the goddess of creation. However, after the Assyrian conquest, she was demoted and considered the primary force of chaos. The myth of her destruction by Marduk served to vilify the old goddesses and support the gods of the conquerors.

A similar motif occurs in Greek mythology. Apollo killed Gaia's python at Delphi and Perseus cut off the head of the snake-haired Medusa. Mythologist Robert Graves believes that such myths reflect how the patriarchal Hellenes invaded Greece in the second millennium BC, challenging the power of the triple goddess.

Serpents in Dreams

These early images and myths illustrate the transformative nature of the serpent. They can help us understand the role of this image in our dreams. Snakes are among the most common symbols in dreams.

Although the meaning of any dream depends upon the context of the dream (among other factors), a common interpretation of a dream about a serpent is that it indicates metamorphosis and transformation. Snakes symbolize change because they shed their skins.

The healing power of a dream about serpents dates from ancient Greece. Serpents were kept in the temples of Asclepius, where they were encouraged to lick the patients as part of the "sleeping cure." It was believed that they would heal the dreamers. Serpents were also associated with fertility. There is an inscription at Epidaurus from a grateful woman who conceived twins after dreaming of intercourse with a snake—a major life transformation.

Psychologist Carl Jung considered the snake to be a potent archetype of psychic energy, power, and psychic and spiritual transformation. In dreams, the snake may indicate that a transformative process is already underway, or it may be calling attention to the need to move to a new level of consciousness. Rather than evoking the fear of change, the dreamer should recognize that change is called for at this time.

Serpents in Ritual

Snakes were common in religious ceremonies in ancient cultures such as in Greece. The fear brought on by snakes, and the effects of their venom, may have figured prominently in their spiritual function.

A major Greek ritual practiced at the Thesmophoria festival celebrated the Mother Goddess, Demeter, and her daughter, Persephone. During this festival, exclusively for women, figures of serpents made of flour were thrown into a snake-invested chamber. The Thesmophoria was enacted to restore the fertility of the fields, with the serpents again representing the energy of transformation.

Snakes are very common in hallucinations as well as in myths and dreams. When the shamans of the Amazon jungle drink the hallucinogen *ayahuasca*, their most common visions are of serpents.

Near-death experiences can lead one to spiritual awakening. People who have survived the bite of venomous snakes often report that they felt passive and unconcerned about their life and safety after the initial feeling of fear and panic. It is quite possible that snake venom, because of its tendency to force an opening in awareness and consciousness, was used in ancient times to initiate a spiritual connection to the expansion that occurs in death.

You may wish to use images of serpents in your ritual where change is indicated. Some practitioners use actual serpents in honor of the Goddess.

In prehistoric times, people associated the snake with the power of the Goddess, symbolizing the transformative cycle of nature. Nature is never static or linear. It continually renews itself in changed form. The symbol of the snake captures this essence.

Welsh Beltane Customs

by Sorita

Beltane is known in Wales as *Calan Mai*, the first day of May, and was formerly known as *Calan Haf*, the first day of Summer. It was one of the *ysprydnos* or "spirit nights," when the fairy and spirits of the dead roamed the land. Protection bonfires were made on May Eve in a traditional manner that we can still follow today, as this ritual is full of the symbolism of our Pagan ancestors.

Nine men would turn out their pockets, removing all money and every piece of metal from their persons. They would then go to the nearest woods and collect sticks from nine different types of trees. The sticks were carried to the place where the fire would be built, a circle having been cut out of the turf. The sticks were set crosswise, effectively making a wheel of different woods. When this was built up, one of the men would rub two pieces of oak together until he kindled a flame. He would light the *coelcerth* (bonfire) from the burning oak.

This removal of metal was performed as a gesture to the fairies or spirits of the woods. The symbolism of nine men and nine sacred woods also honors the spirits. It is interesting to see that crosses were made across the circle, for this recalls the symbol we now use for planet Earth. It also resembles the Wheel of the Year.

Other customs surrounded the Beltane coelcerth. Round cakes made from oatmeal and brown meal were broken into quarters and placed in a bag. Everyone present had to pick out a piece, the last piece being taken by the bag-holder. Every person who picked a piece of brown meal cake had to leap three times over the flames, or run three times between the fires if there were two.

This ensured a plentiful harvest for the coming autumn. The people who picked pieces of oatmeal cake sang, danced, and clapped to encourage the people who had to brave the fires.

When two bonfires were made, flocks of sheep and herds of cows were also driven between the fires to purify them and ensure there was no disease in the animals. This may also have been done to encourage fertility and ensure a plentiful supply of meat, milk, and wool in the coming months.

The ashes from the fires were taken home to protect the hearth from disease and negative magic. Placing a few ashes in a shoe was thought to protect the wearer from any great sorrows in the coming year.

A curious custom practiced by jilted lovers was playing the straw man (*gware gr gwellt*). A young man who had lost his sweetheart to another would make a straw effigy of the new lover and place it near the window of the unfaithful girl, or in a prominent place near her house. A letter was often pinned onto the effigy, resulting in a fight at the May fair. This custom echoes the battle of Gwynn Ap Nudd and Gwythyr, and of Lleu and Gronw over the flower maiden Blodeuwedd in the Mabinogion.

Hawthorn (*draenen wen*, or whitethorn) trees or boughs from them were often planted outside the home at Beltane as a protection from the fairy folk. Although it was unlucky to take this tree into the home, putting the "fairy tree" outside the home was thought to help one avert the mischief of the fairies. Houses were also adorned with greenery and flowers on the outside, in order to celebrate the coming of summer and the new growth in nature. This included the Mayflower (probably the cowslip, *briallu Mair*), rowan (*cerdinen*) and birch (*bedwen*) twigs.

Carols were also sung on Beltane morning. Singers would visit families early in the morning and sing happy songs celebrating the approach of summer and the expectations of fruitful times ahead. This was known as "singing under the wall" (*canu dan y pared*) or "summer singing" (*canu haf*). Talented singers would also incorporate major events that had occurred to the family during the past year, making a ballad of positive reflection to lead the way for more good times to come. If the family enjoyed the singing, the singers would be invited in for food and drink—and possibly money.

The custom of erecting a Maypole was known in South Wales as raising the birch (*Codi'r Bedwen*). Some parts of Wales concentrated more on the Summer Solstice, raising their "summer branch" (*y gangen haf*) at this time of year. The maypoles would be brightly decorated with different colors of paint, flowers, and ribbons. Several maypoles were raised in different parts of a town or village, and the young men and women would dance from pole to pole, "threading the needle" as it was known.

The role of the Fool (*Cadi*) leading these celebrations was considered a great honor. Men would adorn themselves with as many brightly colored ribbons as possible in order to be chosen. The man who got to play the part would wear a mixture of men's and women's clothing. His top half would be dressed in men's clothes, and he wore petticoats around his waist. The Cadi would also wear a mask or have his face blackened. The role of the Cadi was to act as marshal, orator, buffoon, and money collector.

May Day was the official opening of the *twmpath chwarae*, or the tump for playing (a tump being a small hillock or mound). Through the summer months, villagers could gather on the twmpath chwarae in the evenings to dance and play various sports. The green was usually situated on the top of a hill, and musicians sat on a mound. Branches of oak were sometimes used to decorate the mound, and the people would dance in a circle around it.

A custom that was thought to bring much good luck on Beltane morning was the skimming of the wells. Because the earth was thought to be particularly charged with magic at this time, wells at sacred sites were particularly fortunate. The water skimmed from the top of the well after sunrise was thought to have healing and protective properties, blessing the luck and fortune of the person who partook of it. This caused many farmers to guard their wells, as it was believed that other people could steal your luck and fortune if they skimmed the water off before you did.

Another Beltane morning custom concerning water was the use of the morning dew. It was believed that if a woman washed her face with the first dew of Beltane morning it would ensure her beauty remained with her throughout her life.

Magical Amulets for Babies

by Dallas Jennifer Cobb

As parents, we have an instinctual need to protect our children. As Pagans we often use magic and ritual in our daily workings. The practice of using amulets to protect and bless babies and children is as ancient as the roots of Paganism.

Specifically intended for Pagan parents and parents-to-be, this article will help you explore some of the ancient magical traditions for protecting children.

What Is an Amulet?

An amulet is an object that has been ritually charged with energy and is believed to have magical powers. The object is then placed near the person or place it is meant to protect. It can be carried by a person, worn as jewelry, hung near cradles or beds, placed on an altar or mantel, or mounted over the door of a house.

Many amulets for babies and young children are worn on the body and are charged with positive energy to protect against evil and to prolong their lives.

Historically, most amulets were made of simple organic materials such as animal skins, bones, pottery bits, shells, or plant matter. Herbs were also used as amulets or in amulets. Rue (*Ruta graveolens*) was commonly used in children's amulets. The strong smell of rue was thought to ward off illness, and the eye-shaped fruits invoked the Mother Goddess's protection. A sprig of rue was hung over the cradle or pinned to clothing.

Over time, the materials have evolved to include metals, glass, stone, and highly artistic designs. Many people still practice the historic tradition of wearing an amulet bag made of soft leather into which they place their own magical objects and sacred items.

Amulets for babies and children were historically used to ward off the evil eye—a traditional belief that people have the power in their gaze alone to injure or destroy people or possessions dear to someone else. In Arabic the word for evil eye means "envy." Because children are valued and loved dearly, they were considered to be something that someone could envy. Hence, children needed protection.

The *mano fico* has traditionally been used for magical protection from the evil eye, as it resembles ancient hand gestures that ward off evil. With index and baby finger extended and the other fingers curled in, the hand is made to look like the *labia* or lips of the vulva through which the child passed into life, or the sacred Yoni of the Mother Goddess, bestowing protection and creative energy.

In the Middle East, the hand is known as "hamsa hand" or "hamesh hand." Among Arabs, it is known as the hand of Fatima, and among Jews, the hand of Miriam.

Amulets Around the World

Amulets have been found in virtually every country of the world. In Greece, Turkey, Egypt, and parts of the Middle East, the most common form is a blue glass eye charm that "mirrors back" the blue of the evil eye, thus "confounding" it. The shape represents the all-seeing eye, eye-in-hand, and the eye of the god Horus. This was commonly worn for magical protection.

In Roman society, the hand of power was often formed into a sculpture that was placed on the home altar to protect the home and the entire family. It was often made of metal and incorporated sacred writings and stones. In North Africa, an eye-shaped agate stone is used in conjunction with the hamsa hand design.

In India, the blue bead is combined with a cord charm and placed on newborn babies. In time, the cord wears and breaks, and the blue bead is lost. At this time, the child is considered old enough to protect him- or herself to some degree. In India, among the Kalbeliya Gypsies, there is also a practice of sewing small pieces of mirror into clothing in order to mirror back any negative energy or spells.

In Europe and North America, it is common to find tiger's-eye stones or cat's-eye shells made into jewelry and worn as magical protection charms.

In China, the practice of giving children amulets of red cord is common. These are often combined with sacred symbols tied on a red cord and hung near the cradle. Red clothing is believed to bring good fortune and prosperity.

A Short History of Magical Amulets for Babies

Called an apotropaic charm (from the word *apotropous*, which means "to turn away"), many amulets for babies and children have their roots specifically in warding off negative or evil energy.

The Kelsey Museum of Archaeology has a collection of amulets dating back as far as the Neolithic era. The amulets were invocations to the Mother Goddess to protect the energy of creation and procreation: breast-feeding mothers and their babies, fruit-bearing trees, milk-giving animals, and the sperm of men. The mother is known as Isis, Diana, and Selene. Her color is red like the birth blood that gives life to all.

Traditionally, amulets were made of a variety of materials. Silver was sacred to the Moon goddess Luna. Blood coral was sacred to the sea goddess Venus and representative of the blood of Isis. Horn or tusk represented the Moon due to its a lunar shape, and glass or clay beads (sometimes dyed with ochre) were reminiscent of blood and earth.

The shape of amulets varies widely. Historically, the shape of the vulva, representing the Mother Goddess, was used. This shape morphed into the mano fico, or fig hand, in areas influenced by the later waves of Christianity. In areas where Catholicism was predominant, the shape became known as "the most powerful hand of God" or *mano poderosa.*

The horseshoe has its origins as a symbol of luck and protection in the invocation of the protective and fertile vulva of the Mother Goddess who guarded against loss or damage to the energy of creation. The Moon goddess was invoked to protect babies, nursing mothers, and milk animals, so the shape of her lunar crescent was used as an apotropaic charm.

Making and Using an Amulet

Making an amulet to protect your baby or young child is a very personal rite. Ultimately, the amulet is as effective as the intention we put into it, as powerful as our love for our children.

The simplest amulet is made from thread or cord. Red is the most commonly used color, with blue running second.

Choose a cord made from natural fibers that is relatively soft to the baby's skin, yet durable. Take your time choosing the cord, and find something that feels right.

Carry the cord with you for several days and start to charge it with your energy of love and protection. Carry it perhaps in a pocket over your heart to absorb the fiercely protective love that parents feel for their children. Meditate often on the cord, its role as protector, and envision the strength of your love flowing into the cord.

Many people like to make a knotted cord protection charm. Each time they tie a knot into the cord they incant protection, safety, and abundance, speaking always in the positive and never naming the negative energies they are trying to protect their child from.

You may choose to tie a symbolic shape to the cord—something that represents protection to you, be it the sacred vulva of the Mother Goddess, a sprig of rue, or some rowan wood.

You may also write blessings and incorporate the written spells into the amulet or charm.

Do not limit yourself. Throughout history amulets have been worn as necklaces, incorporated into clothing, painted on buildings, or hung in in personal spaces.

Cord Magic

There are many rituals of protection involving cords or threads:

Red cords are placed around the neck or wrist of babies in eastern Europe, China, and India to protect them.

In an old Jewish custom, a red thread was placed on a baby to protect it from evil.

In Mexico a "deer's eye" seed is hung on a tasseled red cord over a baby's crib to ward off the evil eye.

At a ritual gathering, each of the people close to the infant bring a bead, and as they state their blessing tie the bead onto a cord that will become a bracelet, necklace, or ritual charm for the child.

You may wish to organize a formal baby blessing or welcoming of spirit.

Making Vine Pentacles

by Granny Green Witch

Her very essence sings pure beauty. Her newly opened blossoms hypnotize us with their aromas and her ground cover greets our feet as we gently walk upon it.

How often do we take time out to explore all the breathtaking beauty of Mother Nature? Have you ever explored the inside and outside of a seed pod? Have you touched and studied her vines? Have you painted her rocks or woven her leaves? If any of these things sounds interesting or fun to you, then join me on a journey of spirituality through nature crafts.

In this creation segment, we are going to create a vine pentacle to adorn your altar room or personal oasis. Remember as you create your vine pentacle, it does not by any means need to be perfect. It is rather a symbol of your joining with the Goddess, and imperfections often only add to the beauty.

A Few Things You Will Need

A pair of handclippers

A twenty-foot piece of vine

A ten-foot piece of vine

A one-foot piece of jute rope or twine

For this project your vine pentacle is going to be about eighteen inches wide, so the vine will need to be between one-half and three-quarters of an inch in diameter.

In the future, you will be able to make size adjustments to your vine pentacles by just adding and subtracting the vine and its width.

Step 1: Hold one end of your vine and circle it over to make an eighteen-inch circle. You will have plenty of vine left.

Step 2: Now take the other end of the vine and wrap it in and out of the circle you made three times. Cut off any excess vine and place your circle in front of you.

Step 3: Cut five pieces from your ten-foot piece of vine about three inches wider than your circle on both sides. Then run the cut pieces through the wraps on the vine circle to form a pentacle.

Step 4: Take your piece of jute, small rope, or twine and tie it on the top of your pentacle as a hanger.

Here are a few other ideas you can add to fancy up your pentacle wreath.

Add colored ribbons to the corresponding points.

Add strings of bells.

Hang a crystal or gem in the center.

Add fresh flowers, leaves, or seed pods.

Or just get downright creative!

Folklore and Legends of Wales

by Sharynne NicMhacha

The folklore and legends of Wales are beautiful and mysterious, and offer a very rich source of information about the Celtic otherworld.

To the Celts, the otherworld was all around us. It always existed but was easier to access at certain times of year or at certain places. It was located either underground or underwater, on an island across the water, or under the sea. In Wales, the otherworld was known as *Annwn* or *Annwfn*, which may mean "inner" or "under" world, or even "not-world" (referring to the mirror-like aspects of the Celtic divine realms, which are different from our own).

Annwn could be accessed by visiting sacred bodies of water (lakes, rivers, wells) or fairy mounds (*sedd* in Welsh, *síd* in Irish). Sacred assemblies were held at these sites, and there were traditions that if one slept on a fairy mound, one would have an otherworld encounter for good or for bad (depending on one's relationship with the spirits).

The old gods and goddesses were the original inhabitants of the fairy mounds, later becoming the "fairies" of folklore tradition. However, the Celts didn't refer to them as fairies. In Wales, they were called *plant Annwn* ("the children of the other-/under-world"), *gwragedd Annwn* ("the women of Annwn") or *plant Rhys ddwfn* ("the children of Rhys the deep").

In later times, they were called *y yylwyth teg*, the "fair/beautiful family/tribe" (which may be a word play or misunderstanding of the English word fairy). They were sometimes also called *tylwyth Gwynn,* the tribe of Gwynn (a word meaning "white," "fair" or "sacred"). Gwynn ap Nudd was an early ruler of Annwn, and he led the wild hunt for the supernatural boar known as Torc Trwyth. In one tale, he abducts a beautiful woman called Creiddylad. Arthur decides that Gwynn and another suitor must fight for her every May Day until the end of time.

The old gods and goddesses of Wales (or early Britain) were also called *plant Dôn,* the children of Dôn, who was a primal goddess or ancestress. She had a number of divine offspring, including Arianrhod ("silver wheel," a Moon goddess), Gwydion (a divine magician), Amaethon ("divine ploughman"), and Gofannon ("divine smith"). Other early British gods and goddesses may have been ancient inhabitants of Annwn as well. This list includes Epona ("divine horse goddess"), Maponus ("divine son"), Belenus ("bright or healing one"), Cernunnos ("horned one"), and Taranis ("the thunderer").

One of the most famous Welsh legends about Annwn is a kind of Welsh version of the Lady of the Lake legend. Female spirits or goddesses were believed to inhabit most bodies of water (including lakes, wells, and rivers). In this tale, "Llynn y Fan Fach," a young man is tending his cattle on the banks of a lake on the Black Mountain. He sees a beautiful young woman combing her hair, appearing to sit right on the surface of the water. She is so beautiful that he doesn't know what to say or do. He offers her some of his barley bread, but she rejects it, saying:

Cras dy fara, nid hawdd fy nala. ("Hard is thy bread, it is not easy to catch me.")

The lad goes home and tells his mother what he has seen. She makes moist bread for him, which he offers to the fairy maiden the next day. This time, though, she says:

Llaith dy fara, ti ni fynna. ("Moist is thy bread, I do not want thee.")

He goes home, crestfallen. This time, his mother makes half-baked bread. After the lad waits all day, finally the woman appears just before sunset. She accepts the bread and agrees to his offer of marriage on one condition: If he strikes her three times without just cause, she will leave him forever. They are married and live happily for many years. The woman bears him three fine sons.

Years later, when they are going to a baby blessing, the young man taps her to hurry—this is the first causeless blow. Another time, she cries at a wedding, and he taps her again. She replies that she was crying for the young couple's upcoming troubles. Finally, he taps her when she is laughing at a funeral (the person's troubles were over), and she disappears into the lake. The husband and sons are heartbroken, and wander a long time searching for her.

One day she appears to the eldest son, and tells him that his path is to heal the sick. She gives him a bag full of medical cures and herbs and reveals to him the healing properties of the plants. This eldest son and his three sons become famous healers. They write down their medical knowledge (which came from Annwn) in three medieval manuscripts in the twelfth century called *Meddygon Myddfai*. This family remains powerful healers for the next five hundred years, and distant descendants of the family still uphold the tradition to this day.

As late as the 1800s, people visited the site on August 1, the day that signalled the coming of the Lady of the Lake. This date corresponds with a Celtic feast day known elsewhere as Lugnasad, the beginning of the harvest. Other wonderful folk customs took place in Wales during the year.

Candlemas: Candles were lit in the windows to symbolize the coming of spring. Sometimes two candles were lit on the table, and each member of the family would take turns sitting on a chair between the candles. After taking a drink from a drinking horn or goblet, they would throw the vessel backwards over their head. If it landed upright, it meant long life.

May Day (*Calan Haf*): People gathered on a hilltops or village green and created a small mound on which a musician sat. It was decorated with oak branches, and people danced in a circle around the mound. Fires were lit from nine types of sacred wood, and the house was decorated with hawthorn, rowan, or birch.

Midsummer: A sacred pole or tree called the "summer birch" was raised in each area and guarded all night long against theft by another village. In the morning, people danced around the birch. There were also bonfires and divination. St. John's wort and mugwort were used to purify the home.

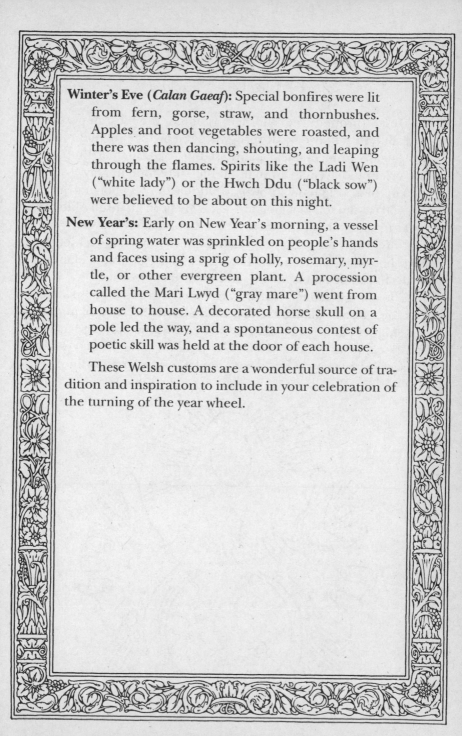

Winter's Eve (*Calan Gaeaf*): Special bonfires were lit from fern, gorse, straw, and thornbushes. Apples and root vegetables were roasted, and there was then dancing, shouting, and leaping through the flames. Spirits like the Ladi Wen ("white lady") or the Hwch Ddu ("black sow") were believed to be about on this night.

New Year's: Early on New Year's morning, a vessel of spring water was sprinkled on people's hands and faces using a sprig of holly, rosemary, myrtle, or other evergreen plant. A procession called the Mari Lwyd ("gray mare") went from house to house. A decorated horse skull on a pole led the way, and a spontaneous contest of poetic skill was held at the door of each house.

These Welsh customs are a wonderful source of tradition and inspiration to include in your celebration of the turning of the year wheel.

Wesak, World Peace Festival

by Elizabeth Hazel

Wesak (pronounced WE-sock) is one of the most important Buddhist holy days. It recognizes the birth, enlightenment, and release from physical manifestation of Gautama Buddha. This celebration is held annually at the Full Moon in May.

The man originally known as Siddhartha was born around 580–560 BC, the son of a king in Nepal. He lived an insular life for any years, unaware of the sorrows of others. Deeply moved by the sight of an old beggar and a dead man, Siddhartha decided to leave his home and family. He undertook a quest, seeking a means to escape illness, death, and the wheel of karma.

The quest lasted many years. He joined a group of monks and took the name Gautama. He did not find what he was looking for in deep meditation or austerities, so he continued to wander. He finally came to a deer park at Isipatana, near modern-day Benares. After many days of contemplation under a Bodhi tree,

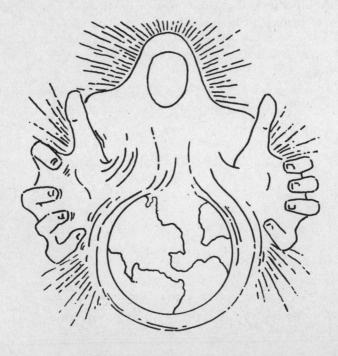

he reached enlightenment and became Buddha, the "Awakened One." He spent the remaining forty-five years of his life teaching what he had learned.

During his eightieth year, Gautama Buddha was released from earthly karma at his death and surrounded by his *sangha,* a religious community that included both men and women. His teachings are preserved in the *Mahavagga,* a document written by his disciples. His Wheel of Teaching includes the doctrine of the Four Truths—ideas about karma, rebirth, and dharma. Liberation from karma can be achieved by following the Eight-Fold Path: right vision, purpose, speech, action, livelihood, effort, awareness, and concentration.

For nearly 2,500 years, Wesak has been a favorite holy day in countries with large Buddhist populations. It is estimated that eight-hundred million people worldwide celebrate Wesak every year. Each branch of Buddhism has its own customs and rituals. Chinese Buddhists "bathe the Buddha." A statue is splashed with water as a reminder to purify the mind from evil. Tibetan Buddhists practice deep meditation and extended mantra chanting. Mainstream Buddhists and Hindus (who recognize Buddha as an enlightened master) organize community parades with dancing, singing, and vegetarian food. Charity and service to humanity include gifts of food and clothing for the poor. Hospitals and orphanages are cleaned.

The Full Moon in Scorpio, which is usually in May, is a deeply compelling event. Scorpio is the sign that rules critical transformations and sexuality. The Sun is in the equally powerful sign of Taurus, which rules fecundity and the will to survive. Both signs are very potent and are ruled by the love planets, Venus and Mars. This profound astrological significance reflects an esoteric focus of birth, death, and regeneration.

This is not merely a memorial holiday, but a yearly manifestation of divine power distributed to the inhabitants of Earth. It is believed that a veil is opened during the Full Moon. The awakened ones, bodhisattvas and avatars, descend to Earth through the veil. Light and love emanate from them, and these vibrations are channeled into receptive celebrants. This blessing gift of divine energy is given to lift the spirit of humanity, cleanse the planet, and promote the evolution of the Earth. The complete ritual takes five days. On the two days before the Full Moon, rituals of purification, prayers, mantras, and deep meditations are performed. The body and its aura are cleansed. The mind is turned inward and prepared for receptivity.

The day of the Full Moon is called the "Day of Safeguarding." The veil is fully opened to release the illumination of light and the embodiment of love. Alice Bailey's booklet about the Wesak festival describes the descent of the awakened ones to earth. Buddha and Christ perform a sacred ceremony in a hidden valley high in the Himalayan Mountains. Religious masters witness the ceremony and chant during the blessing. The Earth is cleansed of negative thought-forms created during the past twelve months of sorrow, war, illness, and disaster.

Each celebrant becomes a receptacle for as much of this spiritual force as they can hold. They must maintain complete inner peace and then continue to meditate on two things: the need to be a receptacle for spirit energy and the needs of humanity. The celebrant must be silent and forget the self in serving the divine.

The two days that follow the Full Moon have an outward focus. The stored energy is ready to be shared with others. These are the "Days of Distribution." This sharing is not to be examined for results or goals. It is a selfless sharing of divine energy. This is a time that the divine works through humans to improve the state of the world for the next twelve months. It is thought that the strength of the Wesak celebration determines the fate of the world in the coming year.

At Buddhist temples, community gatherings, and private enclaves, people from diverse faiths spend the entire day of the Full Moon working toward the evolution of humanity and the Earth. Prayers used at these gatherings include mantras in both ancient and modern languages.

One Tibetan mantra for Wesak is *hung vajra peh*. This mantra invokes Vajrapani, the god who protects dharma and prepares celebrants for holy work. *Om vajra sattwa hung* cleanses the aura of dirt, and infuses it with white light emanating from the crown chakra, purifying the seeker to receive the energy of the awakened ones.

A traditional Hindu Sanskrit mantra is *Om nama shivaya.* It unfolds the path to achieve a state of perfect being. The Mantra of Avaloketeshwara (in China, known as Quan Yin) is *Om mani padme hum,* which translates to "the jewel of consciousness is in the heart's lotus." This mantra accelerates spiritual development and opens a channel for energy that benefits all life on Earth. The Chinese Quan Yin mantra is *namo kwan shi yin pu sa,* which evokes mercy and compassion so the Earth and her inhabitants will be assisted by the awakened ones in attaining a state of grace.

A Hebrew mantra is *baruch atoh adonai elohenu mehloch aholum.* It means "blessed art thou, O Lord our God, king of the universe." A simple Greek mantra is *soma Christu.* This draws the light of illumination from Christ into the soul.

Upcoming Wesak dates are May 13, 2006 and May 2, 2007. The internet has copious information about celebrations and locations. If you wish to participate in Wesak, consider organizing a group to pray for world peace. Use the mantras, or simply perform a deep meditation on the day of the Full Moon in May. Celebrate with vegetarian food and inspirational music. On the following days, offer kindness and generosity to others.

Wesak, also known as Nirvana Day, makes the world a better place, and continues to nourish the hope of planetary evolution. As we approach the challenging planetary alignments that take place during the years from 2010 to 2012, the Earth will need as much help as she can get from her inhabitants. It is no longer enough to hope for world peace. People of good heart must actively work for it, so that, in the words of John Lennon, "the world will live as one."

Loch Lomond

by Muse

By yon bonnie banks and by yon bonnie braes,
Where the sun shines bright on Loch Lomond,
Where me and my true love were ever wont to gae
On the bonnie, bonnie banks o' Loch Lomond.

O ye'll take the high road and I'll take the low road,
An' I'll be in Scotland afore ye;
But me and my true love will never meet again
On the bonnie, bonnie banks o' Loch Lomond.

As I stood on the banks of the largest loch in Scotland, it was easy to see why the Jacobite soldier who wrote the famous song quoted above, "By Yon Bonnie Banks," chose Loch Lomond as his final destination. The loch glistens with life. The water ripples and flashes echoes of the lush plant life on its shores. The Sun shines brightly from a crystal clear sky and dances on the deep gray water.

When I visited the loch, the vision in front of me was a far cry from the gloomy stereotype of Scotland. Excited to experience more of the famous loch, my friends and I hired a boat to take us on a tour, and history unfolded before our eyes.

The famous song about the loch has historic, and heartbreaking, roots. Legend has it that during the Jacobite uprisings in the seventeenth and eighteenth centuries (some think this song was written close to 1745), a Scottish soldier and his brother were captured and left behind in Carlisle. The Redcoats sentenced one to death; the other would be allowed to go free. The choice was given to the brothers as to which one would go to the gallows.

The younger brother stepped forward, sacrificing himself because the older brother had a family and a home to take care of. The boys had grown up near Loch Lomond, and the younger one had a sweetheart there. On the eve of his execution, he penned the now-famous song. The "low road" is a reference to the spiritual road. The younger brother would reach "home" first but would never be with his true love again.

Loch Lomond, about an hour's drive from Glasgow, is twenty-four miles long and up to six-hundred feet deep. Its banks stretch upward to create steep mountains, the most famous of which is Ben Lomond. On the eastern side of the loch, Ben Lomond is Scotland's tallest mountain at 3,192 feet. Loch Lomond also has thirty-eight islands, each with a history of its own. Wildlife abounds on the banks of the loch, as well as on the many islands that exist throughout the waters.

After the Norman invasion, the Earldom of Lennox took hold of the lands surrounding the loch. These powerful leaders ruled through 1748, the most famous earl being Lord Darnley, Mary Stuart's (Mary, Queen of Scots) second husband.

Another famous Earl of Lennox was Earl Duncan, who was beheaded, along with his sons and his father, after the restoration of James I. Isabella, his widow, lived her last remaining years withdrawn on Inchmurrin, the largest island on the loch. Inchmurrin is now preserved for deer, but the ruins of her stronghold still stand today.

There are many ghosts on the banks and islands of Loch Lomond, but not all come from sad endings. The hamlet of Inversnaid was the home of the Jacobite stand led by Rob Roy Macgregor in 1715 against a Hanoverian force. Macgregor was immortalized by Sir Walter Scott's novel, *Rob Roy*. At his death in 1734, Rob Roy Macgregor was laid to rest in the local churchyard at Balquidder, near the northern tip of the loch. Opposite Wallace Island, in Inversnaid, lies Rob Roy's Cave. Inversnaid seems to have been a popular place for Highland heroes, as Robert the Bruce is said to have found refuge in the cave there in 1306.

Deep in the Lowlands, caught between the border of England and the Highlands of Scotland, Loch Lomond has seen its share of history unfold. From my perch on the deck of the small chartered boat, the chill wind fairly hummed with energy. The day I spent on the loch carved a place in my soul, and I walked back to the car singing under my breath, "Ye'll take the high road and I'll take the low road…"

Harnessing Rainbows

by Tammy Sullivan

In ancient myths the rainbow is represented as a bridge that crosses over into the land of death. It was a path for the gods to come into our world and a one-way walk for the dead to enter their new realm. This philosophy is found in Nordic, Polynesian, Greek, and Japanese myths. Below the equator, beliefs were a bit different. Many cultures once believed that the world was created by a rainbow serpent.

Universally, old lore asserts that rainbows were dangerous. They were known to drink the water beneath them. If a ship happened to be sailing underneath, it would be sucked up as well. Today, the rainbow stands for acceptance of all cultures, races, religions, and sexual persuasions. It is a symbol of our freedom from the prejudices of our ancestors.

Technically speaking, a rainbow is refraction and reflection of light as magnified by raindrops present in the air. While the explanation is perfectly scientific, the rainbow retains much of its mystery due to the fact that it is only visual. One cannot touch, taste, hear, or smell a rainbow. We can only observe it. However, some believe the rainbow is a direct link to the great spirit and carries a message. We can access this message within.

Each of us is in possession of our own personal rainbow in the form of chakras. Wiccan belief states, "As above, so below"; this also translates to "as within, so without." All colors exist within, therefore they exist without. A human person is not simply black, brown, or white, but is rainbow-colored. This aspect of the rainbow is most revealing, for it can heal us as a planet if applied properly.

Metaphysically, the properties of the rainbow relate best to magical work in healing, laughter, joy, equality, growth, strength, composure, and dealing with grief. Rainbow magic is powerful, but it cannot compensate for a good purge.

Deep meditation allows us to walk the rainbow path. Each journey is different and carries a unique message. In fact, rainbow bridge meditations are famous and widely available. Try one to see if you can divine your rainbow's personal message.

Prisms create rainbows without the presence of water in the air. They can be used indoors; however, when water is not used for rainbow effects, the magic does not deal with emotional issues as well. It is more suited to dealing with strength and composure. Keep this in mind when choosing your charging method.

Crystals can be energized with rainbow power and used as a harness. Certain crystals respond best to this type of energy, especially pearl, mother-of-pearl, rainbow moonstone, opal, clear quartz, and diamonds. Any stone that is clear, but produces colored effects when light shines through it, or any stone that already encompasses the color spectrum of the rainbow, may be used with good results.

In order to empower the stones, set them beneath a prism for a rainbow light bath, or place them at the bottom of a fountain in the sunlight. You may also use your garden hose to create the rainbow. It does not take long for the stones to absorb the energy. Then tuck it into your pocket or a sachet, or wear it to feel the effects of the rainbow. Rainbows appear and disappear quickly, and when they go they often take their energy with them. Charging a stone with rainbow power usually only lasts about a day.

To consume the effects of the rainbow there are two methods. The dry method is simple. Place your food underneath a prism, allowing it to absorb the energy—then enjoy your meal. The wet method is a bit more complicated, but well worth the effort. To make use of it, you will need seven colored bottles or jars, including red, orange, yellow, green, blue, indigo, and violet. Beginning with red, fill the jar with pure, blessed water and allow it to sit for an hour. Transfer the water sequentially from bottle to bottle, allowing each to rest for an hour. When the final bottle has rested, the rainbow water is ready to be consumed or used to charge crystals.

Rainbow candles bring laughter and happiness to the home. If you cannot find one in your area, light one of each color in succession. To invoke the power of the rainbow, call upon a related deity. The list spans many cultures and includes: Iris (Greek); Nuwa (Chinese); Anyiewo, Ayido, Hwedo, Gunab (African); Ix Chel (Mayan); Anuenue (Hawaiian); Heimdall (Norse); K'uychi (Incan); Amitolane (Zuni); Indra (Indian).

Celtic and Native American cultures have legends about the end of the rainbow. Celtic legends speak of Leprechauns and finding a pot of gold at the end of a rainbow, while Navajo belief speaks of a turquoise house where the Sun god and the water god greet their sons. Considering those two examples, it appears as if the rainbow ends in joy.

We can envision a rainbow bridge to help us cross over troubled times and reach the laughter that resides at the end. A simple visualization of a rainbow beneath the feet can speak to the subconscious enough to say, "There is an end in sight; keep going."

That is often exactly what one needs to hear. In that aspect, the rainbow teaches us inspiration, determination, and, most of all, perseverance.

Harnessing the power of the rainbow for personal use is life-affirming and nurturing. It's hard not to smile when you know you have a piece of a rainbow tucked in your pocket. Allowing the rainbow to buffer, heal, and bring your world into harmony ensures a bright and colorful day.

The Alchemy of Fragrance

by Lynne Sturtevant

Smell is the most primitive of our five senses. Aromas have the power to uncover buried memories, trigger emotions, alter moods, and ignite sexual passion. Scents also have the power to connect us to the spiritual realm. Fragrance has been an invisible element in magical ceremonies and religious rituals for at least 5,000 years. The smoke of incense has carried messages to the gods, cleared negative influences from sacred spaces, helped mystics achieve altered states of consciousness, and lifted the souls of the dead to paradise.

The ancient Egyptians used vast quantities of incense and other aromatics. Priests anointed themselves with perfumes, fragrant unguents, and scented oils several times a day. Flowers, spices, and herbs were essential elements in the sacred art of mummifying the dead. When King Tut's tomb was opened early in the twentieth century, 3,000 years after it had been sealed, the faint aroma of perfume still hung in the air.

The most famous Egyptian scent was *kyphi,* a very intense concoction with the power to induce hypnotic states. Kyphi contained sixteen ingredients—including honey, wine, bitumen, and frankincense. The number sixteen was significant in Egyptian magic because it is the square of a square (four times four). Only priests were allowed to make and use Kyphi. They mixed it according to a secret ritual while chanting sacred texts. Each day at dawn, the priests offered frankincense to the Sun god Re. At noon they burned myrrh. Kyphi was saved for the daily sunset, when it was ignited with great ceremony to encourage the God to return to the sky the following morning.

Egyptians also used perfumes as cosmetics. Women placed scented cones of wax on their heads. As their body heat warmed the cones, the wax melted down over them and scented their hair and bodies. Young men wore as many as fifteen different scents at once, and Cleopatra perfumed the sails of her royal barge.

The Greeks and Romans were as addicted to fragrance as the Egyptians were. The Greeks roasted spices on braziers, used aromatic oil in lamps, poured rose water on hot rocks to produce fragrant steam, and filled fountains with perfume. The intoxicating fumes inhaled by priestesses at Delphi allowed them to predict the future of kings and empires. Romans burned incense to the Lares, their household gods, and before civic ceremonies. The Emperor Nero used more incense every few months than Saudi Arabia could produce in an entire year. The most extravagant use of fragrance was reserved for grand Roman Imperial banquets. Dinner guests rinsed their hands and feet in perfume when they arrived. Mists of fragrance and showers of rose petals drifted down on them from time to time as they ate. Doves whose wings had been saturated with perfume flew overhead, further scenting the air.

Throughout the ancient world, incense meant frankincense, a resin that comes from trees. Its spicy, sensuous smoke filled temples from Babylon to China. Frankincense quieted overactive minds and focused mental energies. Ascetics in India inhaled its smoke to achieve deeper levels of meditation. Its value was surpassed only by myrrh, another resinous substance obtained from shrubs. Myrrh calmed turbulent emotions and provided strength and endurance during times of difficulties. Reactions to individual fragrances are highly personal. To some, the scent of myrrh is vaguely medicinal. To others, its smoky-sweet aroma evokes the very essence of spirituality. Myrrh was so expensive that only the very wealthy had access to it, and so precious that men addressed their sweethearts as "my myrrh."

After the Roman Empire fell, people continued to use herbs and flowers to scent their homes, clothing, and bodies. Wealthier churches still burned frankincense, but the art of perfume making was virtually forgotten in Europe. The Persians, who believed a flower's fragrance was its soul, continued working on ways to extract botanical essences. Attar of roses, an intensely fragrant scent that is still used in perfume making, was developed in Persia during the Dark Ages.

Although attar of roses is powerful, most agree that the ultimate floral fragrance is jasmine. In India, jasmine is known as the "Queen of the Night," because its creamy white blossoms open in the moonlight. Its sweet scent is so intoxicating and so sensual that it borders on the erotic. It is entirely too much for some, but for others it is as addictive as a narcotic. Everywhere it grows, jasmine is considered an aphrodisiac. Inhaling its fragrance strengthens intuition, encourages artistic creativity, and elevates the mood. In the last fifty years, natural jasmine has become so expensive it is now out of reach for all but a few. It is the myrrh of our time.

The knowledge of perfume-making returned to Europe with the Crusaders in the late Middle Ages. At this time, perfume shops began to open in Paris and London. The perfume-makers cultivated auras of mystery around their establishments and themselves. Most dabbled in alchemy, astrology, and the occult. Their dimly lit shops were filled with drying flowers, rare spices, and odd-looking roots. Bits of mummies were strategically placed here and there to remind customers of perfume's historic connection to ancient Egyptian magic. The strong scent of camphor and thick frankincense smoke added to the exotic atmosphere.

People were convinced that certain perfumes possessed magical properties. Some made the wearer irresistible to members of the opposite sex. Other scents guaranteed eternal youth. Still others had the power to destroy one's enemies. The names of today's perfumes—Beautiful, Eternity, Obsession—would have made as much sense in the sixteenth century as they do in the twenty-first.

A simple way to incorporate fragrance into your rituals is by making and using solid perfumes. Focus on a single aroma, perhaps used in the ancient world, or combine different scents to create your own special blend. Use the perfume to purify your space and to create a sacred atmosphere. Scent an entire room or just an object or piece of fabric. Rub the scent on your hands and temples. If you use a particular fragrance consistently and only for ritual purposes, it will gain the power to transport your mind to the proper state for magical work.

Solid Perfume

To make a magical solid perfume to use in ritual, you will need the ingredients listed below.

Petroleum or non-petroleum jelly.

Grated beeswax: Beeswax sheets and pellets are available in the candlemaking section of crafts stores.

Essential or fragrance oils: Essential oils are concentrated natural botanical extracts. Fragrance oils are synthetic and much less expensive.

Small containers with lids: Baby food jars, pillboxes, empty compacts, and small containers for sorting beads all work well.

A cooking pan.

A heatproof measuring cup.

Bring about one inch of water to boil in the pan. Put one tablespoon of grated beeswax and two tablespoons of petroleum jelly in a heatproof measuring cup. Carefully place the measuring cup in the pan of boiling water. Beeswax will ignite, so do not leave the melting wax unattended. In about five minutes, the wax and petroleum jelly will melt completely. Remove the measuring cup from the pan and add one-half ounce of essential or fragrance oil, half a standard-size bottle. If the oil solidifies when you add it to the wax, stir it a little. Pour the mixture into the containers. The perfume will be solid to the touch within ten minutes and will continue to harden over several hours. The finished product should have the consistency of lip balm. If you want it softer, use a little more petroleum jelly. For a firmer product, use a little more beeswax. This recipe will fill ten pillboxes with solid perfume.

The Origin of Anubis

by Denise Dumars

The image of Anubis, the Egyptian jackal-headed god, is familiar to most people. He is an very popular ancient deity among Isians, Pagans, and the Gothic community. His origins, however, may not be familiar to everyone—especially the story of his paternity.

In the Heliopolitan cosmogony (relating to the gods of Heliopolis, Egypt) Isis, Osiris, Set, Nephthys, and Horus the Elder are all born of the same parents, Geb and Nuit. The myth states that Isis and Osiris fell in love in the womb and were later married.

Set and Nephthys, Isis's twin, are also portrayed as husband and wife. Isis conceives her son Horus through magical means after Osiris is killed by his jealous brother Set. Anubis is the son of Nephthys and Set, but wait a minute—we need to back up.

Nephthys is wed to Set, who is described as a cruel, philandering, often drunken husband. Set is sometimes called "the dry god," implying that he is either sterile or impotent.

Meanwhile, Nephthys is in love with her sister's husband, Osiris. One version of the story of Anubis's paternity cites the story of Nephthys, who disguises herself as Isis and seduces Osiris. One source calls Anubis the result of that mating.

It would make sense, then, that Anubis serves Osiris by guiding the soul safely in its transition from a living body to meet Osiris in the afterlife.

Another similar tale tells of Anubis being hidden in the bulrushes, so that an angry Set won't find him and kill the son of the man who cuckolded him. There are many versions of this story. In one version, baby Anubis is left to die in the desert by Nephthys and is rescued by Isis. In another, Isis herself assists Nephthys in hiding Anubis and keeping him from harm.

The family scandals of this group of Egyptian *neteru* are endlessly fascinating, and would rival any soap opera in their plot twists and turns. But we must look to the iconography as well as the stories to discover the truth.

Anubis is portrayed as a jackal-headed man, but many have said that this figure merely represents an embalmer wearing an Anubis mask while doing "Anubis's work." Therefore, the "true" representation of Anubis would be his form as a black, jackal-like dog.

Some writers on magic, such as Konstantinos, feel that this is his true form and that it is, in fact, dangerous to invoke him in this form. Why? It could be because in this form he looks a lot like the Set beast. This animal is also usually portrayed as black, with Set's unusual head, a forked tale that stands straight up, and a very dog-like black body. Are we then to see Anubis as the true son of Set after all?

Indeed, there are many dog-, jackal-, and even wolf-headed Egyptian *neter*. There are no wolves in Egypt, so wolf-headed Wepwawet, often thought of as an aspect of Anubis or an earlier version of him, may be a foreign god. Set is sometimes seen as a foreign god as well, as he is "different" from his siblings. Representations of Anubis may even predate the Heliopolitan gods, suggesting that his adoption (literally and figuratively) into this family came at a later date.

Anubis is usually portrayed as black, though jackals are not black. The color black to the Egyptians did not connote death as it sometimes does to us. In fact, it was a color of fertility, as it represented the rich black silt that was deposited on the banks of the Nile by the yearly inundation. This flooding made agriculture possible for the Egyptians. Osiris, then, as a fertility god, was often portrayed as black. Is Anubis, then, Osiris's son?

Clearly, both sides seem to have evidence linking Anubis to either Set or Osiris, but you should know by now that soap opera stories are never so cut and dried!

One of the stories of Isis hiding baby Anubis in the bulrushes strangely lists him as the child of Isis and Set. In the myth of the assassination of Osiris, Set does indeed attempt to capture and rape Isis, but Isis eludes him by disguising herself as a beggar in foreign lands. Could then Anubis be the offspring of a consensual coupling of Isis and Set?

Isis, called Great of Magic, conceived Horus (the hawk-headed warrior who defeated Set and regained the throne of Egypt), through a phallus she fashioned when the sundered parts of Osiris's body were found, but his generative organ wasn't (the myth says it was eaten by a fish). While her son Horus is the active principle in her family, perhaps she saw the need to have another son, one who would be more of a subordinate and assistant to Osiris in his role as king of the underworld. Is this how Anubis, psychopomp and divine embalmer, came to be after all?

It is easiest to accept the simplest version of the story, which has Horus as son of Isis and Osiris and Anubis as son of Nephthys and Set. But clearly there is more to the story. The copious information we have from many sites in Egypt—each with its own interpretation of the myths—makes for fascinating study.

Anubis is his Greco-Roman name. The Egyptians called him Anpu or Ienpu. Another of his ancient names is Khenty-Amentiu, or "foremost of westerners," indicating his position as the guardian of the cemetery and the portal which we enter from life into death.

To "go toward the west" meant to go toward death, as the west represented the setting or "dying" Sun. Ancient Egyptian cemeteries were located on the west side of the Nile. Some research has shown that he is an older god than the gods of the Heliopolitans, and that many of his functions relating to death and the afterlife were taken on by Osiris later on. Anubis took a somewhat lesser role in assisting Osiris after being "adopted" into the pantheon.

Author Lori Nyx has no problem invoking Anubis in his dog-like form. She sees him as a protective "guard dog" and provides instructions for invoking his aid in her chapter on him in *The Dark Archetype* (New Page Books, 2003).

As for me, well, I'm afraid of dogs. Is it any wonder, since as an Isian I can expect Anubis to come to me as a psychopomp to announce the arrival of my time of death?

Planet Magic

by Diana Rajchel

With all the time that ancestral ceremonial magicians invest in invoking, understanding, and categorizing planetary energies, you'd think nowadays NASA would require a Golden Dawn initiation for all working astronauts. Enough study certainly has gone into these dots of night sky to keep the Earth turning. While the results of these studies have not directly launched any would-be Neil Armstrongs into the night sky, the modern day occultist can still know that planetary energies pack a significant punch.

Despite some dubious arguments at UFO conventions, the planets do not call us, we call them—or more specifically, we call upon their unique energy distributions. Each planet in the astrologically identifiable solar system proffers a long-term source of energy to tap into and draw from the universe each time a circle is cast. Planetary energy may be invoked and mastered in the highly disciplined and complex manner of ceremonial orders such as the Golden Dawn, or may be called into power through straightforward invocation.

The planets of the solar system offer a powerful (planet size) boost to most magical workings. Understand that while compared to humans, planets may last forever, just like all things in the material universe, they are finite resources that should have energy cycled back to them. At the end of magical workings, always direct any excess to the planet in order to keep the energy cycling for long term use.

Magicians can align any of their workings with a planet. In fact, one of the simplest ways to plan a ritual working is to determine its ruling planet or appropriate influencing planets. Even ritualists that primarily call upon deities may find that a planet's association enhances a working. For instance, Sekhmet is associated with the Sun, Zeus with Jupiter, and Kali-Ma with Pluto. Please note that outside of Western culture, planetary associations can differ.

Getting the bearings of basic planet associations takes little effort. Most introductory books on magic offer a chart listing the planets and providing a cursory overview of their associations. Bill Whitcomb's *A Magician's Companion* (Llewellyn, 1993) is particularly handy for determining planet and ritual symbol associations. The basic list below gives a starting point for understanding planetary associations.

Sun: Growth, illumination, burning away

Moon: Emotions and cycles

Mercury: Communication

Venus: Love relationships, healing

Mars: Aggression and fast action

Jupiter: Business success

Saturn: Obstacles, suffering to learn

As those with telescopes may know, the Sun and Moon are not planets. To clarify, the term "planet" in the occult sense means "stable body of celestial energy." The Sun, that giant gas ball that gives the Earth life, is actually a star. The Moon is the Earth's satellite. The Moon's reflection of light differs no more than any planet's illumination by the Sun; Moon energy is as unique as the energy of any other planet in the solar system.

When medieval astrologers first began to theorize about a universe beyond Earth, they proposed that planets revolved around the Earth. This kept with the early church doctrine that man was meant to rule all God's creation. To these earlier minds, it only made sense that God's Earth stood at the center of it all.

Thanks to Copernicus and Galileo, science no longer fixates on this incorrect theory. The greater universe doesn't revolve around the Earth, just as the planets do not orbit around each magician. Only six of the nine known planets could be observed in the night sky without the advantages of modern equipment. Consequently, rulerships over zodiac signs were affixed to those six recognizable planets. This leaves some debate as to whether or how to include Neptune, Uranus, and Pluto. While the mythos behind each name gives some clues as to how to incorporate and use these less-known planets, not all astrologers and magicians have come to agreement as to whether and how these planets may be used.

But the fact remains you need to have a reason to use a planet in a magical working. Say you decide to add some astral "oomph" to a job interview. You pick Jupiter for success. Just in case, you may also want some Mercury energy to make sure you communicate well. In this example, say you're applying for a counseling position, so you desire Venus energy to make your healing qualities readily apparent.

You can go ahead and construct a ritual with your deity of choice or, upon consulting a reference book, perform a battery of rituals in the astrologically correct hours to obtain your job.

Simple folk magic works for those with less time to prepare. For a simple spell, take a taper or votive candle of the dominant planet's color (in this case rich blue for Jupiter), and carve the object of the spell on the candle along with the sigils for Jupiter, Mercury, and Venus. For added impact, anoint the candle with a Jupiter-ruled oil such as olive oil. Cast a circle, and call any chosen guardians. Pause after this, seeing the circle as a universe-in-a-universe.

Consider yourself the Sun as planets rotate around you, and call your desired planets into line by simply saying: "I call upon and align the powers of Mercury, Venus, and Jupiter."

If you invoke, be polite to your guest and manage the orbits while giving your guest center stage. Light the candle and speak your desire with fervor. When all emotional energy is spent, make your polite departure and allow the candle to burn down. For safety's sake, be sure to set the candle on a plate or other non-flammable container.

Planetary energies are better understood than controlled. If you become a fan of planet energy, ceremonial magic offers a wide world of seals, symbols, and mathematical formulas that call upon many energies and aspects of the planets. As a symbolic foundation, planet magic offers a sound and simple method for magical working—just remember to give back any excess. Recall too that the worlds revolve around far more than just one magician waving a wand at the sky.

Bone Magic

by Lily Gardner

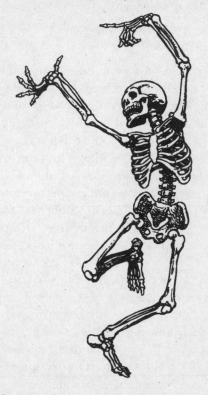

A Blackfoot myth tells the story of a young woman whose father was trampled to bits by a herd of buffalo. A friendly magpie helps the woman find a tiny bone from the father's corpse. The woman covers the bone with her robe, sings a magical song over it, and the body of her beloved father is restored.

A version of this story exists all over the world because of the primal belief that our beingness is retained in our bones. Catholics make pilgrimages to sacred sites where holy relics (that is, a saint's bones) bestow blessings. When well-meaning monks moved the bones of Saint Swithin from his humble churchyard to a magnificent shrine they had built especially for him, the saint wept in protest. It rained for forty days straight. Eleven-hundred years later, July 15, Saint Swithin's Day, remains a weather marker:

Saint Swithin's Day, if thou dost rain
Full forty days it will remain.

There are many customs associated with bones. The most northern tribes were careful not to break any of the bones of the game they killed. They believed if the skeleton was kept intact, the animal could come back to life, ensuring future game for the tribe. One myth recounts Thor resurrecting three goats that were sacrificed to him. The men who had feasted on the goat broke the shin bone of one of the goats to suck the marrow from it. When that goat was resurrected, he was lame, much to Thor's chagrin. Siberians hung the skull of the bear they killed in a nearby tree. If a passerby greeted the bear skull with respect, he would be protected from other bears.

Bones were commonly used in healing work in western Europe. If one carries the knuckle of a sheep in a pocket, that person will be free from rheumatic pain and cramp. Mixing red wine with powdered bone cures dysentery. Headaches can be cured, it is said, by driving a nail into a dead man's skull. Epilepsy can be cured by drinking from the skull of someone who has committed suicide.

The oldest and most common practice of all is using bones as a divination tool. Throwing the bones was a precursor to throwing dice, as dice were originally made from bone. The method I have developed is a combination of African and Thai bone throwing. The African method uses a combination of bones and stones which seems more practical in modern times.

The biggest challenge is to collect enough bones. As a city dweller, the butcher and the rock shop are my best sources. Most rock shops sell fossilized bones of animals that are not available at the meat market. Be sure to put the word out to everyone in your acquaintance that you're looking for bones.

Each bone will contain the totem energies of the animal it came from. The following are a few examples of bones easy to obtain. The chicken is a solar animal and thus associated with light and resurrection. Cows are Moon animals representing fertility. The horse is a messenger between heaven and earth, consciousness and unconsciousness, living and dead.

In addition to using the totem energies of the bones, determine whether the bone is closer to the head, which represents intellect, or to the foot, which represents physicality.

I'm fortunate to own a skull and a shin bone. Because of their size and fragility, these two bones are the stationary pieces on my divination board. The skull represents matters of the intellect, the shin represents matters of physicality. In addition to these bones, I use fossilized teeth (thoughts or projects), a piece of spine (support), a wishbone (matters of the heart), smaller leg bones (work or travel), two red stones (bad fortune), two tigers' eye (wisdom or the ability to perceive), two rose quartz (love), and five shark teeth (facing challenges).

To throw the bones, close your eyes and rotate the divination table so that you don't know which direction the stationary bones lie. Shake the smaller bones and stones in your cupped hands in the same way you would throw a handful of dice. The interpretation is based on the proximity of the stones and bones to the stationary pieces.

To increase the power of your divination, bless your bones over the next four Full Moons. Bathe the bones in the moonlight, thanking the spirits of the animals for the use of their bodies. In addition to the moonlight, use the power of the element of the Moon's current sign to purify your bones. Thus, if the Moon is full in Aries, a fire sign, pass the bones over a flame.

May many new insights come to you with this oldest divinatory tool.

Seasonal Tree Meditation

by Sedwyn

We modern Pagans continually seek ways to honor the natural world and live more closely with the rhythms and spirit of the land. Many of us find that drawing close to nature allows us to access different levels of energy and awareness, which can bring deeper meaning and spiritual satisfaction. Trees can function as a gateway to these different levels, drawing us closer to the green world, as well as providing a better understanding of ourselves and our ancestors.

The tree calendar and the Ogham alphabet have been so widely adopted and integrated into modern Pagan practice that they have become a system of symbols. Like all symbols, their purpose is to aid us in accessing deeper levels of energy and consciousness.

Most well known are the thirteen "month" or lunar trees of the tree calendar. In addition, there are five season or solar trees. Together, these month/lunar and season/solar trees are symbolic of the Moon and Sun. The Moon's thirteen lunations are contained within the five seasons of the year. This concept of the thirteen within the five comes from the Coligny calendar, which was discovered in 1897 near Lyons, France. It is a lunar calendar believed to have been used by the Celts of Gaul. In this calendar, a year consisted of thirteen 28-day months with one extra day (the nameless day) at mid-winter. There was a broader division of the year into five parts, which, it has been argued, made perfect sense for our agrarian ancestors.

Two of the season trees stand on either side of the Winter Solstice. Because we live in a glaringly bright world with electric light available anytime we want it, we tend to forget the deep significance of daylight to ancient people. These two trees represent a powerful threshold. Once the longest night of the year passes, the days gradually lengthen. It is as if the breath of nature is suspended between these two trees waiting for the Sun to begin its return journey.

Tree	Season	Character	Attributes	Action
Yew	Winter Solstice	Iodho Iodhadh	Death, transition, endings	Resting
Fir	Post-Winter Solstice	Ailm Ailim	Perspective, rising above, reaching	Sowing
Gorse	Spring Equinox	Onn Ohn	Hope, persistence	Growing
Heather	Summer Solstice	Ur Ura	Passion, generosity	Ripening
Aspen	Autumn Equinox	Eadhadh Eadha	Endurance, courage, communication	Harvesting

To fully appreciate the energy of a season, take time to focus on the energy of its associated tree, and ponder the tree's attributes. One way to focus on a tree and invite its energy into your life is to light a candle, then meditate or sit quietly as you think about the season and the gifts or lessons that particular tree imparts.

Before beginning your meditation, carve the name of the tree or its Ogham character into the candle. In addition, you may want to write the name of the tree on a slip of paper or find a picture of that type of tree. You could also use an object such as a leaf, needle, or flower from the tree. Light the candle on the first night of the tree's season.

Take time to think about the tree's characteristics that may have meaning for you. If you are using a picture, place it beside the candle and softly focus your eyes on the tree. If you are using something from the tree, hold it between your hands as you envision it still being part of the tree. Whenever possible, use both pictures and items from the tree in order to engage as many of your senses as you can in the process.

Throughout the season, light the candle so it will finish by the end of that tree's time. Alternatively, you could prepare one tall candle with all names and/or Oghams. Let the candle burn down as the year progresses.

To gain insight into the energy of the Wheel of the Year and how the seasonal tree energy spirals through it, you may want to try a full circle meditation. For this you will need candles, objects, and slips of paper with the names of each of the five season trees.

Place a chair or cushion on the floor in the center where you will imagine a circle surrounding you. You may want to cast a circle as you would for ritual. Determine which way is north, and place the candle for yew there with the candle for fir to its right. Place the paper with the tree's name, or a picture or object in front of each candle. The candle, object, picture or name for heather goes in the south position at the opposite side of your circle. Place gorse in the east and aspen in the west. Take your seat in the center.

From inside the circle, face the direction that corresponds to the current season. If it is midway through a season, face the midway point. Begin as with other meditations, focusing on your breath and calming your energy. When you are ready, shift your focus to the tree of the current season. For example, if you are facing east, think about springtime and the attributes of gorse.

Allow yourself to feel and experience the energy of the season and tree. Let the energy of the tree guide you. Moving clockwise, repeat this process for each of the other seasons. If it is winter, start with yew if it is before the solstice and fir if it is after the solstice. The spring and autumn equinoxes are days of balance when light and dark are equal. Take time to feel the equilibrium of these seasons. Spend as much time as you feel is appropriate on each one.

With this meditation you are connecting with the natural world and the cycle of the year. It provides an awareness of the whole of life outside the circle of time, while at the same time helping your energy spiral inward. Trees provide a way to tap into the web of all existence for magical and spiritual purposes, as well as simply to embrace and enhance life. Like music, trees speak to something deep and primal within us.

The more we open to the energy around us, the more mystical our relationship with the land and elements becomes. As we work with tree energy, we are able to see and appreciate the mysteries of the natural world and the wisdom of the soul.

Female Fertility Magic
by Michelle Santos

There comes a point in the quest for having a child when the medical establishment can no longer help. You're trying everything the doctors suggest and are still not achieving your goal of a conceiving a baby. The doctors can provide no reason for the hold-up, and you receive your Moon time every month, on schedule, just like clock-work. You are sad, frustrated, and losing hope quickly.

Still, you must remember, you are a magical person. And in fact we are all magical people if we simply choose to tap into our innate power.

You shouldn't just pin your hopes on the medical profession. Listen to what your doctors say, follow their advice, and supplement their ideas with some of your own.

Set up an Altar

You can use any flat surface in your home, from a spare end table to a section of your book shelf. If you don't feel like you can have an open altar, you can easily make one in a shoe box and store it away under the bed or in the closet. Large trunks or chests work in the same way.

On the altar, place anything that reminds you of fertility, childbirth, or babies. You might want to use pictures of babies in your family or women in your life who are extremely fertile. Spirals are a great depiction of goddess and mothering energy, as are sea shells of any kind (but especially those with a womb-like appearance). Images of the Moon are also excellent for a fertility altar, as the Moon is linked to feminine power and fertility. The semi-precious gemstone moonstone is an excellent representation of the Moon and is known to help in the birthing process. Other crystals and gemstones to use include those connected to the second chakra (the chakra related to the female reproductive organs). Some second chakra stones are carnelian, pink Botswana agate, and golden topaz. Another gemstone to use is rose quartz as it brings unconditional love to all your work. One final addition to your altar would be an item or statue representing a goddess who is associated with fertility.

Fertility Goddesses

Fertility goddesses from around the world number in the hundreds. Not all of them can be named here, so please view this as a partial (even microscopic) list of goddesses who can assist you in becoming pregnant. I recommend that you do some research on a goddess before deciding she is the one with whom you want to work. Also, don't feel like you have to limit yourself to only one of these goddesses. Most of them work very well together.

Celtic-Irish

Aine: As a maiden goddess of sexuality, fertility, and husbandry, Aine is a Sun goddess who is also connected to the Moon and the fairy realms. She brings fruitfulness to the land and guards humans against illness and infertility. Midsummer (around June 21) is her festival day.

Brigid: A three-fold fire goddess of the hearth, poetry, and smithcraft, Brigid is often called upon to awaken the "fire within" in order to start the fertility process. Her holiday is February 1, also known as Imbolc.

Egyptian

Heket: A mother goddess, Heket rose from the primordial waters to give life. She presides over creation, regeneration, and fertility. She helped Osiris rise from the dead. Heket is often depicted as a frog or a woman with a frog head.

Greek

Demeter: As a grain goddess, Demeter brings productivity to the earth, tending the plants and making sure they grow. One myth describes how she wrapped the world in winter because her daughter Persephone was taken away by the god Hades. When Persephone returns every year, spring warms the earth. Demeter is one of the twelve Olympian deities.

Hindu

Maya: As a creativity goddess, Maya gives the spark of life and the desire to live. She is known as the "Mother of Creation" and is connected to the sea, magic, and witchcraft.

Middle Eastern

Asherah: A Canaanite great mother goddess, Asherah helps the crops to grow. She is considered to be the "Living Tree," and shrines were erected to her in nearly every household. A very fertile goddess, Asherah is the mother of seventy deities.

Innana: A Mesopotamian mother goddess, Innana is called upon for crop, animal, and human fertility. She is ruler of the sky and the earth.

Norse

Frigga: Frigga is a mother goddess, known as "beloved" and "wife." She oversaw the running of the household and the fruitfulness of marriage beds. She is a weaver and a seer, connected to the Norns, the Norse Fates. Frigga sees all but says little.

Roman

Diana: Goddess of the Moon and wild animals, Diana is a paradoxical goddess who celebrates chasteness yet is called upon for help with procreation and birthing. Her chief festival is called the Festival of Candles (or Torches), celebrated on August 15.

Candle Magic

Once you have chosen your goddess or goddesses, decide on a candle color that best represents her. You might chose white for the Moon, green for the earth and plants, yellow for the Sun, or red for fire. It doesn't matter which color you choose, as long as it symbolizes the Goddess to you.

This candle will represent your desire for procreation. Since you will be using it over a period of time, a large pillar or similar candle will work best. Anoint the candle with oil by holding the candle by its ends and rubbing the oil onto the candle. Start in the middle and run your finger to the top of the candle, twirling it in a clockwise motion as you go. Once you have reached the part you've already anointed, repeat the procedure from the middle of the candle to the candle's bottom. Any oil will work—including herbal oil, new age "wishing oil," or even the olive oil in your kitchen cabinet—as long as you keep your intention firmly in mind.

Place your fertility goddess candle on your altar. This is where you will honor the Goddess of your choice and let her know your fervent desire for a child.

Whenever you feel the need—every day, once a week, or somewhere in between—kneel or sit in front of your fertility altar and light the candle. Focus on your sincere hope for a child, communing with your goddess and feeling the love that she has for you, her child of the universe.

Speak the following chant (or a similar one) while you sit in front of your candle.

I am the giver of life, universal vessel, womb of the world.
Life flows through my veins and pulses in my blood.
I create,
I am.

Rivers flow through me,
Space heals me.
Creativity is my name,
I am she and I am proud.

Butterflies kiss my lips and alight on my fingers,
Grass sprouts beneath my feet.
I give,
I am.

Stars shine upon me,
Light heals me.
Growth is my name.
I am she and I am proud.

Black soil muddies my feet and seeps up my legs.
Animals play underneath my skirts.
I produce,
I am.

Whispers swirl around me,
Love heals me.
Fertility is my name,
I am she and I am proud.

I am the womb of the goddess,
Creation made incarnate.

As I say it, so shall it be.

Keep the candle lit for an hour or so, making sure that it is in a safe spot to avoid starting a fire. When you feel the time is right, snuff out the candle flame and go about your everyday activities.

Mundane Activities

I recommend augmenting this magic with everyday activities that will help you to get to know your body better. Learn the cycles of your body—not everyone has a perfectly regular twenty-eight–day menstruation cycle. Know when you are ovulating and so at your most fertile. Be able to read your body's signals, your temperature, and your fluid production, in order to know when your body will most likely be ready for procreation.

Visit your local herb shop to get your body ready for fertilization. Red raspberry leaf, nettles, and red clover are excellent tonic herbs for women. Red raspberry leaf helps to tone the uterus, and nettles adds vitamin C and iron. Both are excellent herbs for women, whether trying to get pregnant or not.

Red clover is one of the best herbs to take when attempting to conceive. It tones the uterus, relaxes the nervous system, and balances hormones. Make a tea with equal parts of these three herbs, and then throw in a dash of chamomile (for relaxation) or a pinch of mint (for sexual stimulation), and you've got yourself a great tea to help with conception!

Remember that some herbs will react with some medicines, so please consult your doctor beforehand. Also, just because something is "all natural" does not mean that you can't be allergic to it. Be sure to talk to your local herbalist and start by trying herbs in small doses.

Above all, keep a positive attitude and know that all paths are equal and divine in the eyes of the Goddess.

Wishing Herbs

by Sheri Richerson

When it comes to wishes, the best advice is to be careful what you wish for—you just might get it! While there are numerous spells designed specifically to carry your wish into the universe and to the powers that can make it come true, using herbs as well as the four elements in your spell can help to ensure its success.

It is common knowledge that herbs possess many properties—including numerous magical powers. Herbs add their energy to the spell, which in turn adds an extra dimension of power. While many people believe that using a specific herb is the only way to make a spell come true, today we know that sometimes it is not always possible to get enough of one particular herb, especially if it is hard to find. A mix of herbs can work, too.

If you choose to use a mixture of herbs, be sure that none of the herbs in the mixture will counteract your wish. Vervain is a good herb to use in almost all wish spells, because its properties are very general as well as protective. Cinnamon, however, would not be a good choice if your wish is to release your power. It would counteract the wish and instead grant you additional power.

You also need to make sure you use the correct ink. For example, Dove's Blood Ink is the common ink used in wishing spells. However, if your wish is destructive in nature, you would use Dragon's Blood Ink instead. A word of caution here is that whatever you wish onto another will come back to you sevenfold, so, again, be careful what you wish for.

When you need a special wish granted, write the wish out in Dove's Blood Ink on parchment paper. Make three folds in the paper and place it in a red flannel bag. Then fill the bag with dandelion petals, sew it closed with red thread, and wear it around your neck for three days. Although this spell is not recommended for acquiring money or property, it is quite effective when used in situations when you are in danger of losing something or having it taken from you by outside influences.

You can also write your wish on a piece of parchment paper using Dove's Blood Ink. While the ink is still fresh sprinkle on some peony petals. Roll the paper up, and seal it with melted red wax from a candle. Hide the talisman in your home, making sure to change the hiding place every third day. Repeat the spell as you remove and hide the bag. After your wish has been granted, destroy the token by burning it.

Here is a common spell that can be chanted three times in succession as you perform your ritual. You may adapt it to suit your specific needs. For example, you can replace the word "wish" with your specific request.

Powers that be grant me a wish today,
Large, small, tiny, or huge.
Let my wish grow here, there, and everywhere,
North, south, east, and west.
Carry my wish through your quarter to the powers that be,
Grant me this wish so that we may rejoice together.
So mote it be.

Here are some popular herbs used in wishing spells.

Basil is an easy herb to obtain or grow yourself. If your wish is to be protected from negativity or to be cleansed, then basil is the herb to use.

Bay laurel, commonly known as bay leaf, is used in success and prestige wishes. Although this is a tender perennial, it does grow well indoors in a pot.

Calendula leaves and dried flowers placed under the bed are said to make one's dreams come true. This is an easy flower to grow. It adds extra punch to your herb garden with its bright orange, yellow, and pink petals.

Cinnamon is the spice of choice for wishes dealing with power.

Hyssop is effective when used in wishing spells for spiritual calmness.

Job's tears, sewn inside your pillow, are said to make a wish come true within seven days.

Mustard seed has always had special properties. To make a wishing bag of your own for a particular objective, place into a drawstring pouch one rabbit's foot, five new nails, nine mustard seeds, and thirteen pennies. Anoint the bag with Mojo Oil and then rub the bag between your palms as you make your wish.

Parsley is best used in wishing spells by women. Parsley is effective for wishes involving calming an atmosphere or protecting a specific place.

Peppermint is best used for money and prosperity wishes. Peppermint is said to give a mentally stimulating vibration. When growing your own peppermint be sure to put it in a large pot and bury the entire pot. Peppermint is very invasive.

Rosemary is most effective when used in promotion or advancement wishes. In cooler climates, rosemary can be overwintered in a pot indoors.

Rue is an excellent herb to add to your wish spell mixture, because it provides protection. It is also a spiritualizing herb that adds a calming vibration to spells. A note of caution: If you are allergic to rue, it can cause boils on your skin when you touch it.

Sage is good if you wish to resolve a problem. It is also a good choice for wishing spells that deal with mental clarity. Sage is a very easy herb to grow.

Vervain is good for making your dreams or wishes come true. Steep the vervain, covered, in warm water for five minutes. Strain and add the water to your bath. The carrying or wearing of vervain places one under the protective influences of the Love Goddess. Vervain is also considered a protective herb that will guard the wearer from enchantments on them. This is the best herb to use for general wishes.

Yarrow leaves and flowers are often used in wishing spells that deal with love. A word of caution here: One should not perform a love spell. These spells are known to backfire, and one should not try to control the will of another. However the sprinkling of yarrow can increase human love.

Once you have decided which herbs you will be using and are ready to complete your spell, you will need to measure out the correct amount of herbs. Generally a small amount, such as a tablespoon, of each herb is sufficient. However, for talismans you may need a bit more in order to fill your container. If you are using fresh herbs, be sure to dry them first—especially if they will be put into a talisman.

Protective Pentacle Stepping Stone

by Olivia O'Meir

After moving into my first home, I wanted to create a unique and beautiful protection talisman for the space and all of its inhabitants. After some thought, the inspiration for this talisman came to me from a clearance bin slate-circle found at a local crafts store.

If you want a protective pentacle, I suggest you begin this project by determining the talisman's true purpose and placement. I decided to decorate a slate as a stepping-stone talisman of protection in the garden. The talisman can be used as an altar plate or tile, as a gift, or simply as a decoration. It can be made to mark any goal or to commemorate a special event, such as a birth, death, or Wiccaning.

Starting Your Pentacle

The first step in making your protective pentacle stepping stone is planning the design. Take a piece of paper and sketch an outline of the talisman on it. The outline should be similar in size to the actual talisman—this way, you can play with the design and symbols as many times as you want without running the risk of ruining the project.

The great thing about this project is that you can make the design as simple or complex as you want. I made mine complex, as I wanted to include multiple symbols for the elements and deities. Some symbols you can use include pentacles, astrological signs, elemental signs, runes, magical tools, deity symbols, numbers, and names.

I started my design by drawing a pentacle inside the circle to represent the Pagan ideal of "as above, so below," which teaches that the spiritual and mundane are connected within all of nature. I outlined the pentacle in the color black for two reasons. First, black defines and outlines boundaries. Second, black ink contains all the colors of the rainbow—so it seems inclusive of all the powers I wanted to evoke.

Next, I marked the elemental quarter directions (north/earth, east/air, south/fire, west/water) on the outer circle band with alchemical triangles and their alternate circular symbols. I wrote the names of the elements around the outer circle between the symbols, using four different magical languages. I wrote "earth" in brown using the Celtic tree alphabet, known as the Ogham. Then, I wrote "air" in light blue using Germanic runes. "Fire" was written in a deep red-brown using the Theban script. I finished the elements by writing "water" in blue-green with the English alphabet.

On the inside pentagram, I drew the Hindu Tattwas symbols for the elements on their respective triangles, which are (from top and going clockwise) spirit, water, fire, earth, and air. These positions are the traditional starting points for the invoking pentacles used when calling the elements. The colors I used were purple for spirit, silver for water, rust for fire, deep brown-red for earth, and light blue for air.

In the middle of the pentacle I placed a black dot, which represents the womb—as the place of creation. Next to the dot, I put the traditional Wiccan symbols of the Lord and Lady, with the Goddess on the left and the God on the right. I also placed the traditional Wiccan names of the deities below the symbols. I felt that the black color added a nice contrast to help draw attention to the deity symbols.

Around the triangles on the inside of the circle, I added the blessings that I wished for my home and its inhabitants. The words I chose were: understanding, love, strength, knowledge, and power, all written in black. In addition, I drew the symbols of the planet that best represents each key word in the corresponding triangle.

I picked the Moon for understanding, Venus for love, Mars for strength, Mercury for knowledge, and the Sun for power. The colors of the planet sigils matched its key word. I used silver for the Moon, bright red for Venus, rust for Mars, yellow for Mercury, and gold for the Sun. I added zodiac glyphs around the inside of the circle and matched up the symbols to the corresponding keyword:

Understanding: Pisces, Libra, Aquarius

Love: Cancer, Virgo

Strength: Taurus, Capricorn

Knowledge: Gemini, Sagittarius

Power: Leo, Aries, Scorpio

I colored each astrological sign according to its sign element. The earth signs (Taurus, Virgo, Capricorn) were painted green. The air signs (Gemini, Libra, Aquarius) are in yellow. The fire signs (Aries, Leo, Sagittarius) are in bright red. The water signs (Cancer, Scorpio, Pisces) are in blue.

To strengthen the talisman's protective qualities, I added the following prayer on the back.

Lord and Lady, protect and bless this home's owners and visitors with understanding, love, strength, knowledge, and power. So mote it be!

Transferring the Talismanic Magic

These are just suggestions to help you get started. Remember that your magic and creativity is only limited by your imagination. Once you are happy with the design, it is time to collect all the materials you need to create the talisman.

This project's supplies are easy to get at any crafts or home and garden store. As I mentioned, the slate was bought at a craft store, but most likely can be found for less at a home and garden store. You can paint the symbols on with acrylic paint and a brush. I used paint pens, which are only a couple of dollars each and are easier and neater to use. There is also a wide assortment of paint pen colors to choose from.

When your design is completed, you can transfer it to the talisman. After I finished painting on my slate, I coated the talisman with an acrylic sealant because I planned to put it outside. The sealant is inexpensive and will extend the project's life by protecting the design. You can purchase the sealant at any crafts or hardware store.

There are many ways to take this idea and personalize it. The most powerful magic is the kind you create yourself. The colors can be changed to match your décor or simply your heart's desire. You can change the materials to suit your own style. You can use tile, wood, fabric, cardboard, window cling-ons, or anything else you can think of.

The symbolism can be changed to match your spiritual path or personal preference. A Celtic pentacle might incorporate more knot work or zoomorphic shapes. The claddagh might be used in the center instead of the God and Goddess symbols. Rich colors, like deep greens and golds, could accent the design. A Dianic pentacle might incorporate the Nile River goddess in the center with Moon phases replacing the quarter symbols. The names of the Goddess can be written around the pentacle. The colors can be bright and vibrant or deep and dark, depending on your preferences.

Almanac Section

Calendar

Time Changes

Lunar Phases

Moon Signs

Full Moons

Sabbats

World Holidays

Incense of the Day

Color of the Day

Almanac Listings

In these listings you will find the date, day, lunar phase, Moon sign, color and incense for the day, and festivals from around the world.

The Date

The date is used in numerological calculations that govern magical rites.

The Day

Each day is ruled by a planet that possesses specific magical influences:

MONDAY (MOON): Peace, sleep, healing, compassion, friends, psychic awareness, purification, and fertility.

TUESDAY (MARS): Passion, sex, courage, aggression, and protection.

WEDNESDAY (MERCURY): The conscious mind, study, travel, divination, and wisdom.

THURSDAY (JUPITER): Expansion, money, prosperity, and generosity.

FRIDAY (VENUS): Love, friendship, reconciliation, and beauty.

SATURDAY (SATURN): Longevity, exorcism, endings, homes, and houses.

SUNDAY (SUN): Healing, spirituality, success, strength, and protection.

The Lunar Phase

The lunar phase is important in determining the best times for magic.

THE WAXING MOON (from the New Moon to the Full) is the ideal time for magic to draw things toward you.

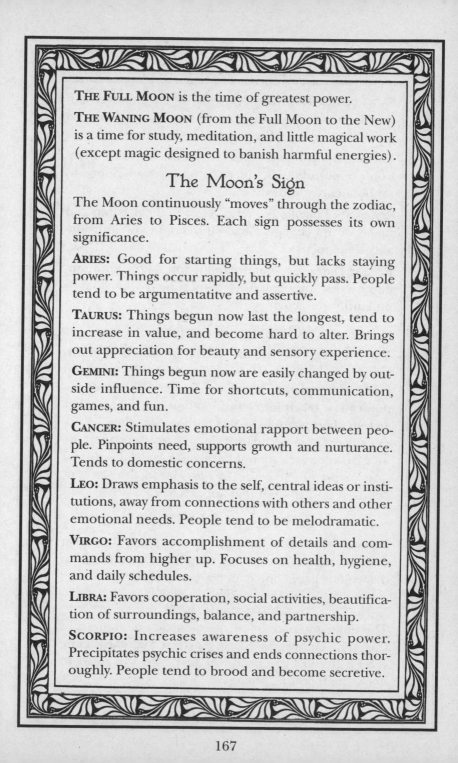

THE FULL MOON is the time of greatest power.

THE WANING MOON (from the Full Moon to the New) is a time for study, meditation, and little magical work (except magic designed to banish harmful energies).

The Moon's Sign

The Moon continuously "moves" through the zodiac, from Aries to Pisces. Each sign possesses its own significance.

ARIES: Good for starting things, but lacks staying power. Things occur rapidly, but quickly pass. People tend to be argumentatitve and assertive.

TAURUS: Things begun now last the longest, tend to increase in value, and become hard to alter. Brings out appreciation for beauty and sensory experience.

GEMINI: Things begun now are easily changed by outside influence. Time for shortcuts, communication, games, and fun.

CANCER: Stimulates emotional rapport between people. Pinpoints need, supports growth and nurturance. Tends to domestic concerns.

LEO: Draws emphasis to the self, central ideas or institutions, away from connections with others and other emotional needs. People tend to be melodramatic.

VIRGO: Favors accomplishment of details and commands from higher up. Focuses on health, hygiene, and daily schedules.

LIBRA: Favors cooperation, social activities, beautification of surroundings, balance, and partnership.

SCORPIO: Increases awareness of psychic power. Precipitates psychic crises and ends connections thoroughly. People tend to brood and become secretive.

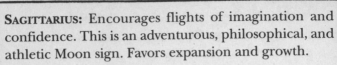

SAGITTARIUS: Encourages flights of imagination and confidence. This is an adventurous, philosophical, and athletic Moon sign. Favors expansion and growth.

CAPRICORN: Develops strong structure. Focus on traditions, responsibilities, and obligations. A good time to set boundaries and rules.

AQUARIUS: Rebellious energy. Time to break habits and make abrupt change. Personal freedom and individuality is the focus.

PISCES: The focus is on dreaming, nostalgia, intuition, and psychic impressions. A good time for spiritual or philanthropic activities.

Color and Incense

The color and incense for the day are based on information from *Personal Alchemy* by Amber Wolfe, and relate to the planet that rules each day. This information can be taken into consideration along with other factors when planning works of magic or when blending magic into mundane life. Please note that the incense selections are not hard-and-fast. If you can not find or do not like the incense listed for the day, choose a similar scent that appeals to you.

Festivals and Holidays

Festivals are listed throughout the year. The exact dates of many of these ancient festivals are difficult to determine; prevailing data has been used.

Time Changes

The times and dates of all astrological phenomena in this almanac are based on **Eastern Standard Time (EST)**. If you live outside of EST, you will need to make the following changes:

PACIFIC STANDARD TIME: Subtract three hours.

MOUNTAIN STANDARD TIME: Subtract two hours.

CENTRAL STANDARD TIME: Subtract one hour.

ALASKA/HAWAII: Subtract five hours.

DAYLIGHT SAVING TIME: Add an hour. Daylight Saving Time runs from April 2 to October 29, 2006.

2006 Sabbats and Full Moons

January 14	Full Moon 4:48 am
February 2	Imbolc
February 12	Full Moon 11:44 pm
March 14	Full Moon 6:25 pm
March 20	Ostara (Spring Equinox)
April 13	Full Moon 12:40 pm
May 1	Beltane
May 13	Full Moon 2:51 am
June 11	Full Moon 2:03 pm
June 21	Litha (Summer Solstice)
July 10	Full Moon 11:02 pm
August 1	Lammas
August 9	Full Moon 6:54 am
September 7	Full Moon 2:42 pm
September 23	Mabon (Fall Equinox)
October 6	Full Moon 11:13 pm
October 31	Samhain
November 5	Full Moon 7:58 am
December 4	Full Moon 7:25 pm
December 21	Yule (Winter Solstice)

Capricorn ♑

1 Sunday
New Year's Day • Kwanzaa ends
Waxing Moon
Moon Phase: First Quarter
Color: Yellow

Moon Sign: Capricorn
Moon enters Aquarius 7:14 am
Incense: Poplar

2 Monday
First Writing (Japanese)
Waxing Moon
Moon Phase: First Quarter
Color: Gray

Moon Sign: Aquarius
Incense: Maple

3 Tuesday
St. Genevieve's Day
Waxing Moon
Moon Phase: First Quarter
Color: Red

Moon Sign: Aquarius
Moon enters Pisces 7:43 am
Incense: Gardenia

4 Wednesday
Frost Fairs on the Thames
Waxing Moon
Moon Phase: First Quarter
Color: Brown

Moon Sign: Pisces
Incense: Cedar

5 Thursday
Epiphany Eve
Waxing Moon
Moon Phase: First Quarter
Color: Green

Moon Sign: Pisces
Moon enters Aries 9:44 am
Incense: Evergreen

◐ Friday
Epiphany
Waxing Moon
Moon Phase: Second Quarter 1:56 pm
Color: White

Moon Sign: Aries
Incense: Ginger

7 Saturday
Rizdvo (Ukrainian)
Waxing Moon
Moon Phase: Second Quarter
Color: Indigo

Moon Sign: Aries
Moon enters Taurus 2:09 pm
Incense: Jasmine

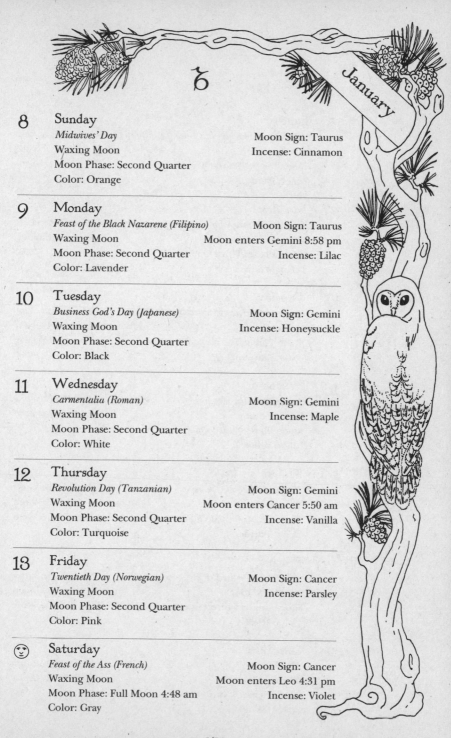

ʒ January

8 Sunday
Midwives' Day
Waxing Moon
Moon Phase: Second Quarter
Color: Orange

Moon Sign: Taurus
Incense: Cinnamon

9 Monday
Feast of the Black Nazarene (Filipino)
Waxing Moon
Moon Phase: Second Quarter
Color: Lavender

Moon Sign: Taurus
Moon enters Gemini 8:58 pm
Incense: Lilac

10 Tuesday
Business God's Day (Japanese)
Waxing Moon
Moon Phase: Second Quarter
Color: Black

Moon Sign: Gemini
Incense: Honeysuckle

11 Wednesday
Carmentalia (Roman)
Waxing Moon
Moon Phase: Second Quarter
Color: White

Moon Sign: Gemini
Incense: Maple

12 Thursday
Revolution Day (Tanzanian)
Waxing Moon
Moon Phase: Second Quarter
Color: Turquoise

Moon Sign: Gemini
Moon enters Cancer 5:50 am
Incense: Vanilla

13 Friday
Twentieth Day (Norwegian)
Waxing Moon
Moon Phase: Second Quarter
Color: Pink

Moon Sign: Cancer
Incense: Parsley

Saturday
Feast of the Ass (French)
Waxing Moon
Moon Phase: Full Moon 4:48 am
Color: Gray

Moon Sign: Cancer
Moon enters Leo 4:31 pm
Incense: Violet

15 Sunday
Martin Luther King, Jr.'s Birthday (actual)   Moon Sign: Leo
Waning Moon   Incense: Sage
Moon Phase: Third Quarter
Color: Gold

16 Monday
Birthday of Martin Luther King, Jr. (observed)   Moon Sign: Leo
Waning Moon   Incense: Coriander
Moon Phase: Third Quarter
Color: White

17 Tuesday
St. Anthony's Day (Mexican)   Moon Sign: Leo
Waning Moon   Moon enters Virgo 4:49 am
Moon Phase: Third Quarter   Incense: Poplar
Color: Maroon

18 Wednesday
Assumption Day   Moon Sign: Virgo
Waning Moon   Incense: Pine
Moon Phase: Third Quarter
Color: Yellow

19 Thursday
Kitchen God Feast (Chinese)   Moon Sign: Virgo
Waning Moon   Moon enters Libra 5:49 pm
Moon Phase: Third Quarter   Incense: Sandalwood
Color: Purple

20 Friday
Breadbasket Festival (Portuguese)   Moon Sign: Libra
Waning Moon   Sun enters Aquarius 12:15 am
Moon Phase: Third Quarter   Incense: Rose
Color: Rose

21 Saturday
St. Agnes Day   Moon Sign: Libra
Waning Moon   Incense: Cedar
Moon Phase: Third Quarter
Color: Black

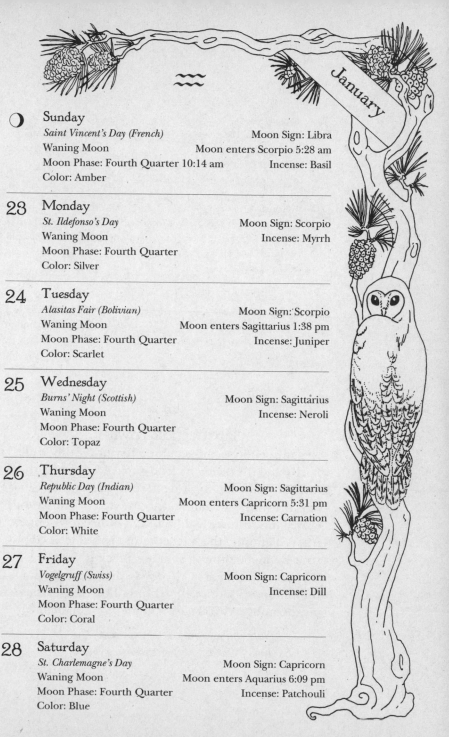

○ Sunday
Saint Vincent's Day (French)
Waning Moon
Moon Phase: Fourth Quarter 10:14 am
Color: Amber

Moon Sign: Libra
Moon enters Scorpio 5:28 am
Incense: Basil

---

23 Monday
St. Ildefonso's Day
Waning Moon
Moon Phase: Fourth Quarter
Color: Silver

Moon Sign: Scorpio
Incense: Myrrh

---

24 Tuesday
Alasitas Fair (Bolivian)
Waning Moon
Moon Phase: Fourth Quarter
Color: Scarlet

Moon Sign: Scorpio
Moon enters Sagittarius 1:38 pm
Incense: Juniper

---

25 Wednesday
Burns' Night (Scottish)
Waning Moon
Moon Phase: Fourth Quarter
Color: Topaz

Moon Sign: Sagittarius
Incense: Neroli

---

26 Thursday
Republic Day (Indian)
Waning Moon
Moon Phase: Fourth Quarter
Color: White

Moon Sign: Sagittarius
Moon enters Capricorn 5:31 pm
Incense: Carnation

---

27 Friday
Vogelgruff (Swiss)
Waning Moon
Moon Phase: Fourth Quarter
Color: Coral

Moon Sign: Capricorn
Incense: Dill

---

28 Saturday
St. Charlemagne's Day
Waning Moon
Moon Phase: Fourth Quarter
Color: Blue

Moon Sign: Capricorn
Moon enters Aquarius 6:09 pm
Incense: Patchouli

Aquarius

≈≈≈

Sunday
Chinese New Year (dog)
Waning Moon
Moon Phase: New Moon 9:15 am
Color: Orange

Moon Sign: Aquarius
Incense: Coriander

---

30 Monday
Three Hierarchs' Day (Eastern Orthodox)
Waxing Moon
Moon Phase: First Quarter
Color: Ivory

Moon Sign: Aquarius
Moon enters Pisces 5:32 pm
Incense: Maple

---

31 Tuesday
Islamic New Year
Waxing Moon
Moon Phase: First Quarter
Color: Black

Moon Sign: Pisces
Incense: Chrysanthemum

Purification Powder

Negative energy can accumulate during the winter. Purify and protect your living space from negativity with this powder. In a dish combine one crushed bay leaf with one-half teaspoon each of cinnamon, clove, and nutmeg, and a pinch of dried rosemary. After blending the ingredients, sprinkle it about your home beginning at an east-facing door or window and moving in a clockwise direction. Sprinkle on window sills, door thresholds, fireplaces, attics—any opening. As you sprinkle the powder, chant:

Sacred dust, protect this space,
Every crack, every crevice, everyplace.

—James Kambos

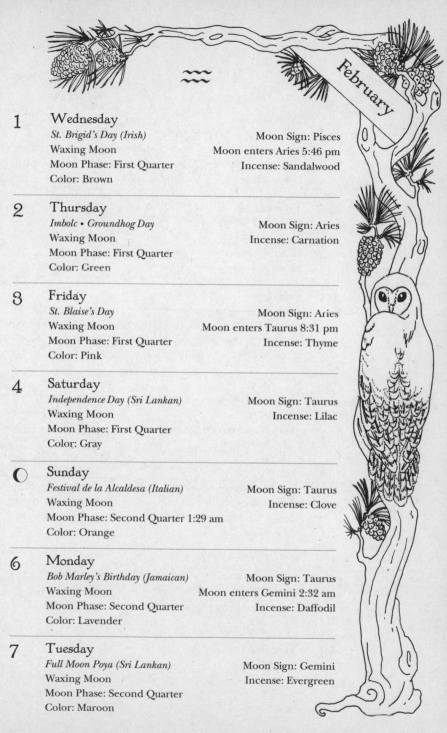

1 Wednesday

St. Brigid's Day (Irish)
Waxing Moon
Moon Phase: First Quarter
Color: Brown

Moon Sign: Pisces
Moon enters Aries 5:46 pm
Incense: Sandalwood

2 Thursday

Imbolc • Groundhog Day
Waxing Moon
Moon Phase: First Quarter
Color: Green

Moon Sign: Aries
Incense: Carnation

3 Friday

St. Blaise's Day
Waxing Moon
Moon Phase: First Quarter
Color: Pink

Moon Sign: Aries
Moon enters Taurus 8:31 pm
Incense: Thyme

4 Saturday

Independence Day (Sri Lankan)
Waxing Moon
Moon Phase: First Quarter
Color: Gray

Moon Sign: Taurus
Incense: Lilac

◖ Sunday

Festival de la Alcaldesa (Italian)
Waxing Moon
Moon Phase: Second Quarter 1:29 am
Color: Orange

Moon Sign: Taurus
Incense: Clove

6 Monday

Bob Marley's Birthday (Jamaican)
Waxing Moon
Moon Phase: Second Quarter
Color: Lavender

Moon Sign: Taurus
Moon enters Gemini 2:32 am
Incense: Daffodil

7 Tuesday

Full Moon Poya (Sri Lankan)
Waxing Moon
Moon Phase: Second Quarter
Color: Maroon

Moon Sign: Gemini
Incense: Evergreen

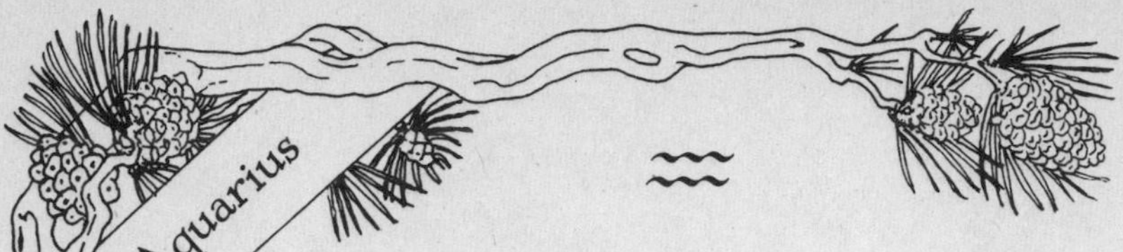

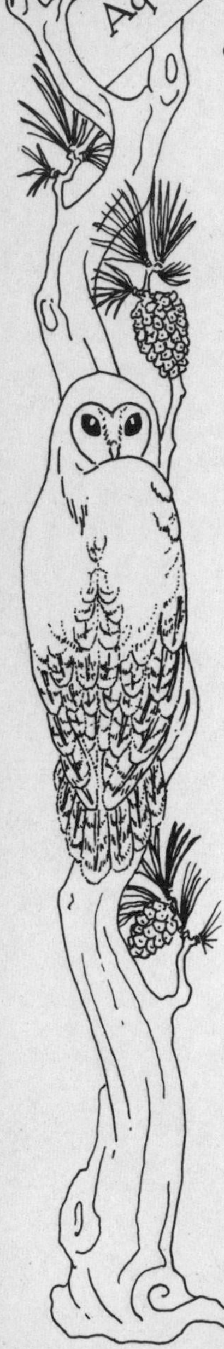

≈≈

8 Wednesday
Mass for Broken Needles (Japanese)
Waxing Moon
Moon Phase: Second Quarter
Color: Yellow

Moon Sign: Gemini
Moon enters Cancer 11:33 am
Incense: Coriander

9 Thursday
St. Marion's Day (Lebanese)
Waxing Moon
Moon Phase: Second Quarter
Color: White

Moon Sign: Cancer
Incense: Geranium

10 Friday
Gasparilla Day (Florida)
Waxing Moon
Moon Phase: Second Quarter
Color: Rose

Moon Sign: Cancer
Moon enters Leo 10:44 pm
Incense: Sandalwood

11 Saturday
Foundation Day (Japanese)
Waxing Moon
Moon Phase: Second Quarter
Color: Brown

Moon Sign: Leo
Incense: Juniper

Sunday
Lincoln's Birthday (actual)
Waxing Moon
Moon Phase: Full Moon 11:44 pm
Color: Gold

Moon Sign: Leo
Incense: Poplar

13 Monday
Parentalia (Roman)
Waning Moon
Moon Phase: Third Quarter
Color: Silver

Moon Sign: Leo
Moon enters Virgo 11:13 am
Incense: Rose

14 Tuesday
Valentine's Day
Waning Moon
Moon Phase: Third Quarter
Color: Gray

Moon Sign: Virgo
Incense: Sage

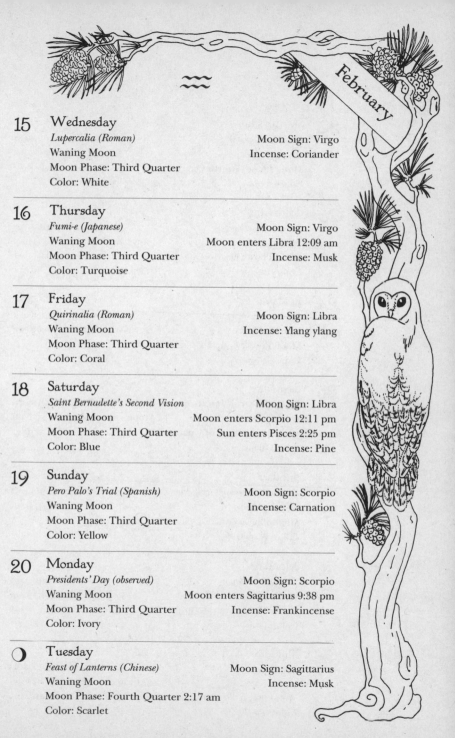

15 Wednesday

Lupercalia (Roman)
Waning Moon
Moon Phase: Third Quarter
Color: White

Moon Sign: Virgo
Incense: Coriander

16 Thursday

Fumi-e (Japanese)
Waning Moon
Moon Phase: Third Quarter
Color: Turquoise

Moon Sign: Virgo
Moon enters Libra 12:09 am
Incense: Musk

17 Friday

Quirinalia (Roman)
Waning Moon
Moon Phase: Third Quarter
Color: Coral

Moon Sign: Libra
Incense: Ylang ylang

18 Saturday

Saint Bernadette's Second Vision
Waning Moon
Moon Phase: Third Quarter
Color: Blue

Moon Sign: Libra
Moon enters Scorpio 12:11 pm
Sun enters Pisces 2:25 pm
Incense: Pine

19 Sunday

Pero Palo's Trial (Spanish)
Waning Moon
Moon Phase: Third Quarter
Color: Yellow

Moon Sign: Scorpio
Incense: Carnation

20 Monday

Presidents' Day (observed)
Waning Moon
Moon Phase: Third Quarter
Color: Ivory

Moon Sign: Scorpio
Moon enters Sagittarius 9:38 pm
Incense: Frankincense

◐ Tuesday

Feast of Lanterns (Chinese)
Waning Moon
Moon Phase: Fourth Quarter 2:17 am
Color: Scarlet

Moon Sign: Sagittarius
Incense: Musk

Pisces

♓

22 Wednesday
Caristia (Roman)
Waning Moon
Moon Phase: Fourth Quarter
Color: Topaz

Moon Sign: Sagittarius
Incense: Cedar

23 Thursday
Terminalia (Roman)
Waning Moon
Moon Phase: Fourth Quarter
Color: Purple

Moon Sign: Sagittarius
Moon enters Capricorn 3:16 am
Incense: Jasmine

24 Friday
Regifugium (Roman)
Waning Moon
Moon Phase: Fourth Quarter
Color: White

Moon Sign: Capricorn
Incense: Nutmeg

25 Saturday
Saint Walburga's Day (German)
Waning Moon
Moon Phase: Fourth Quarter
Color: Black

Moon Sign: Capricorn
Moon enters Aquarius 5:14 am
Incense: Lavender

26 Sunday
Zamboanga Festival (Filipino)
Waning Moon
Moon Phase: Fourth Quarter
Color: Amber

Moon Sign: Aquarius
Incense: Basil

☽ Monday
Threepenny Day
Waning Moon
Moon Phase: New Moon 7:31 pm
Color: Gray

Moon Sign: Aquarius
Moon enters Pisces 4:56 am
Incense: Peony

28 Tuesday
Mardi Gras
Waxing Moon
Moon Phase: First Quarter
Color: Red

Moon Sign: Pisces
Moon enters Scorpio 7:21 am
Incense: Gardenia

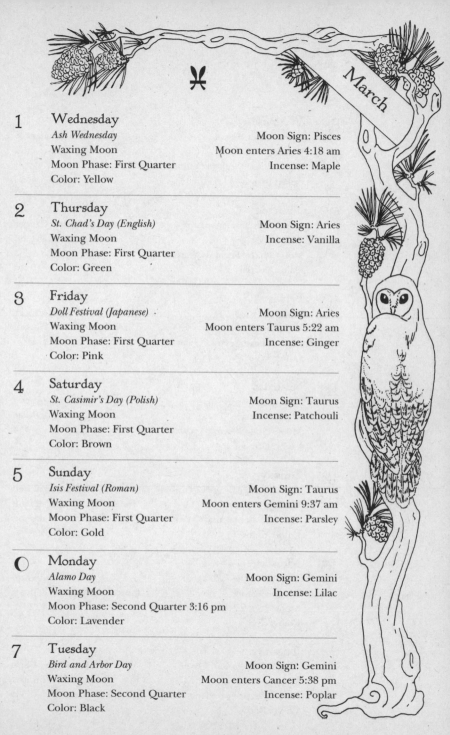

1 Wednesday
Ash Wednesday
Waxing Moon
Moon Phase: First Quarter
Color: Yellow

Moon Sign: Pisces
Moon enters Aries 4:18 am
Incense: Maple

2 Thursday
St. Chad's Day (English)
Waxing Moon
Moon Phase: First Quarter
Color: Green

Moon Sign: Aries
Incense: Vanilla

3 Friday
Doll Festival (Japanese)
Waxing Moon
Moon Phase: First Quarter
Color: Pink

Moon Sign: Aries
Moon enters Taurus 5:22 am
Incense: Ginger

4 Saturday
St. Casimir's Day (Polish)
Waxing Moon
Moon Phase: First Quarter
Color: Brown

Moon Sign: Taurus
Incense: Patchouli

5 Sunday
Isis Festival (Roman)
Waxing Moon
Moon Phase: First Quarter
Color: Gold

Moon Sign: Taurus
Moon enters Gemini 9:37 am
Incense: Parsley

6 ☽ Monday
Alamo Day
Waxing Moon
Moon Phase: Second Quarter 3:16 pm
Color: Lavender

Moon Sign: Gemini
Incense: Lilac

7 Tuesday
Bird and Arbor Day
Waxing Moon
Moon Phase: Second Quarter
Color: Black

Moon Sign: Gemini
Moon enters Cancer 5:38 pm
Incense: Poplar

8 Wednesday
International Women's Day
Waxing Moon
Moon Phase: Second Quarter
Color: Brown

Moon Sign: Cancer
Incense: Pine

---

9 Thursday
Forty Saints' Day (Romanian)
Waxing Moon
Moon Phase: Second Quarter
Color: Purple

Moon Sign: Cancer
Incense: Sandalwood

---

10 Friday
Tibet Day
Waxing Moon
Moon Phase: Second Quarter
Color: Rose

Moon Sign: Cancer
Moon enters Leo 4:42 am
Incense: Rose

---

11 Saturday
Feast of Gauri (Hindu)
Waxing Moon
Moon Phase: Second Quarter
Color: Gray

Moon Sign: Leo
Incense: Lilac

---

12 Sunday
Receiving the Water (Buddhist)
Waxing Moon
Moon Phase: Second Quarter
Color: Yellow

Moon Sign: Leo
Moon enters Virgo 5:23 pm
Incense: Cinnamon

---

13 Monday
Purification Feast (Balinese)
Waxing Moon
Moon Phase: Second Quarter
Color: Gray

Moon Sign: Virgo
Incense: Chrysanthemum

Tuesday
Mamuralia (Roman) • *Purim*
Waxing Moon
Moon Phase: Full Moon 6:35 pm
Color: Maroon

Moon Sign: Virgo
Incense: Juniper

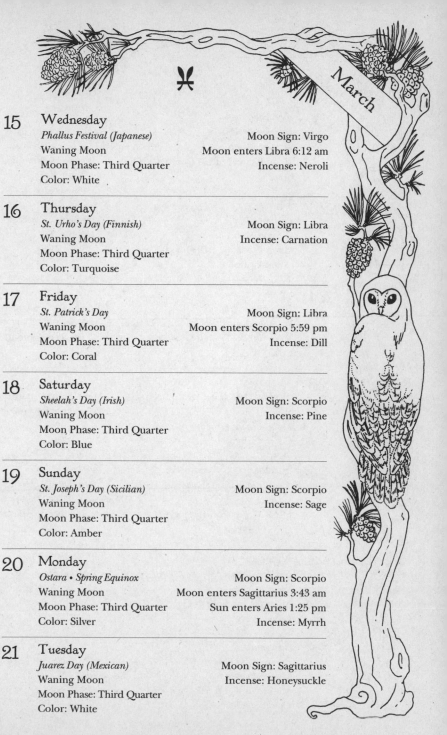

♓

15 Wednesday
Phallus Festival (Japanese)
Waning Moon
Moon Phase: Third Quarter
Color: White

Moon Sign: Virgo
Moon enters Libra 6:12 am
Incense: Neroli

16 Thursday
St. Urho's Day (Finnish)
Waning Moon
Moon Phase: Third Quarter
Color: Turquoise

Moon Sign: Libra
Incense: Carnation

17 Friday
St. Patrick's Day
Waning Moon
Moon Phase: Third Quarter
Color: Coral

Moon Sign: Libra
Moon enters Scorpio 5:59 pm
Incense: Dill

18 Saturday
Sheelah's Day (Irish)
Waning Moon
Moon Phase: Third Quarter
Color: Blue

Moon Sign: Scorpio
Incense: Pine

19 Sunday
St. Joseph's Day (Sicilian)
Waning Moon
Moon Phase: Third Quarter
Color: Amber

Moon Sign: Scorpio
Incense: Sage

20 Monday
Ostara • Spring Equinox
Waning Moon
Moon Phase: Third Quarter
Color: Silver

Moon Sign: Scorpio
Moon enters Sagittarius 3:43 am
Sun enters Aries 1:25 pm
Incense: Myrrh

21 Tuesday
Juarez Day (Mexican)
Waning Moon
Moon Phase: Third Quarter
Color: White

Moon Sign: Sagittarius
Incense: Honeysuckle

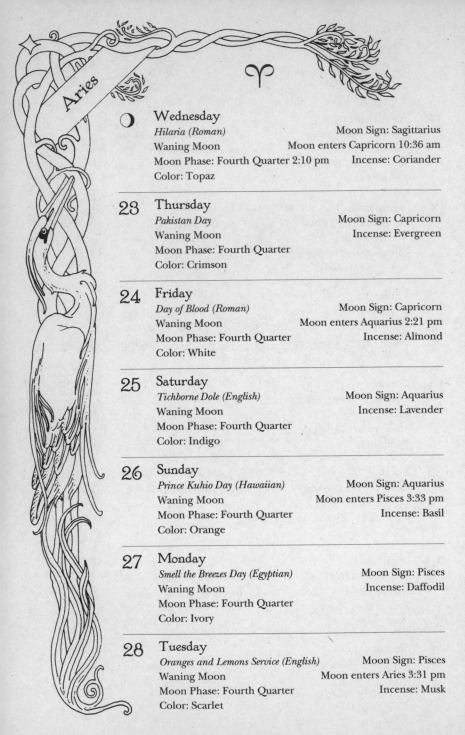

♈

◐ **Wednesday**
Hilaria (Roman)
Waning Moon
Moon Phase: Fourth Quarter 2:10 pm
Color: Topaz

Moon Sign: Sagittarius
Moon enters Capricorn 10:36 am
Incense: Coriander

23 **Thursday**
Pakistan Day
Waning Moon
Moon Phase: Fourth Quarter
Color: Crimson

Moon Sign: Capricorn
Incense: Evergreen

24 **Friday**
Day of Blood (Roman)
Waning Moon
Moon Phase: Fourth Quarter
Color: White

Moon Sign: Capricorn
Moon enters Aquarius 2:21 pm
Incense: Almond

25 **Saturday**
Tichborne Dole (English)
Waning Moon
Moon Phase: Fourth Quarter
Color: Indigo

Moon Sign: Aquarius
Incense: Lavender

26 **Sunday**
Prince Kuhio Day (Hawaiian)
Waning Moon
Moon Phase: Fourth Quarter
Color: Orange

Moon Sign: Aquarius
Moon enters Pisces 3:33 pm
Incense: Basil

27 **Monday**
Smell the Breezes Day (Egyptian)
Waning Moon
Moon Phase: Fourth Quarter
Color: Ivory

Moon Sign: Pisces
Incense: Daffodil

28 **Tuesday**
Oranges and Lemons Service (English)
Waning Moon
Moon Phase: Fourth Quarter
Color: Scarlet

Moon Sign: Pisces
Moon enters Aries 3:31 pm
Incense: Musk

Wednesday
St. Eustace's Day
Waning Moon
Moon Phase: New Moon 5:15 am
Color: Brown

Moon Sign: Aries
Incense: Sandalwood

30 Thursday
Seward's Day (Alaskan)
Waxing Moon
Moon Phase: First Quarter
Color: White

Moon Sign: Aries
Moon enters Taurus 4:00 pm
Incense: Carnation

31 Friday
The Borrowed Days (Ethiopian)
Waxing Moon
Moon Phase: First Quarter
Color: Purple

Moon Sign: Taurus
Incense: Thyme

Primrose Lore

Primroses (*Primula vulgaris*) are well-known shade-loving plants that brighten the early spring garden with their cheerful flowers in a variety of colors: red, purple, blue, white, and yellow. They also have a long history as a healing and magical plant. Extracts obtained from the roots are added to cough medications. The flowers yield a bitter tea that is an age-old treatment for calming the nerves. In magic, primroses attract love, aid in protection, and draw fairies to the garden. Used in love spells they attract loyalty and devotion. The red and blue varieties are thought to be most powerful. Planted in average soil, in light shade, they'll give years of carefree beauty.

—James Kambos

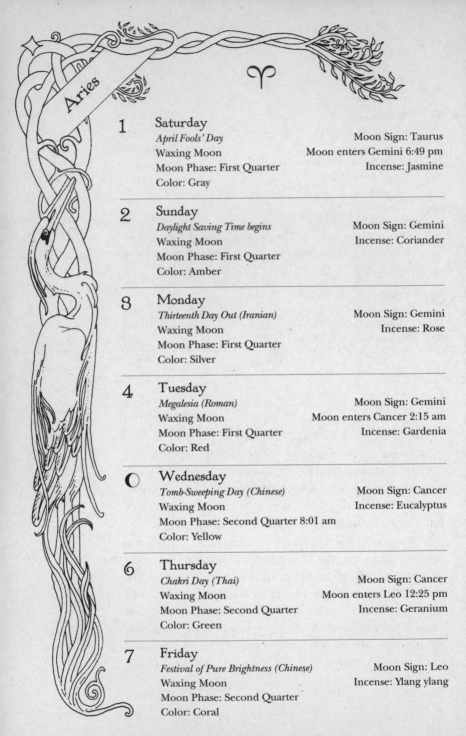

Aries ♈

1 **Saturday**
April Fools' Day
Waxing Moon
Moon Phase: First Quarter
Color: Gray

Moon Sign: Taurus
Moon enters Gemini 6:49 pm
Incense: Jasmine

2 **Sunday**
Daylight Saving Time begins
Waxing Moon
Moon Phase: First Quarter
Color: Amber

Moon Sign: Gemini
Incense: Coriander

3 **Monday**
Thirteenth Day Out (Iranian)
Waxing Moon
Moon Phase: First Quarter
Color: Silver

Moon Sign: Gemini
Incense: Rose

4 **Tuesday**
Megalesia (Roman)
Waxing Moon
Moon Phase: First Quarter
Color: Red

Moon Sign: Gemini
Moon enters Cancer 2:15 am
Incense: Gardenia

☾ **Wednesday**
Tomb-Sweeping Day (Chinese)
Waxing Moon
Moon Phase: Second Quarter 8:01 am
Color: Yellow

Moon Sign: Cancer
Incense: Eucalyptus

6 **Thursday**
Chakri Day (Thai)
Waxing Moon
Moon Phase: Second Quarter
Color: Green

Moon Sign: Cancer
Moon enters Leo 12:25 pm
Incense: Geranium

7 **Friday**
Festival of Pure Brightness (Chinese)
Waxing Moon
Moon Phase: Second Quarter
Color: Coral

Moon Sign: Leo
Incense: Ylang ylang

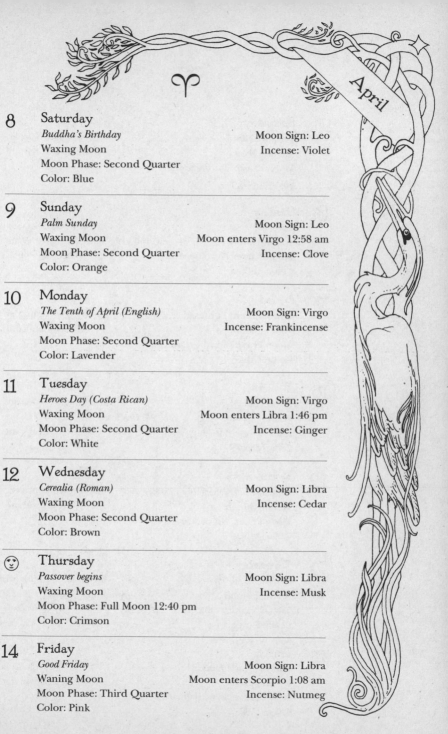

8 Saturday
Buddha's Birthday
Waxing Moon
Moon Phase: Second Quarter
Color: Blue

Moon Sign: Leo
Incense: Violet

---

9 Sunday
Palm Sunday
Waxing Moon
Moon Phase: Second Quarter
Color: Orange

Moon Sign: Leo
Moon enters Virgo 12:58 am
Incense: Clove

---

10 Monday
The Tenth of April (English)
Waxing Moon
Moon Phase: Second Quarter
Color: Lavender

Moon Sign: Virgo
Incense: Frankincense

---

11 Tuesday
Heroes Day (Costa Rican)
Waxing Moon
Moon Phase: Second Quarter
Color: White

Moon Sign: Virgo
Moon enters Libra 1:46 pm
Incense: Ginger

---

12 Wednesday
Cerealia (Roman)
Waxing Moon
Moon Phase: Second Quarter
Color: Brown

Moon Sign: Libra
Incense: Cedar

☺ Thursday
Passover begins
Waxing Moon
Moon Phase: Full Moon 12:40 pm
Color: Crimson

Moon Sign: Libra
Incense: Musk

---

14 Friday
Good Friday
Waning Moon
Moon Phase: Third Quarter
Color: Pink

Moon Sign: Libra
Moon enters Scorpio 1:08 am
Incense: Nutmeg

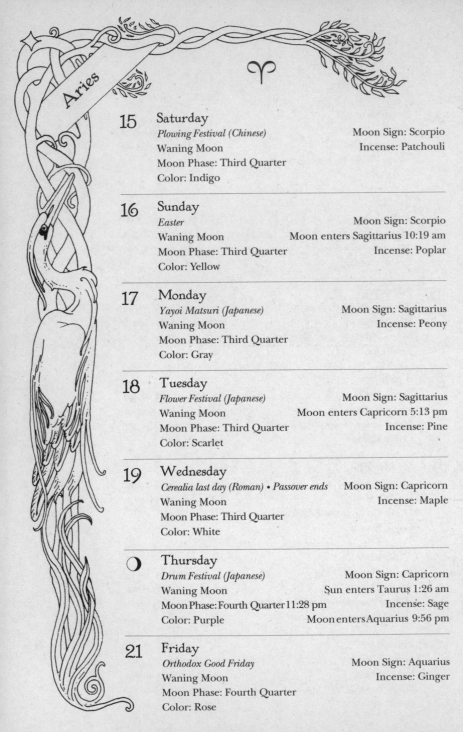

♈

15 Saturday
Plowing Festival (Chinese)
Waning Moon
Moon Phase: Third Quarter
Color: Indigo

Moon Sign: Scorpio
Incense: Patchouli

16 Sunday
Easter
Waning Moon
Moon Phase: Third Quarter
Color: Yellow

Moon Sign: Scorpio
Moon enters Sagittarius 10:19 am
Incense: Poplar

17 Monday
Yayoi Matsuri (Japanese)
Waning Moon
Moon Phase: Third Quarter
Color: Gray

Moon Sign: Sagittarius
Incense: Peony

18 Tuesday
Flower Festival (Japanese)
Waning Moon
Moon Phase: Third Quarter
Color: Scarlet

Moon Sign: Sagittarius
Moon enters Capricorn 5:13 pm
Incense: Pine

19 Wednesday
Cerealia last day (Roman) • Passover ends
Waning Moon
Moon Phase: Third Quarter
Color: White

Moon Sign: Capricorn
Incense: Maple

☽ Thursday
Drum Festival (Japanese)
Waning Moon
Moon Phase: Fourth Quarter 11:28 pm
Color: Purple

Moon Sign: Capricorn
Sun enters Taurus 1:26 am
Incense: Sage
Moon enters Aquarius 9:56 pm

21 Friday
Orthodox Good Friday
Waning Moon
Moon Phase: Fourth Quarter
Color: Rose

Moon Sign: Aquarius
Incense: Ginger

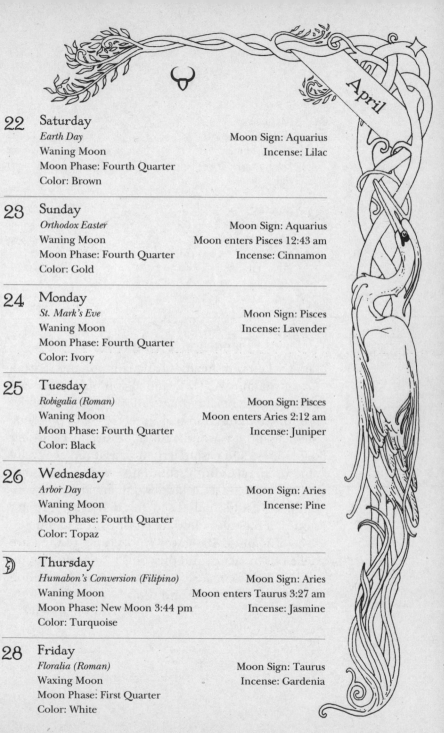

22 Saturday
Earth Day
Waning Moon
Moon Phase: Fourth Quarter
Color: Brown

Moon Sign: Aquarius
Incense: Lilac

23 Sunday
Orthodox Easter
Waning Moon
Moon Phase: Fourth Quarter
Color: Gold

Moon Sign: Aquarius
Moon enters Pisces 12:43 am
Incense: Cinnamon

24 Monday
St. Mark's Eve
Waning Moon
Moon Phase: Fourth Quarter
Color: Ivory

Moon Sign: Pisces
Incense: Lavender

25 Tuesday
Robigalia (Roman)
Waning Moon
Moon Phase: Fourth Quarter
Color: Black

Moon Sign: Pisces
Moon enters Aries 2:12 am
Incense: Juniper

26 Wednesday
Arbor Day
Waning Moon
Moon Phase: Fourth Quarter
Color: Topaz

Moon Sign: Aries
Incense: Pine

Thursday
Humabon's Conversion (Filipino)
Waning Moon
Moon Phase: New Moon 3:44 pm
Color: Turquoise

Moon Sign: Aries
Moon enters Taurus 3:27 am
Incense: Jasmine

28 Friday
Floralia (Roman)
Waxing Moon
Moon Phase: First Quarter
Color: White

Moon Sign: Taurus
Incense: Gardenia

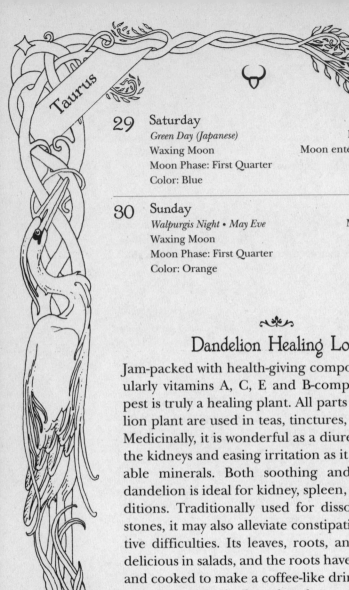

29 **Saturday**
Green Day (Japanese)
Waxing Moon
Moon Phase: First Quarter
Color: Blue

Moon Sign: Taurus
Moon enters Gemini 5:58 am
Incense: Juniper

30 **Sunday**
Walpurgis Night • May Eve
Waxing Moon
Moon Phase: First Quarter
Color: Orange

Moon Sign: Gemini
Incense: Sage

Dandelion Healing Lore

Jam-packed with health-giving components, particularly vitamins A, C, E and B-complex, this yard pest is truly a healing plant. All parts of the dandelion plant are used in teas, tinctures, and powders. Medicinally, it is wonderful as a diuretic, cleansing the kidneys and easing irritation as it replaces valuable minerals. Both soothing and stimulating, dandelion is ideal for kidney, spleen, and liver conditions. Traditionally used for dissolving urinary stones, it may also alleviate constipation and digestive difficulties. Its leaves, roots, and flowers are delicious in salads, and the roots have been ground and cooked to make a coffee-like drink. Dandelion wine is good for body and soul.

—Kristin Madden

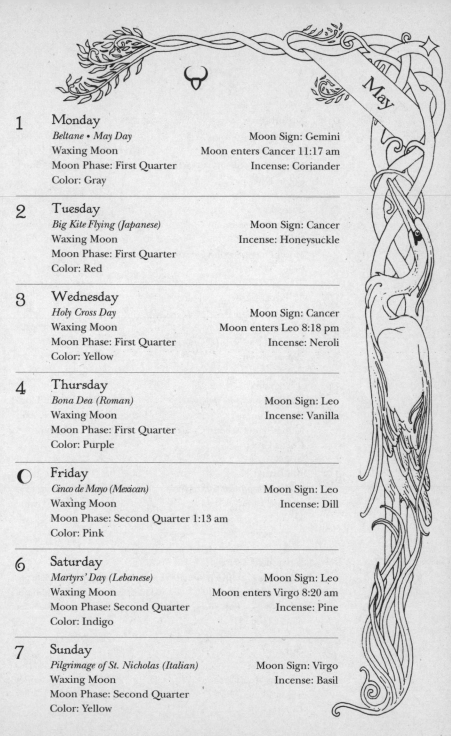

1 Monday
Beltane • May Day
Waxing Moon
Moon Phase: First Quarter
Color: Gray

Moon Sign: Gemini
Moon enters Cancer 11:17 am
Incense: Coriander

2 Tuesday
Big Kite Flying (Japanese)
Waxing Moon
Moon Phase: First Quarter
Color: Red

Moon Sign: Cancer
Incense: Honeysuckle

3 Wednesday
Holy Cross Day
Waxing Moon
Moon Phase: First Quarter
Color: Yellow

Moon Sign: Cancer
Moon enters Leo 8:18 pm
Incense: Neroli

4 Thursday
Bona Dea (Roman)
Waxing Moon
Moon Phase: First Quarter
Color: Purple

Moon Sign: Leo
Incense: Vanilla

◐ Friday
Cinco de Mayo (Mexican)
Waxing Moon
Moon Phase: Second Quarter 1:13 am
Color: Pink

Moon Sign: Leo
Incense: Dill

6 Saturday
Martyrs' Day (Lebanese)
Waxing Moon
Moon Phase: Second Quarter
Color: Indigo

Moon Sign: Leo
Moon enters Virgo 8:20 am
Incense: Pine

7 Sunday
Pilgrimage of St. Nicholas (Italian)
Waxing Moon
Moon Phase: Second Quarter
Color: Yellow

Moon Sign: Virgo
Incense: Basil

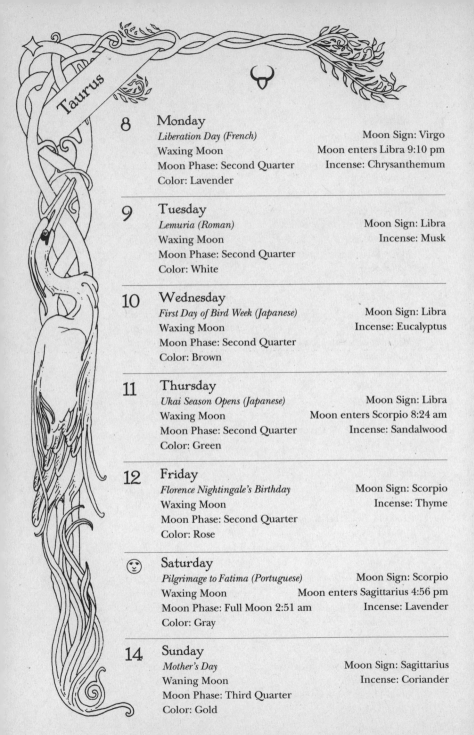

8 Monday
Liberation Day (French)
Waxing Moon
Moon Phase: Second Quarter
Color: Lavender

Moon Sign: Virgo
Moon enters Libra 9:10 pm
Incense: Chrysanthemum

9 Tuesday
Lemuria (Roman)
Waxing Moon
Moon Phase: Second Quarter
Color: White

Moon Sign: Libra
Incense: Musk

10 Wednesday
First Day of Bird Week (Japanese)
Waxing Moon
Moon Phase: Second Quarter
Color: Brown

Moon Sign: Libra
Incense: Eucalyptus

11 Thursday
Ukai Season Opens (Japanese)
Waxing Moon
Moon Phase: Second Quarter
Color: Green

Moon Sign: Libra
Moon enters Scorpio 8:24 am
Incense: Sandalwood

12 Friday
Florence Nightingale's Birthday
Waxing Moon
Moon Phase: Second Quarter
Color: Rose

Moon Sign: Scorpio
Incense: Thyme

Saturday
Pilgrimage to Fatima (Portuguese)
Waxing Moon
Moon Phase: Full Moon 2:51 am
Color: Gray

Moon Sign: Scorpio
Moon enters Sagittarius 4:56 pm
Incense: Lavender

14 Sunday
Mother's Day
Waning Moon
Moon Phase: Third Quarter
Color: Gold

Moon Sign: Sagittarius
Incense: Coriander

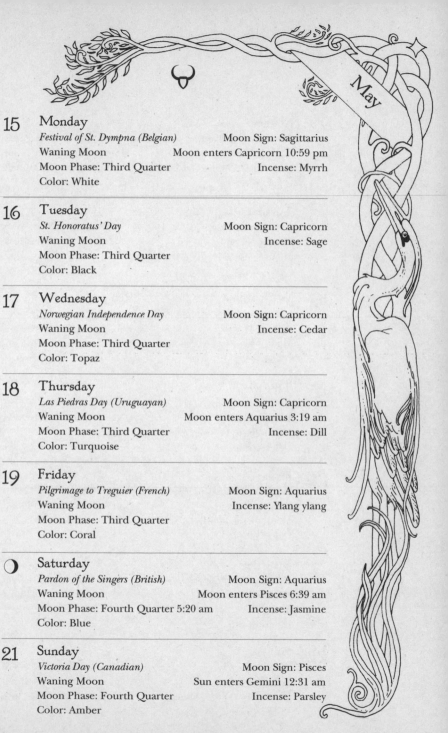

15 Monday
Festival of St. Dympna (Belgian)
Waning Moon
Moon Phase: Third Quarter
Color: White

Moon Sign: Sagittarius
Moon enters Capricorn 10:59 pm
Incense: Myrrh

16 Tuesday
St. Honoratus' Day
Waning Moon
Moon Phase: Third Quarter
Color: Black

Moon Sign: Capricorn
Incense: Sage

17 Wednesday
Norwegian Independence Day
Waning Moon
Moon Phase: Third Quarter
Color: Topaz

Moon Sign: Capricorn
Incense: Cedar

18 Thursday
Las Piedras Day (Uruguayan)
Waning Moon
Moon Phase: Third Quarter
Color: Turquoise

Moon Sign: Capricorn
Moon enters Aquarius 3:19 am
Incense: Dill

19 Friday
Pilgrimage to Treguier (French)
Waning Moon
Moon Phase: Third Quarter
Color: Coral

Moon Sign: Aquarius
Incense: Ylang ylang

Saturday
Pardon of the Singers (British)
Waning Moon
Moon Phase: Fourth Quarter 5:20 am
Color: Blue

Moon Sign: Aquarius
Moon enters Pisces 6:39 am
Incense: Jasmine

21 Sunday
Victoria Day (Canadian)
Waning Moon
Moon Phase: Fourth Quarter
Color: Amber

Moon Sign: Pisces
Sun enters Gemini 12:31 am
Incense: Parsley

Gemini ♊

22 Monday
Heroes' Day (Sri Lankan)
Waning Moon
Moon Phase: Fourth Quarter
Color: Silver

Moon Sign: Pisces
Moon enters Aries 9:24 am
Incense: Daffodil

23 Tuesday
Tubilustrium (Roman)
Waning Moon
Moon Phase: Fourth Quarter
Color: Gray

Moon Sign: Aries
Incense: Musk

24 Wednesday
Culture Day (Bulgarian)
Waning Moon
Moon Phase: Fourth Quarter
Color: White

Moon Sign: Aries
Moon enters Taurus 12:00 pm
Incense: Maple

25 Thursday
Lady Godiva's Day
Waning Moon
Moon Phase: Fourth Quarter
Color: Crimson

Moon Sign: Taurus
Incense: Carnation

26 Friday
Pepys' Commemoration (English)
Waning Moon
Moon Phase: Fourth Quarter
Color: Purple

Moon Sign: Taurus
Moon enters Gemini 3:19 pm
Incense: Almond

Saturday
St. Augustine of Canterbury's Day
Waning Moon
Moon Phase: New Moon 1:25 am
Color: Brown

Moon Sign: Gemini
Incense: Violet

28 Sunday
St. Germain's Day
Waxing Moon
Moon Phase: First Quarter
Color: Orange

Moon Sign: Gemini
Moon enters Cancer 8:33 pm
Incense: Clove

29 Monday
Memorial Day (observed)
Waxing Moon
Moon Phase: First Quarter
Color: Ivory

Moon Sign: Cancer
Incense: Rose

30 Tuesday
Memorial Day (actual)
Waxing Moon
Moon Phase: First Quarter 7:47 am
Color: Maroon

Moon Sign: Cancer
Incense: Gardenia

31 Wednesday
Flowers of May
Waxing Moon
Moon Phase: First Quarter
Color: Yellow

Moon Sign: Cancer
Moon enters Leo 4:51 am
Incense: Pine

Fern Magic

Nothing is more mysterious or beautiful than a fern unfurling in the sun-dappled shade of the woodland on a spring afternoon. Ferns are the ancient ones of the plant kingdom, unchanged in appearance for millions of years. Ferns have long been linked to magic in the garden and the home, particularly valued for their protective vibrations. Thrown on a fire or smoldering embers, dried fern repels all evil. Adepts of long-ago included ferns in luck and prosperity magic. Include a bit of fern leaf in a money-attracting bundle. To attract the fairy folk, place a small shiny object among a clump of ferns at Beltane or Midsummer.

—James Kambos

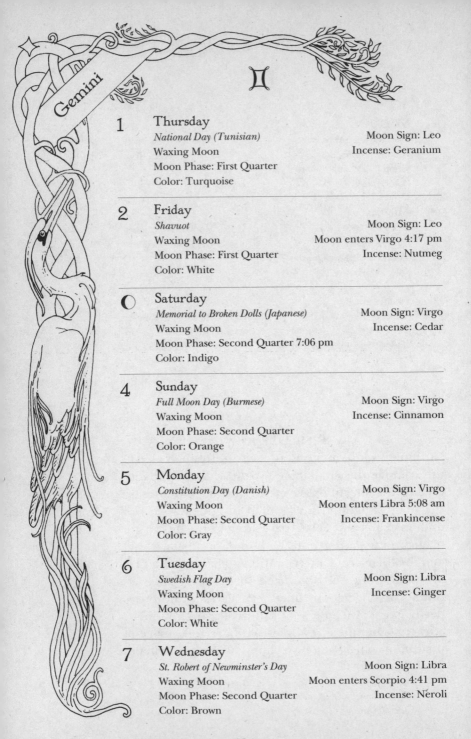

Gemini ♊

1 Thursday
National Day (Tunisian)
Waxing Moon
Moon Phase: First Quarter
Color: Turquoise

Moon Sign: Leo
Incense: Geranium

2 Friday
Shavuot
Waxing Moon
Moon Phase: First Quarter
Color: White

Moon Sign: Leo
Moon enters Virgo 4:17 pm
Incense: Nutmeg

☾ Saturday
Memorial to Broken Dolls (Japanese)
Waxing Moon
Moon Phase: Second Quarter 7:06 pm
Color: Indigo

Moon Sign: Virgo
Incense: Cedar

4 Sunday
Full Moon Day (Burmese)
Waxing Moon
Moon Phase: Second Quarter
Color: Orange

Moon Sign: Virgo
Incense: Cinnamon

5 Monday
Constitution Day (Danish)
Waxing Moon
Moon Phase: Second Quarter
Color: Gray

Moon Sign: Virgo
Moon enters Libra 5:08 am
Incense: Frankincense

6 Tuesday
Swedish Flag Day
Waxing Moon
Moon Phase: Second Quarter
Color: White

Moon Sign: Libra
Incense: Ginger

7 Wednesday
St. Robert of Newminster's Day
Waxing Moon
Moon Phase: Second Quarter
Color: Brown

Moon Sign: Libra
Moon enters Scorpio 4:41 pm
Incense: Neroli

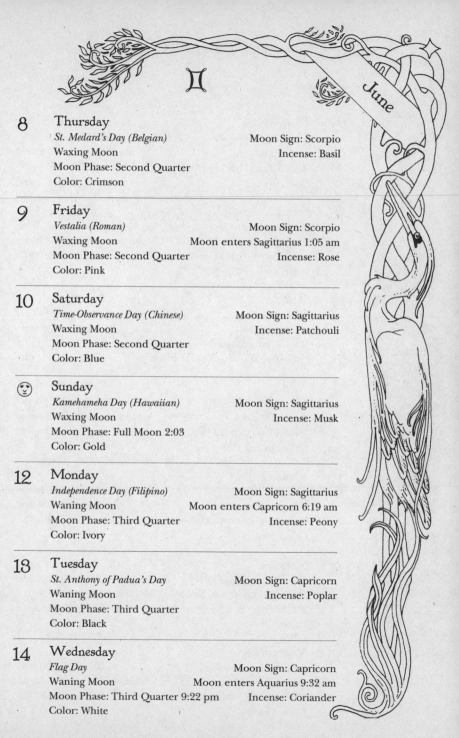

8 Thursday
St. Medard's Day (Belgian)
Waxing Moon
Moon Phase: Second Quarter
Color: Crimson

Moon Sign: Scorpio
Incense: Basil

9 Friday
Vestalia (Roman)
Waxing Moon
Moon Phase: Second Quarter
Color: Pink

Moon Sign: Scorpio
Moon enters Sagittarius 1:05 am
Incense: Rose

10 Saturday
Time-Observance Day (Chinese)
Waxing Moon
Moon Phase: Second Quarter
Color: Blue

Moon Sign: Sagittarius
Incense: Patchouli

☺ Sunday
Kamehameha Day (Hawaiian)
Waxing Moon
Moon Phase: Full Moon 2:03
Color: Gold

Moon Sign: Sagittarius
Incense: Musk

12 Monday
Independence Day (Filipino)
Waning Moon
Moon Phase: Third Quarter
Color: Ivory

Moon Sign: Sagittarius
Moon enters Capricorn 6:19 am
Incense: Peony

13 Tuesday
St. Anthony of Padua's Day
Waning Moon
Moon Phase: Third Quarter
Color: Black

Moon Sign: Capricorn
Incense: Poplar

14 Wednesday
Flag Day
Waning Moon
Moon Phase: Third Quarter 9:22 pm
Color: White

Moon Sign: Capricorn
Moon enters Aquarius 9:32 am
Incense: Coriander

Gemini ♊

15 Thursday
St. Vitus's Day Fires
Waning Moon
Moon Phase: Third Quarter
Color: Green

Moon Sign: Aquarius
Incense: Sage

16 Friday
Bloomsday (Irish)
Waning Moon
Moon Phase: Third Quarter
Color: Rose

Moon Sign: Libra
Moon enters Pisces 12:05 pm
Incense: Dill

17 Saturday
Bunker Hill Day
Waning Moon
Moon Phase: Third Quarter
Color: Gray

Moon Sign: Pisces
Incense: Maple

☽ Sunday
Father's Day
Waning Moon
Moon Phase: Fourth Quarter 10:08 am
Color: Amber

Moon Sign: Pisces
Moon enter Aries 2:54 pm
Incense: Parsley

19 Monday
Juneteenth
Waning Moon
Moon Phase: Fourth Quarter
Color: Silver

Moon Sign: Aries
Incense: Lavender

20 Tuesday
Flag Day (Argentinian)
Waning Moon
Moon Phase: Fourth Quarter
Color: Gray

Moon Sign: Aries
Moon enters Taurus 6:23 pm
Incense: Juniper

21 Wednesday
Litha • Summer Solstice
Waning Moon
Moon Phase: Fourth Quarter
Color: Topaz

Moon Sign: Taurus
Sun enters Cancer 8:26 am
Incense: Sandalwood

22 Thursday
Rose Festival (English)
Waning Moon
Moon Phase: Fourth Quarter
Color: Crimson

Moon Sign: Taurus
Moon enters Gemini 10:49 pm
Incense: Carnation

23 Friday
St. John's Eve
Waning Moon
Moon Phase: Fourth Quarter
Color: Purple

Moon Sign: Gemini
Incense: Thyme

24 Saturday
St. John's Day
Waning Moon
Moon Phase: Fourth Quarter
Color: Brown

Moon Sign: Gemini
Incense: Lilac

Sunday
Fiesta of Santa Orosia (Spanish)
Waning Moon
Moon Phase: New Moon 12:05 pm
Color: Yellow

Moon Sign: Gemini
Moon enters Cancer 4:48 am
Incense: Cinnamon

26 Monday
Pied Piper Day (German)
Waxing Moon
Moon Phase: First Quarter
Color: Lavender

Moon Sign: Cancer
Incense: Chrysanthemum

27 Tuesday
Day of the Seven Sleepers (Islamic)
Waxing Moon
Moon Phase: First Quarter
Color: Scarlet

Moon Sign: Cancer
Moon enters Leo 1:09 pm
Incense: Honeysuckle

28 Wednesday
Paul Bunyan Day
Waxing Moon
Moon Phase: First Quarter
Color: Brown

Moon Sign: Leo
Incense: Eucalyptus

29 Thursday
Saint Peter and Paul's Day
Waxing Moon
Moon Phase: First Quarter
Color: Purple

Moon Sign: Leo
Incense: Geranium

30 Friday
The Burning of the Three Firs (French)
Waxing Moon
Moon Phase: First Quarter
Color: Coral

Moon Sign: Leo
Moon enters Virgo 12:15 am
Incense: Sandalwood

Hummingbird Lore

Little jeweled rainbows, hummingbirds bring us the blessings of beauty and wonder. They amaze us with their ability to hover like tiny helicopters, gifting us with a reminder to stop every now and then to take stock of our own paths. As they flit from flower to flower, they teach us about savoring the sweetness in life, and about not getting too attached to things. Diversity is a blessing, and hummingbirds know it. As hummingbirds are extremely territorial, they can teach us about both sides of our protective urges. They may help you find your boundaries and stand up for yourself. They may also be a reminder that we can get stuck within our own shields, preventing true connections.

—Kristin Madden

$\odot$ July

1 Saturday
Canada Day
Waxing Moon
Moon Phase: First Quarter
Color: Gray

Moon Sign: Virgo
Incense: Juniper

2 Sunday
Heroes' Day (Zambian)
Waxing Moon
Moon Phase: First Quarter
Color: Orange

Moon Sign: Virgo
Moon enters Libra 1:06 pm
Incense: Sage

☾ Monday
Indian Sun Dance (Native American)
Waxing Moon
Moon Phase: Second Quarter 12:37 pm
Color: White

Moon Sign: Libra
Incense: Myrrh

4 Tuesday
Independence Day
Waxing Moon
Moon Phase: Second Quarter
Color: Maroon

Moon Sign: Libra
Incense: Evergreen

5 Wednesday
Tynwald (Nordic)
Waxing Moon
Moon Phase: Second Quarter
Color: Yellow

Moon Sign: Libra
Moon enters Scorpio 1:13 am
Incense: Cedar

6 Thursday
Khao Phansa Day (Thai)
Waxing Moon
Moon Phase: Second Quarter
Color: Green

Moon Sign: Scorpio
Incense: Musk

7 Friday
Weaver's Festival (Japanese)
Waxing Moon
Moon Phase: Second Quarter
Color: White

Moon Sign: Scorpio
Moon enters Sagittarius 10:13 am
Incense: Ylang ylang

Cancer ♋

8 Saturday
St. Elizabeth's Day (Portuguese)
Waxing Moon
Moon Phase: Second Quarter
Color: Indigo

Moon Sign: Sagittarius
Incense: Pine

9 Sunday
Battle of Sempach Day (Swiss)
Waxing Moon
Moon Phase: Second Quarter
Color: Amber

Moon Sign: Sagittarius
Moon enters Capricorn 3:25 pm
Incense: Clove

☺ Monday
Lady Godiva Day (English)
Waxing Moon
Moon Phase: Full Moon 11:02 pm
Color: Gray

Moon Sign: Capricorn
Incense: Rose

11 Tuesday
Revolution Day (Mongolian)
Waning Moon
Moon Phase: Third Quarter
Color: Red

Moon Sign: Capricorn
Moon enters Aquarius 5:46 pm
Incense: Clove

12 Wednesday
Lobster Carnival (Nova Scotian)
Waning Moon
Moon Phase: Third Quarter
Color: Brown

Moon Sign: Aquarius
Incense: Maple

13 Thursday
Festival of the Three Cows (Spanish)
Waning Moon
Moon Phase: Third Quarter
Color: Turquoise

Moon Sign: Aquarius
Moon enters Pisces 6:59 pm
Incense: Jasmine

14 Friday
Bastille Day (French)
Waning Moon
Moon Phase: Third Quarter
Color: Pink

Moon Sign: Pisces
Incense: Nutmeg

15 Saturday
St. Swithin's Day
Waning Moon
Moon Phase: Third Quarter
Color: Blue

Moon Sign: Pisces
Moon enters Aries 8:39 pm
Incense: Lavender

16 Sunday
Our Lady of Carmel
Waning Moon
Moon Phase: Third Quarter
Color: Yellow

Moon Sign: Aries
Incense: Basil

☾ Monday
Rivera Day (Puerto Rican)
Waning Moon
Moon Phase: Fourth Quarter 3:12 pm
Color: Silver

Moon Sign: Aries
Moon enters Taurus 11:44 pm
Incense: Daffodil

18 Tuesday
Gion Matsuri Festival (Japanese)
Waning Moon
Moon Phase: Fourth Quarter
Color: Black

Moon Sign: Taurus
Incense: Musk

19 Wednesday
Flitch Day (English)
Waning Moon
Moon Phase: Fourth Quarter
Color: White

Moon Sign: Taurus
Incense: Pine

20 Thursday
Binding of Wreaths (Lithuanian)
Waning Moon
Moon Phase: Fourth Quarter
Color: Purple

Moon Sign: Taurus
Moon enters Gemini 4:38 am
Incense: Chrysanthemum

21 Friday
National Day (Belgian)
Waning Moon
Moon Phase: Fourth Quarter
Color: Rose

Moon Sign: Gemini
Incense: Ginger

Leo ♌

22 Saturday
St. Mary Magdalene's Day
Waning Moon
Moon Phase: Fourth Quarter
Color: Brown

Moon Sign: Gemini
Sun enters Leo 7:18 pm
Moon enters Cancer 11:28 am
Incense: Violet

23 Sunday
Mysteries of Santa Cristina (Italian)
Waning Moon
Moon Phase: Fourth Quarter
Color: Gold

Moon Sign: Cancer
Incense: Coriander

24 Monday
Pioneer Day (Mormon)
Waning Moon
Moon Phase: Fourth Quarter
Color: Ivory

Moon Sign: Cancer
Moon enters Leo 8:24 pm
Incense: Peony

Tuesday
St. James' Day
Waning Moon
Moon Phase: New Moon 12:31 am
Color: White

Moon Sign: Leo
Incense: Gardenia

26 Wednesday
St. Anne's Day
Waxing Moon
Moon Phase: First Quarter
Color: Topaz

Moon Sign: Leo
Incense: Neroli

27 Thursday
Sleepyhead Day (Finnish)
Waxing Moon
Moon Phase: First Quarter
Color: Crimson

Moon Sign: Leo
Moon enters Virgo 7:36 am
Incense: Evergreen

28 Friday
Independence Day (Peruvian)
Waxing Moon
Moon Phase: Fourth Quarter
Color: Purple

Moon Sign: Virgo
Incense: Parsley

29 Saturday
Pardon of the Birds (French)
Waxing Moon
Moon Phase: First Quarter
Color: Black

Moon Sign: Virgo
Moon enters Libra 8:27 pm
Incense: Cedar

30 Sunday
Micmac Festival of St. Ann
Waxing Moon
Moon Phase: First Quarter
Color: Amber

Moon Sign: Libra
Incense: Poplar

31 Monday
Weighing of the Aga Khan
Waxing Moon
Moon Phase: First Quarter
Color: Gray

Moon Sign: Libra
Incense: Lavender

Ant Lore

The lowly ant, following its scent trail as it creates tunnels and provides for its colony, has much to teach us about knowing. Ant can guide you to use your senses and develop nonphysical ways of perceiving. Living in amazingly complex societies, ants can remind us to look at our motivations. Are we being too selfish? Or have we lost sight of ourselves and our individuality? Ant energy brings strength, survival, and endurance. Ant is also an excellent lowerworld guide and can be an ideal ally for exploring your shadow side. Ant is a protector and may bring powerful lessons in standing up for oneself and fighting back when necessary.

—Kristin Madden

Leo ♌

1 Tuesday
Lammas
Waxing Moon
Moon Phase: First Quarter
Color: Black

Moon Sign: Libra
Moon enters Scorpio 9:08 am
Incense: Ginger

☽ Wednesday
Porcingula (Native American)
Waxing Moon
Moon Phase: Second Quarter 4:46 am
Color: Yellow

Moon Sign: Scorpio
Incense: Coriander

3 Thursday
Drimes (Greek)
Waxing Moon
Moon Phase: Second Quarter
Color: Green

Moon Sign: Scorpio
Moon enters Sagittarius 7:13 pm
Incense: Dill

4 Friday
Cook Islands Constitution Celebration
Waxing Moon
Moon Phase: Second Quarter
Color: White

Moon Sign: Sagittarius
Incense: Rose

5 Saturday
Benediction of the Sea (French)
Waxing Moon
Moon Phase: Second Quarter
Color: Indigo

Moon Sign: Sagittarius
Incense: Patchouli

6 Sunday
Hiroshima Peace Ceremony
Waxing Moon
Moon Phase: Second Quarter
Color: Orange

Moon Sign: Sagittarius
Moon enters Capricorn 1:19 am
Incense: Cinnamon

7 Monday
Republic Day (Ivory Coast)
Waxing Moon
Moon Phase: Second Quarter
Color: Lavender

Moon Sign: Capricorn
Incense: Maple

8 Tuesday
Dog Days (Japanese)
Waxing Moon
Moon Phase: Second Quarter
Color: Gray

Moon Sign: Capricorn
Moon enters Aquarius 3:47 am
Incense: Juniper

Wednesday
Nagasaki Peace Ceremony
Waxing Moon
Moon Phase: Full Moon 6:54 am
Color: Brown

Moon Sign: Aquarius
Incense: Sandalwood

10 Thursday
St. Lawrence's Day
Waning Moon
Moon Phase: Third Quarter
Color: Purple

Moon Sign: Aquarius
Moon enters Pisces 4:10 am
Incense: Carnation

11 Friday
Puck Fair (Irish)
Waning Moon
Moon Phase: Third Quarter
Color: Pink

Moon Sign: Pisces
Incense: Thyme

12 Saturday
Fiesta of Santa Clara
Waning Moon
Moon Phase: Third Quarter
Color: Black

Moon Sign: Pisces
Moon enters Aries 4:22 am
Incense: Lilac

13 Sunday
Women's Day (Tunisian)
Waning Moon
Moon Phase: Third Quarter
Color: Amber

Moon Sign: Aries
Incense: Sage

14 Monday
Festival at Sassari
Waning Moon
Moon Phase: Third Quarter
Color: Silver

Moon Sign: Aries
Moon enters Taurus 6:00 am
Incense: Chrysanthemum

Tuesday
Assumption Day
Waning Moon
Moon Phase: Fourth Quarter 9:51 pm
Color: Red

Moon Sign: Taurus
Incense: Honeysuckle

---

16 Wednesday
Festival of Minstrels (European)
Waning Moon
Moon Phase: Fourth Quarter
Color: Topaz

Moon Sign: Taurus
Moon enters Gemini 10:07 am
Incense: Eucalyptus

---

17 Thursday
Feast of the Hungry Ghosts (Chinese)
Waning Moon
Moon Phase: Fourth Quarter
Color: Turquoise

Moon Sign: Gemini
Incense: Geranium

---

18 Friday
St. Helen's Day
Waning Moon
Moon Phase: Fourth Quarter
Color: Coral

Moon Sign: Gemini
Moon enters Cancer 5:03 pm
Incense: Sandalwood

---

19 Saturday
Rustic Vinalia (Roman)
Waning Moon
Moon Phase: Fourth Quarter
Color: Blue

Moon Sign: Cancer
Incense: Juniper

---

20 Sunday
Constitution Day (Hungarian)
Waning Moon
Moon Phase: Fourth Quarter
Color: Yellow

Moon Sign: Cancer
Incense: Clove

---

21 Monday
Consualia (Roman)
Waning Moon
Moon Phase: Fourth Quarter
Color: Ivory

Moon Sign: Cancer
Moon enters Leo 2:33 am
Incense: Frankincense

22 Tuesday
Feast of the Queenship of Mary (English)
Waning Moon
Moon Phase: Fourth Quarter
Color: Scarlet

Moon Sign: Leo
Incense: Evergreen

☽ Wednesday
National Day (Romanian)
Waning Moon
Moon Phase: New Moon 3:10 pm
Color: White

Moon Sign: Leo
Moon enters Virgo 2:08 pm
Sun enters Virgo 2:22 am
Incense: Cedar

24 Thursday
St. Bartholomew's Day
Waxing Moon
Moon Phase: First Quarter
Color: Crimson

Moon Sign: Virgo
Incense: Musk

25 Friday
Feast of the Green Corn (Native American)
Waxing Moon
Moon Phase: First Quarter
Color: Rose

Moon Sign: Virgo
Incense: Ylang ylang

26 Saturday
Pardon of the Sea (French)
Waxing Moon
Moon Phase: First Quarter
Color: Brown

Moon Sign: Virgo
Moon enters Libra 3:01 am
Incense: Pine

27 Sunday
Summer Break (English)
Waxing Moon
Moon Phase: First Quarter
Color: Gold

Moon Sign: Libra
Incense: Basil

28 Monday
St. Augustine's Day
Waxing Moon
Moon Phase: First Quarter
Color: Gray

Moon Sign: Libra
Moon enters Scorpio 3:56 pm
Incense: Myrrh

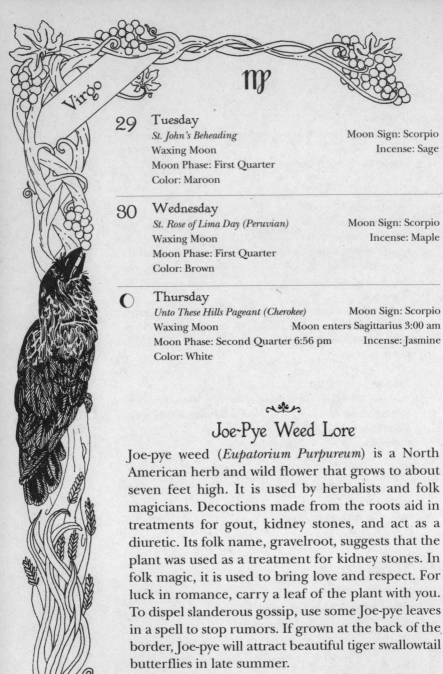

Virgo ♍

29 Tuesday
St. John's Beheading
Waxing Moon
Moon Phase: First Quarter
Color: Maroon

Moon Sign: Scorpio
Incense: Sage

30 Wednesday
St. Rose of Lima Day (Peruvian)
Waxing Moon
Moon Phase: First Quarter
Color: Brown

Moon Sign: Scorpio
Incense: Maple

☾ Thursday
Unto These Hills Pageant (Cherokee)
Waxing Moon
Moon Phase: Second Quarter 6:56 pm
Color: White

Moon Sign: Scorpio
Moon enters Sagittarius 3:00 am
Incense: Jasmine

Joe-Pye Weed Lore

Joe-pye weed (*Eupatorium Purpureum*) is a North American herb and wild flower that grows to about seven feet high. It is used by herbalists and folk magicians. Decoctions made from the roots aid in treatments for gout, kidney stones, and act as a diuretic. Its folk name, gravelroot, suggests that the plant was used as a treatment for kidney stones. In folk magic, it is used to bring love and respect. For luck in romance, carry a leaf of the plant with you. To dispel slanderous gossip, use some Joe-pye leaves in a spell to stop rumors. If grown at the back of the border, Joe-pye will attract beautiful tiger swallowtail butterflies in late summer.

—James Kambos

1 **Friday**
Greek New Year
Waxing Moon
Moon Phase: Second Quarter
Color: Pink

Moon Sign: Sagittarius
Incense: Almond

2 **Saturday**
St. Mamas's Day
Waxing Moon
Moon Phase: Second Quarter
Color: Black

Moon Sign: Sagittarius
Moon enters Capricorn 10:34 am
Incense: Lavender

3 **Sunday**
Founder's Day (San Marino)
Waxing Moon
Moon Phase: Second Quarter
Color: Orange

Moon Sign: Capricorn
Incense: Coriander

4 **Monday**
Labor Day (observed)
Waxing Moon
Moon Phase: Second Quarter
Color: Lavender

Moon Sign: Capricorn
Moon enters Aquarius 2:15 pm
Incense: Rose

5 **Tuesday**
Roman Circus
Waxing Moon
Moon Phase: Second Quarter
Color: Red

Moon Sign: Aquarius
Incense: Musk

6 **Wednesday**
The Virgin of Remedies (Spanish)
Waxing Moon
Moon Phase: Second Quarter
Color: Yellow

Moon Sign: Aquarius
Moon enters Pisces 2:56 pm
Incense: Pine

☺ **Thursday**
Festival of the Durga (Hindu)
Waxing Moon
Moon Phase: Full Moon 2:42 pm
Color: Purple

Moon Sign: Pisces
Incense: Chrysanthemum

8 **Friday**
Birthday of the Virgin Mary
Waning Moon
Moon Phase: Third Quarter
Color: Coral

Moon Sign: Pisces
Moon enters Aries 2:23 pm
Incense: Nutmeg

---

9 **Saturday**
Chrysanthemum Festival (Japanese)
Waning Moon
Moon Phase: Third Quarter
Color: Brown

Moon Sign: Aries
Incense: Jasmine

---

10 **Sunday**
Festival of the Poets (Japanese)
Waning Moon
Moon Phase: Third Quarter
Color: Yellow

Moon Sign: Aries
Moon enters Taurus 2:30 pm
Incense: Parsley

---

11 **Monday**
Coptic New Year
Waning Moon
Moon Phase: Third Quarter
Color: Gray

Moon Sign: Taurus
Incense: Daffodil

---

12 **Tuesday**
National Day (Ethiopian)
Waning Moon
Moon Phase: Third Quarter
Color: Black

Moon Sign: Taurus
Moon enters Gemini 4:59 pm
Incense: Gardenia

---

13 **Wednesday**
The Gods' Banquet (Roman)
Waning Moon
Moon Phase: Third Quarter
Color: White

Moon Sign: Gemini
Incense: Neroli

◑ **Thursday**
Holy Cross Day
Waning Moon
Moon Phase: Fourth Quarter 7:15 am
Color: Turquoise

Moon Sign: Gemini
Moon enters Cancer 10:53 pm
Incense: Evergreen

15 Friday
Birthday of the Moon (Chinese)
Waning Moon
Moon Phase: Fourth Quarter
Color: Rose

Moon Sign: Cancer
Incense: Ginger

16 Saturday
Mexican Independence Day
Waning Moon
Moon Phase: Fourth Quarter
Color: Blue

Moon Sign: Cancer
Incense: Violet

17 Sunday
Von Steuben's Day
Waning Moon
Moon Phase: Fourth Quarter
Color: Gold

Moon Sign: Cancer
Moon enters Leo 8:15 am
Incense: Poplar

18 Monday
Dr. Johnson's Birthday
Waning Moon
Moon Phase: Fourth Quarter
Color: White

Moon Sign: Leo
Incense: Peony

19 Tuesday
St. Januarius' Day (Italian)
Waning Moon
Moon Phase: Fourth Quarter
Color: Maroon

Moon Sign: Leo
Moon enters Virgo 8:07 pm
Incense: Pine

20 Wednesday
St. Eustace's Day
Waning Moon
Moon Phase: Fourth Quarter
Color: Topaz

Moon Sign: Virgo
Incense: Coriander

21 Thursday
Christ's Hospital Founder's Day (British)
Waning Moon
Moon Phase: Fourth Quarter
Color: Green

Moon Sign: Virgo
Incense: Dill

Libra

Friday
St. Maurice's Day (Swiss)
Waning Moon
Moon Phase: New Moon 7:45 am
Color: Purple

Moon Sign: Virgo
Moon enters Libra 9:06 am
Incense: Thyme

---

23 Saturday
Mabon • Fall Equinox • Rosh Hashanah
Waxing Moon
Moon Phase: First Quarter
Color: Indigo

Moon Sign: Libra
Sun enters Libra 12:03 am
Incense: Cedar

---

24 Sunday
Ramadan begins
Waxing Moon
Moon Phase: First Quarter
Color: Amber

Moon Sign: Libra
Moon enters Scorpio 9:54 pm
Incense: Cinnamon

---

25 Monday
Doll's Memorial Service (Japanese)
Waxing Moon
Moon Phase: First Quarter
Color: Ivory

Moon Sign: Scorpio
Incense: Lavender

---

26 Tuesday
Feast of Santa Justina (Mexican)
Waxing Moon
Moon Phase: First Quarter
Color: White

Moon Sign: Scorpio
Incense: Juniper

---

27 Wednesday
Saints Cosmas and Damian's Day
Waxing Moon
Moon Phase: First Quarter
Color: Brown

Moon Sign: Scorpio
Moon enters Sagittarius 9:16 am
Incense: Sandalwood

---

28 Thursday
Confucius' Birthday
Waxing Moon
Moon Phase: First Quarter
Color: Crimson

Moon Sign: Sagittarius
Incense: Carnation

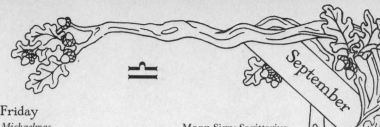

29 Friday

Michaelmas
Waxing Moon
Moon Phase: First Quarter
Color: White

Moon Sign: Sagittarius
Moon enters Capricorn 6:01 pm
Incense: Ylang ylang

☾ Saturday

St. Jerome's Day
Waxing Moon
Moon Phase: Second Quarter 7:04 am
Color: Gray

Moon Sign: Capricorn
Incense: Patchouli

Mabon Cornbread Recipe

1½ cups buttermilk
2   Tbsp. baking powder
2   cups cornmeal
¼   cup sugar
1   tsp. salt
2   eggs
1   cup all-purpose flour
⅓   cup melted butter or bacon fat

Heat oven to 425°F. Mix all ingredients together, beat for 30 seconds and pour into a greased round 9-inch pan. Cut a sun symbol into the center of the bread. Bake for 20 minutes until golden brown, checking at 10 minutes to recut sun symbol if necessary. Optional: stir in one 4-oz can of chopped green chiles or ½ cup shredded cheddar cheese.

—Kristin Madden

Libra

♎

1 Sunday
Armed Forces Day (South Korean)
Waxing Moon
Moon Phase: Second Quarter
Color: Yellow

Moon Sign: Capricorn
Moon enters Aquarius 11:24 pm
Incense: Sage

2 Monday
Yom Kippur
Waxing Moon
Moon Phase: Second Quarter
Color: White

Moon Sign: Aquarius
Incense: Maple

3 Tuesday
Moroccan New Year's Day
Waxing Moon
Moon Phase: Second Quarter
Color: Red

Moon Sign: Aquarius
Incense: Honeysuckle

4 Wednesday
St. Francis' Day
Waxing Moon
Moon Phase: Second Quarter
Color: Topaz

Moon Sign: Aquarius
Moon enters Pisces 1:33 am
Incense: Eucalyptus

5 Thursday
Republic Day (Portuguese)
Waxing Moon
Moon Phase: Second Quarter
Color: Purple

Moon Sign: Pisces
Incense: Geranium

☺ Friday
Dedication of the Virgin's Crowns (English)
Waxing Moon
Moon Phase: Full Moon 11:13 pm
Color: Pink

Moon Sign: Pisces
Moon enters Aries 1:32 am
Incense: Almond

7 Saturday
Sukkot begins
Waning Moon
Moon Phase: Third Quarter
Color: Black

Moon Sign: Aries
Incense: Lilac

≏ October

8 Sunday
Okunchi (Japanese)
Waning Moon
Moon Phase: Third Quarter
Color: Orange

Moon Sign: Aries
Moon enters Taurus 1:04 am
Incense: Sage

9 Monday
Columbus Day (observed)
Waning Moon
Moon Phase: Third Quarter
Color: Lavender

Moon Sign: Taurus
Incense: Chrysanthemum

10 Tuesday
Health Day (Japanese)
Waning Moon
Moon Phase: Third Quarter
Color: White

Moon Sign: Taurus
Moon enters Gemini 2:06 am
Incense: Evergreen

11 Wednesday
Medetrinalia (Roman)
Waning Moon
Moon Phase: Third Quarter
Color: Yellow

Moon Sign: Gemini
Incense: Cedar

12 Thursday
National Day (Spanish)
Waning Moon
Moon Phase: Third Quarter
Color: Turquoise

Moon Sign: Gemini
Moon enters Cancer 6:21 am
Incense: Musk

☾ Friday
Sukkot ends • Fortinalia (Roman)
Waning Moon
Moon Phase: Fourth Quarter 8:25 pm
Color: Rose

Moon Sign: Cancer
Incense: Nutmeg

14 Saturday
Battle Festival (Japanese)
Waning Moon
Moon Phase: Fourth Quarter
Color: Indigo

Moon Sign: Cancer
Moon enters Leo 2:38 pm
Incense: Juniper

Libra ♎

15 Sunday
The October Horse (Roman)
Waning Moon
Moon Phase: Fourth Quarter
Color: Amber

Moon Sign: Leo
Incense: Basil

16 Monday
The Lion Sermon (British)
Waning Moon
Moon Phase: Fourth Quarter
Color: Ivory

Moon Sign: Leo
Incense: Frankincense

17 Tuesday
Pilgrimage to Paray-le-Monial
Waning Moon
Moon Phase: Fourth Quarter
Color: Gray

Moon Sign: Leo
Moon enters Virgo 2:15 am
Incense: Sage

18 Wednesday
Brooklyn Barbeque
Waning Moon
Moon Phase: Fourth Quarter
Color: Brown

Moon Sign: Virgo
Incense: Maple

19 Thursday
Our Lord of Miracles Procession (Peruvian)
Waning Moon
Moon Phase: Fourth Quarter
Color: Green

Moon Sign: Virgo
Moon enters Libra 3:19 pm
Incense: Jasmine

20 Friday
Colchester Oyster Feast
Waning Moon
Moon Phase: Fourth Quarter
Color: White

Moon Sign: Libra
Incense: Ginger

21 Saturday
Feast of the Black Christ
Waning Moon
Moon Phase: Fourth Quarter
Color: Blue

Moon Sign: Libra
Incense: Pine

♏

☽ Sunday

Goddess of Mercy Day (Chinese)
Waning Moon
Moon Phase: New Moon 1:14 am
Color: Gold

Moon Sign: Libra
Moon enters Scorpio 3:54 am
Incense: Coriander

23 Monday

Revolution Day (Hungarian)
Waxing Moon
Moon Phase: First Quarter
Color: Silver

Moon Sign: Scorpio
Sun enters Scorpio 9:26 am
Incense: Myrrh

24 Tuesday

United Nations Day • Ramadan ends
Waxing Moon
Moon Phase: First Quarter
Color: Scarlet

Moon Sign: Scorpio
Moon enters Sagittarius 2:53 pm
Incense: Musk

25 Wednesday

St. Crispin's Day
Waxing Moon
Moon Phase: First Quarter
Color: White

Moon Sign: Sagittarius
Incense: Neroli

26 Thursday

Quit Rent Ceremony (England)
Waxing Moon
Moon Phase: First Quarter
Color: Purple

Moon Sign: Sagittarius
Moon enters Capricorn 11:47 pm
Incense: Vanilla

27 Friday

Feast of the Holy Souls
Waxing Moon
Moon Phase: First Quarter
Color: Coral

Moon Sign: Capricorn
Incense: Parsley

28 Saturday

Ochi Day (Greek)
Waxing Moon
Moon Phase: First Quarter
Color: Black

Moon Sign: Capricorn
Incense: Lavender

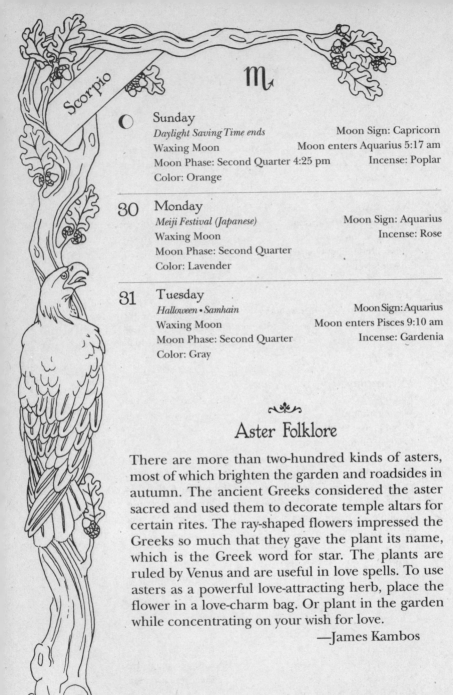

Scorpio

♏

Sunday
Daylight Saving Time ends
Waxing Moon
Moon Phase: Second Quarter 4:25 pm
Color: Orange

Moon Sign: Capricorn
Moon enters Aquarius 5:17 am
Incense: Poplar

30 Monday
Meiji Festival (Japanese)
Waxing Moon
Moon Phase: Second Quarter
Color: Lavender

Moon Sign: Aquarius
Incense: Rose

31 Tuesday
Halloween • Samhain
Waxing Moon
Moon Phase: Second Quarter
Color: Gray

Moon Sign: Aquarius
Moon enters Pisces 9:10 am
Incense: Gardenia

Aster Folklore

There are more than two-hundred kinds of asters, most of which brighten the garden and roadsides in autumn. The ancient Greeks considered the aster sacred and used them to decorate temple altars for certain rites. The ray-shaped flowers impressed the Greeks so much that they gave the plant its name, which is the Greek word for star. The plants are ruled by Venus and are useful in love spells. To use asters as a powerful love-attracting herb, place the flower in a love-charm bag. Or plant in the garden while concentrating on your wish for love.

—James Kambos

1 Wednesday
All Saints' Day
Waxing Moon
Moon Phase: Second Quarter
Color: White

Moon Sign: Pisces
Incense: Coriander

2 Thursday
All Souls' Day
Waxing Moon
Moon Phase: Second Quarter
Color: Turquoise

Moon Sign: Pisces
Moon enters Aries 10:46 am
Incense: Sandalwood

3 Friday
Saint Hubert's Day (Belgian)
Waxing Moon
Moon Phase: Second Quarter
Color: White

Moon Sign: Aries
Incense: Dill

4 Saturday
Mischief Night (British)
Waxing Moon
Moon Phase: Second Quarter
Color: Blue

Moon Sign: Aries
Moon enters Taurus 11:05 am
Incense: Basil

☺ Sunday
Guy Fawkes Night (British)
Waxing Moon
Moon Phase: Full Moon 7:58 am
Color: Amber

Moon Sign: Taurus
Incense: Cinnamon

6 Monday
Leonard's Ride (German)
Waning Moon
Moon Phase: Third Quarter
Color: Lavender

Moon Sign: Taurus
Moon enters Gemini 11:46 am
Incense: Peony

7 Tuesday
Election Day
Waning Moon
Moon Phase: Third Quarter
Color: White

Moon Sign: Gemini
Incense: Ginger

♏

8 Wednesday
The Lord Mayor's Show (English)
Waning Moon
Moon Phase: Third Quarter
Color: Brown

Moon Sign: Gemini
Moon enters Cancer 2:46 pm
Incense: Eucalyptus

---

9 Thursday
Lord Mayor's Day (British)
Waning Moon
Moon Phase: Third Quarter
Color: Purple

Moon Sign: Cancer
Incense: Chrysanthemum

---

10 Friday
Martin Luther's Birthday
Waning Moon
Moon Phase: Third Quarter
Color: Coral

Moon Sign: Cancer
Moon enters Leo 9:34 pm
Incense: Thyme

---

11 Saturday
Veterans Day
Waning Moon
Moon Phase: Third Quarter
Color: Indigo

Moon Sign: Leo
Incense: Violet

☽ Sunday
Tesuque Feast Day (Native American)
Waning Moon
Moon Phase: Fourth Quarter 12:45 pm
Color: Orange

Moon Sign: Leo
Incense: Sage

---

13 Monday
Festival of Jupiter (Roman)
Waning Moon
Moon Phase: Fourth Quarter
Color: Silver

Moon Sign: Leo
Moon enters Virgo 8:18 am
Incense: Lavender

---

14 Tuesday
The Little Carnival (Greek)
Waning Moon
Moon Phase: Fourth Quarter
Color: Black

Moon Sign: Virgo
Incense: Poplar

15 **Wednesday**
St. Leopold's Day
Waning Moon
Moon Phase: Fourth Quarter
Color: White

Moon Sign: Virgo
Moon enters Libra 9:14 pm
Incense: Cedar

---

16 **Thursday**
St. Margaret of Scotland's Day
Waning Moon
Moon Phase: Fourth Quarter
Color: Crimson

Moon Sign: Libra
Incense: Evergreen

---

17 **Friday**
Queen Elizabeth's Day
Waning Moon
Moon Phase: Fourth Quarter
Color: Pink

Moon Sign: Libra
Incense: Sandalwood

---

18 **Saturday**
St. Plato's Day
Waning Moon
Moon Phase: Fourth Quarter
Color: Gray

Moon Sign: Libra
Moon enters Scorpio 9:46 am
Incense: Patchouli

---

19 **Sunday**
Garifuna Day (Belizian)
Waning Moon
Moon Phase: Fourth Quarter
Color: Yellow

Moon Sign: Scorpio
Incense: Parsley

Monday
Commerce God Ceremony (Japanese)
Waning Moon
Moon Phase: New Moon 5:18 pm
Color: Ivory

Moon Sign: Scorpio
Moon enters Sagittarius 8:15 pm
Incense: Maple

---

21 **Tuesday**
Repentance Day (German)
Waxing Moon
Moon Phase: First Quarter
Color: Maroon

Moon Sign: Sagittarius
Incense: Pine

Sagittarius

22 Wednesday
St. Cecilia's Day
Waxing Moon
Moon Phase: First Quarter
Color: Topaz

Moon Sign: Sagittarius
Sun enters Sagittarius 6:02 am
Incense: Neroli

23 Thursday
Thanksgiving Day
Waxing Moon
Moon Phase: First Quarter
Color: Green

Moon Sign: Sagittarius
Moon enters Capricorn 6:02 am
Incense: Dill

24 Friday
Feast of the Burning Lamps (Egyptian)
Waxing Moon
Moon Phase: First Quarter
Color: Rose

Moon Sign: Capricorn
Incense: Ylang ylang

25 Saturday
Saint Catherine of Alexandria's Day
Waxing Moon
Moon Phase: First Quarter
Color: Black

Moon Sign: Capricorn
Moon enters Aquarius 10:41 am
Incense: Lilac

26 Sunday
Festival of Lights (Tibetan)
Waxing Moon
Moon Phase: First Quarter
Color: Gold

Moon Sign: Aquarius
Incense: Basil

27 Monday
Saint Maximus' Day
Waxing Moon
Moon Phase: First Quarter
Color: Gray

Moon Sign: Aquarius
Moon enters Pisces 3:20 pm
Incense: Frankincense

◑ Tuesday
Day of the New Dance (Tibetan)
Waxing Moon
Moon Phase: Second Quarter 1:29 am
Color: Red

Moon Sign: Pisces
Incense: Juniper

29 Wednesday
Tubman's Birthday (Liberian)   Moon Sign: Pisces
Waxing Moon   Moon enters Aries 6:30 pm
Moon Phase: Second Quarter   Incense: Coriander
Color: Brown

30 Thursday
St. Andrew's Day
Waxing Moon   Moon Sign: Aries
Moon Phase: Second Quarter   Incense: Carnation
Color: Purple

Country Apple Pie Recipe

1   cup sugar, divided

1   tsp. ground cinnamon

6–8   tart apples, peeled, cored, sliced

1   9-inch pie shell, unbaked

½   cup flour

½   cup margarine or butter, cold

Combine ½ cup of the sugar and cinnamon; sprinkle about half of this mixture over bottom of pie shell. Place sliced apples in the shell and sprinkle with remaining sugar/cinnamon mixture. Mix together remaining ½ cup sugar and flour, and cut in butter or margarine until crumbly. Sprinkle this topping over the apples. Bake at 375° for about 50 minutes, until golden and bubbly.

—James Kambos

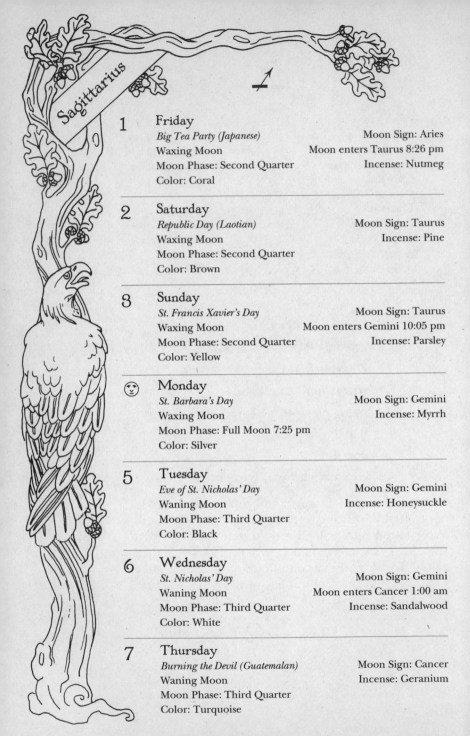

Sagittarius

1 **Friday**
Big Tea Party (Japanese)
Waxing Moon
Moon Phase: Second Quarter
Color: Coral

Moon Sign: Aries
Moon enters Taurus 8:26 pm
Incense: Nutmeg

2 **Saturday**
Republic Day (Laotian)
Waxing Moon
Moon Phase: Second Quarter
Color: Brown

Moon Sign: Taurus
Incense: Pine

3 **Sunday**
St. Francis Xavier's Day
Waxing Moon
Moon Phase: Second Quarter
Color: Yellow

Moon Sign: Taurus
Moon enters Gemini 10:05 pm
Incense: Parsley

☺ **Monday**
St. Barbara's Day
Waxing Moon
Moon Phase: Full Moon 7:25 pm
Color: Silver

Moon Sign: Gemini
Incense: Myrrh

5 **Tuesday**
Eve of St. Nicholas' Day
Waning Moon
Moon Phase: Third Quarter
Color: Black

Moon Sign: Gemini
Incense: Honeysuckle

6 **Wednesday**
St. Nicholas' Day
Waning Moon
Moon Phase: Third Quarter
Color: White

Moon Sign: Gemini
Moon enters Cancer 1:00 am
Incense: Sandalwood

7 **Thursday**
Burning the Devil (Guatemalan)
Waning Moon
Moon Phase: Third Quarter
Color: Turquoise

Moon Sign: Cancer
Incense: Geranium

8 Friday
Feast of the Immaculate Conception
Waning Moon
Moon Phase: Third Quarter
Color: White

Moon Sign: Cancer
Moon enters Leo 6:52 am
Incense: Ginger

9 Saturday
St. Leocadia's Day
Waning Moon
Moon Phase: Third Quarter
Color: Gray

Moon Sign: Leo
Incense: Lavender

10 Sunday
Nobel Day
Waning Moon
Moon Phase: Third Quarter
Color: Orange

Moon Sign: Leo
Moon enters Virgo 4:31 pm
Incense: Poplar

11 Monday
Pilgrimage at Tortugas
Waning Moon
Moon Phase: Third Quarter
Color: Lavender

Moon Sign: Virgo
Incense: Rose

12 Tuesday
Fiesta of Our Lady of Guadalupe
Waning Moon
Moon Phase: Fourth Quarter 9:32 am
Color: Maroon

Moon Sign: Virgo
Incense: Evergreen

13 Wednesday
St. Lucy's Day (Swedish)
Waning Moon
Moon Phase: Fourth Quarter
Color: Brown

Moon Sign: Virgo
Moon enters Libra 5:00 am
Incense: Eucalyptus

14 Thursday
Warriors' Memorial (Japanese)
Waning Moon
Moon Phase: Fourth Quarter
Color: Green

Moon Sign: Libra
Incense: Musk

Sagittarius

15 Friday
Consualia (Roman)
Waning Moon
Moon Phase: Fourth Quarter
Color: Pink

Moon Sign: Libra
Moon enters Scorpio 5:42 pm
Incense: Almond

16 Saturday
Hanukkah begins
Waning Moon
Moon Phase: Fourth Quarter
Color: Blue

Moon Sign: Scorpio
Incense: Pine

17 Sunday
Saturnalia (Roman)
Waning Moon
Moon Phase: Fourth Quarter
Color: Amber

Moon Sign: Scorpio
Incense: Cinnamon

18 Monday
Feast of the Virgin of Solitude
Waning Moon
Moon Phase: Fourth Quarter
Color: Gray

Moon Sign: Scorpio
Moon enters Sagittarius 4:10 am
Incense: Peony

19 Tuesday
Opalia (Roman)
Waning Moon
Moon Phase: Fourth Quarter
Color: Red

Moon Sign: Sagittarius
Incense: Sage

Wednesday
Commerce God Festival (Japanese)
Waning Moon
Moon Phase: New Moon 9:01 am
Color: Yellow

Moon Sign: Sagittarius
Moon enters Capricorn 11:39 am
Incense: Cedar

21 Thursday
Yule • Winter Solstice
Waxing Moon
Moon Phase: First Quarter
Color: Crimson

Moon Sign: Capricorn
Sun enters Capricorn 7:22 pm
Incense: Vanilla

♑   *December*

22 Friday
Saints Chaeremon and Ischyrion's Day   Moon Sign: Capricorn
Waxing Moon   Moon enters Aquarius 4:49 pm
Moon Phase: First Quarter   Incense: Dill
Color: Coral

23 Saturday
Larentalia (Roman) • Hanukkah ends   Moon Sign: Aquarius
Waxing Moon   Incense: Violet
Moon Phase: First Quarter
Color: Indigo

24 Sunday
Christmas Eve   Moon Sign: Aquarius
Waxing Moon   Moon enters Pisces 8:43 pm
Moon Phase: First Quarter   Incense: Sage
Color: Gold

25 Monday
Christmas Day   Moon Sign: Pisces
Waxing Moon   Incense: Chrysanthemum
Moon Phase: First Quarter
Color: Ivory

26 Tuesday
Kwanzaa begins   Moon Sign: Pisces
Waxing Moon   Incense: Gardenia
Moon Phase: First Quarter
Color: Scarlet

◑ Wednesday
Boar's Head Supper (English)   Moon Sign: Pisces
Waxing Moon   Moon enters Aries 12:04 am
Moon Phase: Second Quarter 9:48 am   Incense: Neroli
Color: Topaz

28 Thursday
Holy Innocents' Day   Moon Sign: Aries
Waxing Moon   Incense: Evergreen
Moon Phase: Second Quarter
Color: White

29 Friday
St. Thomas à Becket
Waxing Moon
Moon Phase: Second Quarter
Color: Purple

Moon Sign: Aries
Moon enters Taurus 3:08 am
Incense: Sage

---

30 Saturday
Republic Day (Madagascar)
Waxing Moon
Moon Phase: Second Quarter
Color: Black

Moon Sign: Taurus
Incense: Lavender

---

31 Sunday
New Year's Eve
Waxing Moon
Moon Phase: Second Quarter
Color: Yellow

Moon Sign: Taurus
Moon enters Gemini 6:16 am
Incense: Poplar

Paraffin Leaves

Gather some paraffin (found where candle making supplies are sold), some leaves (likely dried from autumn at this time of year, but also green if you can find them), tongs or tweezers, some wax paper, and a pencil. Place the paraffin in a small pan or tin can. Place that in the center of a larger pan filled with water. Warm the water on medium heat until the paraffin melts. Do not allow the paraffin to boil. Using tongs or tweezers, quickly dip your leaves into the hot paraffin. Set them aside on wax paper to dry. Once they are dry, you can gently inscribe them with your name or special words and symbols. Use them to decorate your home and altar.

—Kristin Madden

Articles for Summer

The Nine Sacred Trees

by Lily Gardner

Most famous among tree worshippers were the druids who worshiped in the sacred groves of Great Britain. They gathered the branches and fruit of their sacred trees to fashion besoms, staffs, wands, and amulets. Nine species of tree were observed as having magical properties: birch, rowan, ash, alder, willow, hawthorn, oak, hazel, and holly.

Birch

Tall and slender with white bark and silvery leaves, the birch is the most graceful tree on earth. Birch is the tree with which to contact the world of spirits. The dead were said to wear birch bark clothing in many tales of spirit visitation.

The birch tree also signifies new beginnings. Birch branches are often used for making wands, because the wand, signifying will, is what drives new projects. Shamans also use a hoop made of birch wood for shape-shifting. Birch twigs are gathered together for the brush of the besom, the female aspect of the witch's broom.

Tying a red ribbon around a birch branch will ward off the evil eye. Birch is also known for its protection. Cradles made from birch wood are believed to protect a sleeping baby, and birch twigs set in the rafters protect the house from lightning strikes.

Rowan

Rowan, or "Witch tree," is the tree most loved by Witches and fairies. Also known as mountain ash, delight of the eye, quickbeam, and whitty tree, rowan is most known for its protective properties. Fortunate is the householder who has a rowan tree planted near his home, for it is said that the rowan will protect the family from fire, theft, and disease. Two twigs of rowan tied in a simple cross with red thread are often hung over the door of a house or barn for good luck. The Scots often carry these crosses in their pockets or sewn into their clothing when they travel.

The rowan's red berries are sometimes strung into necklaces for good luck. Rowan, with its centuries-old association with witchcraft, is an excellent choice for spell work.

Alder

Alder is sometimes known as the king of the waters because it typically grows near lakes or streams. Its association with water makes it a powerful aid in divination, oracles, and healing. Italian Witches combine alder sap with madder plant to produce a red dye for protective cords and ribbon.

Willow

As the alder is known as the king of the waters, the willow is queen. Willow magic is fertility magic. It binds the feminine birch twigs to the male handle of the besom. A very old custom is to place willow branches in the beds of barren women to encourage fertility.

Wands made of willow invoke the Muses. Sacred to poets, the music of the wind through willow leaves provokes inspiration. Orpheus, the most famous of Greek poets, gained his gift of eloquence by carrying willow branches as he journeyed through the underworld. To help with dream work, place a willow twig underneath your pillow.

The weeping willow is associated with grief, especially as it relates to abandonment. A practice that continued for centuries was for jilted lovers to wear willow hats. Willow trees often decorated gravestones; a willow planted on the grave was said to ease the passage of the departed.

Ash

Tall and strong, ash wood is prized for building and firewood. Like many of the sacred trees, all parts of the ash are used for magic. The wood of the ash tree is used for staffs; its seed pods, called "ash keys," are used for protection, and its leaves are used for love charms.

Ash is used as the phallic handle of the besom. After a couple is married, they "jump the broom" to ensure fertility. Perhaps this association with fertility has something to do with its leaves being used in love charms. Carrying ash leaves in your pocket will attract a lover to you.

A staff carved from ash is often hung over the threshold of a home for protection. An equal-armed cross carved from its wood will prevent a traveler from drowning. The only thing the ash will not protect you from is storm. It is said that the ash tree attracts lightning.

Burning ash wood in your Yule fire will bring prosperity to the household for the year.

Hawthorn

Hawthorn is the principal tree used at Beltane and is known for its power to grant fertility. Witches who wash their faces with morning dew from the hawthorn on Beltane will be beautiful throughout the year.

> *The fair maid who*
> *The first of May*
> *Goes to the field at the break of day*
> *And washes in the dew*
> *from the hawthorn tree*
> *will ever after handsome be.*
> *—Mother Goose*

Wearing an amulet made from hawthorn wards off depression and restores happiness. Travelers, when coming upon a hawthorn tree, may wish to tear off a piece of their clothing to hang on the tree as a "wish rag." To do so ensures their wishes will come true.

Oak

The oak tree is associated with the Summer Solstice and the light half of the year. One of the oldest dramas in western Europe is the battle between the Oak King and the Holly King, which takes place each solstice. The Oak King defeats the Holly King at the Winter Solstice, and sunlight begins to return to the north lands. On the Summer Solstice, the Oak King is defeated and the Sun begins its decline.

Carrying a small piece of oak as an amulet protects the wearer. An equal-armed cross, made from oak twigs and tied with a red thread, will protect ones home from fire, theft, and illness. Acorns on the windowsill protect the house from lightning, and an oak fire draws away illness from the household. Catching a falling oak leaf midair will bring good fortune.

Hazel

As oak is known for its strength, hazel is known for its wisdom. The salmon of wisdom, from Celtic myth, gained his insight from swallowing nine hazelnuts.

Hazel is probably even better known as the wood used in dowsing sticks. The dowser uses a forked hazel stick that will point to where there is underground water. Before the seventeenth century, dowsing sticks were used to find both treasure and criminals.

Hazel's ability to find what is hidden makes it the perfect wood for divination. By eating hazelnuts before you practice any form of divination, you will enhance your reading. The nuts themselves are used in an old love charm performed on Samhain night. Place two hazelnuts side by side in the fire as you chant: "If you love me, pop and fly! If you hate me, burn and die."

Crowns of hazel twigs are called wishing caps. When worn while making a heartfelt wish, the wish is said to come true. Wands of hazel wood will provide poetic inspiration.

Holly

Holly is the sacred tree associated with the Winter Solstice. It symbolizes peace, goodwill, and happiness. The custom of

decorating one's house with holly at Yule first began with the Romans who packed their gifts for Saturnalia in holly leaves.

A love spell requires the seeker to go out at midnight, in absolute silence, and gather nine, smooth holly leaves, (known as *she-holly*). The leaves must be folded in a three-cornered handkerchief and tied with nine knots. This packet is placed under the seeker's pillow and, as long as the seeker remains silent until dawn, he or she will dream of their future mate.

The Holly King, who represents dying vegetation, is defeated on the winter solstice by the Oak King. The Holly King, usually depicted as an old man, may be the precursor of Santa Claus.

Knowing and working with the nine sacred trees is a way to deepen our appreciation and further connect us with the green world.

A Family Midsummer Celebration

by Twilight Bard

Heigh ho, my children, a Midsummer blessing upon you! As the Sun Lord reaches the zenith of his power now, we celebrate as our Pagan ancestors have for millennia.

Across all cultures of the Northern hemisphere, this time was known to be the pinnacle of the Sun's journey through the year and was honored with some form of celebration. From the ancient Inca people of South America, to the Iglulingmiut of the polar regions of North America, native cultures gathered to mark the Sun's turning. The Romans, Druids, and Norse people of Europe held fire festivals, built ancient stone structures, and feasted the peak of the Sun's journey. In China, the shift of the yin-yang at this time kept people busy as they performed rituals to keep the balance of the year.

How solstice time was celebrated depended upon the weather, religions, and agricultural cycles of an area. In the north, where the land is cold and barren for most of the year, people found relief in the longer days and ripening Earth. The Sun bathed the growing crops in nourishing light, and abundance dripped from every fertile vine. This was a time to take advantage of the warm weather and the period between planting and harvest with revelry and rest. Those who lived in the warmer climates knew that the peak of Summer would begin the Sun's decline, bringing relief from the relentless heat and droughts. This was a time to give thanks for the shift, look forward to the return of cool breezes and plan for the planting season.

No matter what regional traditions dictated, the solstice was marked almost universally in ancient Pagan cultures as a magical time. And like those who have gone before us, we seize this opportunity to celebrate. In honor of the Sun Father at the summit of his strength, and in honor of the Earth Mother as she reaches full blossom, we feast and make merry with a Midsummer festival.

As Neopagan adults, we try to recreate ancient festivals to remind us of the importance that the earth, and the Sun's journey through time, play in our lives. Long, drawn-out, formal religious ceremonies—complete with a plethora of invocations and dedications—may only serve to bore our new, budding generation of eager young Pagans. The best way for children to truly understand the spirit of the sabbat is to experience it for themselves as it was originally intended.

For this sabbat in particular, we should let actions paint the mental and emotional picture that a thousand incantations may fail to do justice. Midsummer has always been a time for pure, unadulterated joy. Why confine such a day to a circle or a spate of speeches? Actions speak louder than words, especially to children. Actions will steep their minds in the true meaning of the season.

To give children the full scope of Midsummer, it is best to dedicate the full day to celebrating. If you absolutely cannot put off any commitment that falls on the solstice, don't try to squeeze the holiday into a couple of hours after work. It is better to set the ritual for the closest free day.

Don't feel too badly if you're not able to hold your ritual on the exact solstice. Remember, in ancient times the solstice was a season, and the day of celebration could change with the agricultural or lunar cycle from year to year. You honor this tradition by moving the festivity to the most suitable time to take full advantage of the holiday and its energy.

Once your day is set, rise early, and plan to spend the day outdoors. If you don't have a yard, go to a local park or beach for your ritual. Have a picnic or barbecue packed and ready. Try to plan a

bonfire, or if this is not possible, arrange a fire in a large cauldron or barbeque grill. Fire, being the element most closely related to the Sun, is an integral element of Summer Solstice celebrations. If nothing else, a pillar candle decorated with glitter and set prominently in the center of the table will suffice. Fire is fire, no matter how large or small the flame.

Gather the children around and tell them a story of how ancient solstice festivals were celebrated by your ancestors. Drink lemonade, paint each other's faces, and allow the light-hearted mood of the season to take over.

In many northern European cultures, Midsummer was a traditional day for playing games. Feats of strength, speed, and skill are not only fun, but a wonderful way to get across the seasonal feelings of mirth and merriment? Planning games for your celebration will hit that primal chord of joyousness within all present. Traditional camp and country fair games require little preparation, but still are crowd pleasers. Potato sack (or pillow case) races, obstacle courses, tug-of-wars, and water-balloon tossing are all good options. If you are so inclined, don't discount playing a game of baseball—a modern summer tradition that fits nicely with the holiday season.

Rolling a burning wheel down a hillside into a pond (representing the Sun's imminent decline) was a European tradition that survived through medieval times. While this is not a safe (or legal) practice, you can adapt the ritual by rolling red glittery hula-hoops or playing games of ring-toss.

Children enjoy nature crafts, which are more than pertinent to this celebration. Collect moss, leaves, twigs, shells, and small stones for a collage. Gather large stones to be painted and left around the home as household guardians. Perhaps you can assemble a small stick figure to be used as a miniature "Burning Man," and place him upon the fire after the ritual feast.

Children can cut out and decorate animal shapes using felt or cotton material and the treasures they've found on the ground. If doubled and sewn together, children can stuff their animals with dried herbs and "sacrifice" them in the fire at dusk. This will be their offering to the Sun Lord, entreating him to return in another incarnation at the Winter Solstice, just as Pagans did so long ago.

At sunset, the children may enjoy staging a seasonal enactment of the battle between the Oak King and the Holly King. Tradition says that, at the Summer Solstice, the Holly King claims victory and rules the waning half of the year. Perhaps, if a physical enactment is not possible, a puppet show will do.

Dancing and storytelling around the fire should continue into the night. Children may wish to pile a plate with fruits, honey, and milk to leave out for the fairies, who are known to be at their most active on solstice night. Before going to bed, they may be lucky enough to catch a fleeting glimpse of fluttering wings.

By the end of the celebration, children will understand from personal experience the enduring enchantment of this magical time of year.

Mystical Yantras

by S. Y. Zenith

Yantras derive their name from a Sanskrit word meaning "instrument," "machine," or "loom." Yantras are mystical linear diagrams that represent various dimensions of creative energy that radiate from the core of the universe. A yantra is also described as an interlocking matrix of geometric figures, circles, triangles, and floral patterns that form fractal intricacies of elegance and beauty.

Although traditionally found in two-dimensional form, the Yantra signifies a three-dimensional sacred object. Today, three-dimensional yantras are increasingly common as hand-carved designs on quartz crystal, stone, wood, copper, and other metal plates. They are even formulated in solidified mercury and plated in silver by adepts in India. Mystical yantras are also drawn on paper, painted with various mediums using numerous materials such as cloth, walls, sand, and even plastic resins.

Ancient Indian *shilpi-yogins* (makers of ritual arts) believed that yantras reveal the inner basis of all forms and shapes in the universe, and that they function as revelatory symbols of cosmic truths. In practice, a yantra is a holy diagram that usually symbolizes the supreme Mother Goddess. The primal shapes of yantras are also indicative of the attributes and qualities of a deity, whether male or female. Yantras are also significant psychological symbols that correspond to inner states of human consciousness.

It would take a book to explain yantra as a science, a classical tradition, and a ritual application. Thus, this brief article is simply an attempt to share the bare basics for yantra use by interested beginners and intermediate practitioners.

Different Types of Yantras

There are generally four basic categories of yantras. Deity yantras or *shakta* yantras are usually forms of the Great Mother or one of the goddesses of the ten *mahavidyas,* an important group of female deities who are manifestations of the supreme Goddess. These ten aspects of female divinity are Kali, Tara, Chinnamasta, Bhuveneshwari, Bagala, Dhumavati, Kamala, Matangi, Sodashi and Bhairavi.

One of the most famous and sought after yantras is the *shree* yantra, also called *shree chakra* and *shree vidya.* It is often misunderstood to represent just Lakshmi, the goddess of abundance, prosperity, and wealth. The serious and advanced practitioner or initiate reveres shree yantra as transcending every notion of divinity ever conceived in the pantheon of deities relating to the sanatana dharma (commonly known as Hinduism).

The second common group of yantras are astrological or planetary yantras for harnessing energies and placating negative influences of the nine major planets in the *jyotish* astrology system. The nine planets are the Sun, Moon, Mars, Mercury, Venus, Jupiter, Saturn, Ketu, and Rahu. Of the nine, Mars, Saturn, Ketu, and Rahu are generally considered "natural malefics" by astrologers. However, any planet that is ill-placed in the birth chart can also become malefic. *Jyotishis* or Indian astrologers do often prescribe the use of a yantra with an associated mantra for deflecting or stabilizing negative planetary influences. In some cases, planetary yantras are used for strengthening weak but beneficial planets in the individual horoscope.

The third group of general yantras are architectural yantras applied as foundation or ground plans for Indian temples. In the science of *vaastu* (Indian feng shui), architectural yantras are laid at the foundation of a building site before construction takes place. In the home, yantras can be installed on the altar, at the home shrine, or in the prayer room.

Most Indian families of traditional upbringing designate a special room for prayers. Other families observe different and diverse traditional guidelines regarding the placement of yantras for various reasons—such as for use in absorbing opposing energies in a room or house.

The fourth group are numerical yantras: formulas of numbers that serve as talismans. Planetary yantras can also be found in numerical form and etched on copper and other metals.

Uses of Yantra

The *shakti* or power of yantras is available to beginners who are sincere and have disciplined devotion. The novice first concentrates upon a yantra, then closes the eyes, striving to visualize it in the mind's eye. Regular practice of intense meditation culminates in the ability to see every detail of the yantra's outer form. In general, this practice guides the novice towards internalizing the deity contained in a specific mystical diagram.

It is believed that malevolent and evil desires can never bear fruit via the use of yantras. When used as talismans or amulets, yantras are known to produce strong transformational spiritual benefits, such as powering the auric field, acting as shields for deflecting viciousness, malice, and psychic attacks, and preventing the entry of unwanted entities.

There are many ways of utilizing yantras, ranging from spiritual advancement to mundane purposes. Traditional or otherwise, devotees usually obtain yantras for worshipping deities, seeking blessings, achieving success in career or academics, relieving health problems, and improving business, harmony, love, healing, and other desired life aspects. It is said by a respected source in the Indian state of Maharashtra that "there are about 700 million types of yantras originating in India alone due to the multitude of lineage and language diversities." In the Indian subcontinent, yantras hold a supreme status among esoteric or metaphysical sciences and disciplines.

Some Effective Yantras

If you are wondering whether there is any guarantee that desires can be fulfilled while using yantras, the answer is "no." Yantras are arcane diagrams representing spiritual systems of energy that cannot be subverted for negative agendas out of harmony with the laws of nature. With good intent, results generally take thirty to forty days to materialize, but one must not hunger for more than what is not karmically deserved. The yantras described herein are easily available in square copper plates around the world.

Ganesh yantra: For removing obstacles; gaining blessings in new undertakings and beginnings.

Mahalakshmi yantra: For prosperity, abundance, and healthy monetary flow.

Shree yantra: For good fortune, fame, comfort, continuous prosperity, and salvation.

Saraswati yantra: For enhancing intellect, wisdom, focus, creativity, academic achievement, and skills in the arts.

Kubera yantra: For riches and preserving acquired monies.

Vyapar vridhi yantra: For business activity.

Mahamrityunjaya yantra: For protection, healing, and preventing diseases and untimely demise.

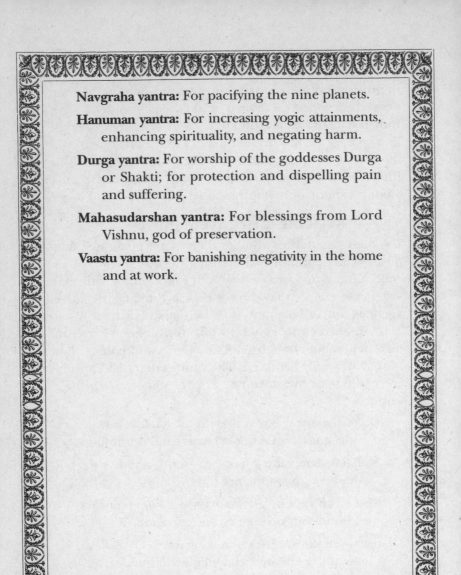

Navgraha yantra: For pacifying the nine planets.

Hanuman yantra: For increasing yogic attainments, enhancing spirituality, and negating harm.

Durga yantra: For worship of the goddesses Durga or Shakti; for protection and dispelling pain and suffering.

Mahasudarshan yantra: For blessings from Lord Vishnu, god of preservation.

Vaastu yantra: For banishing negativity in the home and at work.

Ancient Greek
Festivals of August
by Sorita

The beginning of August marks the harvest of the grain, cele-brated in modern Paganism as Lughnasadh or Lammas. To the Greeks this was a time of transformation, as the harvested crops were transformed into bread and beer. Goddesses of trans-formation were celebrated in August, marking the transition from the birth of a new year toward the mysteries of death and rebirth.

The Greek calendar began in the summer. In the Athenian calendar, the first month was called Hekatombion and ran from the middle of July to the middle of August. The second month was called Metageitnion and ran from the middle of August to the middle of September.

One of the great feasts of Hecate was celebrated on August 13. Hecate was honored on this day as goddess of storms, that she might avert any bad weather that would destroy the crops and cause the harvest to fail. As the goddess of the liminal marking the journeys through life, death, and initiation, Hecate's pres-ence was always felt.

Hecate's symbols of the twin torches, keys, and crossroads show how she has always been seen as a bringer of change. In addition to her major festivals, Hecate was also honored every month with the "Hecate suppers." In these, food would be left at the crossroads in her honor at the dark of the Moon. It was recorded that the poor would eat this food, so we can see that Hecate is one of the original patrons of charity and looking after those less fortunate.

Invocation to Hecate

Lady crowned with the oak leaves of the earth,
Shining your bright torches from the heavens,
Guiding us across the mysteries of the oceans,
Goddess of the sacred crossroads,
Key-holding goddess of the whole world—

Hecate! Hecate! Hecate!
Dark mother, who knows the sacred mysteries—
Hecate! Hecate! Hecate!
Cosmic queen, who guides us through life, death, and rebirth—
Hecate! Hecate! Hecate!
Chthonic lady, with the knowledge of ancient magic,
Saffron-clad goddess, guide and protectress,
Come to me now, in this place between the worlds—
Join me and guide me.

In the middle of August a festival known as the Athenaea was held in honor of Athena. Athena was the goddess of wisdom and disciplined fighting, rather than wild combat. She was the patron of Athens, and was said to have sprung fully armed and fully grown from the head of her father Zeus. The olive tree and its fruit and the owl were especially sacred to her.

The Athenaea was one of the grandest festivals in the whole of Greece. The festival lasted two days, involving processions followed by the sacrifice of animals. Then, epic poems were recited, although this was later replaced by music contests. Athletic competitions were also held, along with nighttime torch-lit processions to the temples on the Acropolis. Around the fifth century BC, a larger festival was instituted every four years called the Great Panathenaea. Lasting five days, it was akin to the modern Olympic Games. At the Panathenaea, women took part in weaving and spinning contests, demonstrating their skill in activities associated with Athena.

Invocation to Athena

Beautiful maiden Athena, wise and just ruler,
Disciplined in war and the pursuits of the mind,
Bearing the serpent of wisdom and the olive branch of peace,
I call to you and ask you to fill me with your inspiration.
Great goddess, you destroy the unworthy
And bring power to those who honor you in truth.
I anoint myself with the oil of your olives
And offer my love and reverence to thee.

The Eleusinia was a thanksgiving festival held every two years on August 15–18 in honor of Demeter. Demeter was the great goddess of fertility and crops. All appealed to her to ensure plentiful harvests. Sacrifices were made to Demeter, and athletic contests were held in her honor. All types of grain were particularly sacred to Demeter, as was the cornucopia or horn of plenty.

Her mysteries were celebrated at Eleusis, where the myth of the descent of her daughter Persephone to the underworld formed part of the initiation rites. This myth, central to the Eleusinian mysteries and celebrated at the Autumn Equinox, has become a major aspect of modern Paganism and Wicca.

Invocation to Demeter

Demeter, thou art the beloved mother
Of the earth and all that grows.

I ask you to fill me with your love of all that lives
That I may be open to the pleasures of life.
Demeter, I offer my love and reverence to thee,
Guide me that I may know the seasons of life—
When to grow, when to nurture, and when to rest.
Fertile goddess of the mysteries of life,
Teach me and bless me with your wisdom.

The festival of Nemesia was celebrated on August 23. It honored the goddess Nemesis and celebrated the memory of the dead, whose memory she protected from insult. Nemesis was the goddess of righteous anger, daughter of Nox, and one of the earliest Greek goddesses.

Unlike many of the other Titans, Nemesis remained part of the pantheon when Zeus and the Olympian gods came to prominence. Nemesis also avenged any slights to Themis, punishing those who acted against the natural balance that Themis embodied.

Invocation to Nemesis

I call thee, Nemesis, almighty queen,
By whom the deeds of mortal life are seen—
Eternal, much revered, of boundless sight,
Alone rejoicing in the just and right,
Changing the counsels of the human breast,
Ever varying, rolling without rest.

The Fates were also honored on August 23. Atropos, Lachesis, and Clotho were the three divine sisters who measured the thread of human life and wove together the tapestry of existence. Even the gods were bound by the actions of the Fates, who spun, measured, and cut the thread of every life. The Fates were responsible for keeping all and everyone within its own proper measure.

Clotho was the first of the Fates. With her spindle, she wove the threads of life. Lachesis with her scroll measured the length of each thread and recorded it. And finally Atropos, with her scales, was responsible for the cutting of the thread, which ended the life of the being it measured.

Invocation to the Fates

Daughters of dark night, much-named, draw near,
Infinite Fates, and listen to my prayer.
Your power extends to all of mortal birth,
Who live and love upon the fertile earth.
Come, awesome powers, benign and famed,
Atropos, Lachesis, and Clotho are you named—
Fates all-producing all-destroying, most fair,
Regard the incense and hear my prayer;
Propitious listen to these rites inclined,
And keep distress far from my mind.

When we walk a spiritual path, it is strangely ironic that change is the one constant. The Greek goddesses celebrated in August help us to come to terms with change.

Through them we examine ourselves and our aims; we evaluate the transformations we need. These transformations can be aided by honoring these ancient goddesses and welcoming their energies into our lives to help us grow into our potential.

Who Were the Druids?

by Sharynne NicMhacha

Modern pagans and spiritual seekers are often fascinated by the image of the Druid, a shadowy figure represented in this day and age by white-robed celebrants at stone circles and sacred sites in Britain (and North America). They seem to possess some mysterious or arcane knowledge—but what is it? Do modern Druid traditions resemble those of the ancient and powerful priests and priestesses of the Celts?

We do know that during one particular ritual, the Druids of ancient Gaul wore white garments. This was a rite in which mistletoe was gathered from the branches of an oak tree on the sixth day of the Moon. Both ancient and modern Celtic traditions concerning the gathering of plants and herbs mention the use of white cloth in these types of rituals. Celtic priestesses in Cimbria wore white when performing sacrifices. However, in another account, when the Romans were pursuing the Druids of Britain, they encountered a group of women dressed in black (who may have been either Druidesses or the wives of the Druids). They were said to be surrounded by a group of Druids.

We have no evidence that the Druids utilized stone circles or any other pre-Celtic sites in their rituals (including Stonehenge). They were said to hold many of their rituals out of doors, particularly in sacred groves. Evidence also shows that they worshiped or made offerings near bodies of water. And in some areas, the Celts used wooden temples.

What did ancient Druids do, and what did they know? Greeks and Romans who actually met Druids provide quite a bit of interesting information about their traditions and knowledge. In Celtic society, there were three groups of sacred people—Druids, Bards, and Seers. The modern word Druid actually represents the plural form of the singular *Druí*. The Celtic name comes from an ancient root word meaning "wisdom of oak." The druids were described as teachers of wisdom, who studied natural and moral philosophy, the motion of the stars and the heavens, and the will of the gods. They were considered experts in communication with the divine.

The Druids were said to have provided lengthy and intensive training to druidic students in secret locations such as caves or groves. They were powerful and honored members of societies, who advised kings (and queens) and provided guidance and healing for members of the community. Druids are described as having knowledge of sacred plants, both in the proper ritual culling of the plants and in their physical and magical uses. They served as judges and arbitrators and were exempt from having to participate in battle. They sometimes appeared between two armies to provide counsel or bring about peace. In addition, they were said to perform magic and make prophesies.

One of the most interesting druidic beliefs was that the soul (like the universe) was immortal. One classical author said that Druids believed that people's souls were immortal—that after a period of years they lived again, the soul entering another body. Reincarnation appears in several Celtic myths. People "die" and are reborn in new forms—sometimes human and sometimes animal. The writer Lucan, in the first century AD, wrote a highly styl-

ized but moving piece referring to this belief of the Druids: "If what you sing of is true, death is but the mid-point of a long existence."

In myths and stories, Druids are honored and respected. They were said to have magical abilities, including power over the elements and the ability to fly or shapeshift (much like shamans in other cultures). They preserved in oral tradition and memory the important sacred knowledge of the tribe—including its mythology, genealogy, poetry, and sacred lore. They also performed divination (frequently using omens from the natural world) and were said to use secret druidic languages.

Were there any historical female Druids? The group of women in black mentioned above could have been female Druids who were also fleeing to Ireland to escape the Romans. Their torches and curses certainly terrified the Roman troops. Several

Classical authors refer to women in various Celtic regions as *dryas* or *dryadas*. One was said to have had an aunt called Dryadia! There are also two accounts of groups of women inhabiting sacred islands off the shore of Britain and Gaul who lived apart from men and seemed to perform priestess-like duties. It is hard to know if these are Druids in the strict, cultural sense, or if they were "wise women" or "female seers" (both of which are known to have existed).

Female Druids do exist in traditional myths and stories. Finn mac Cumhaill was said to have been raised in the forest by two women, at least one of whom is explicitly said to be a Druidess. In one traditional tale, legend had it that a woman called Dreco was "versed in all the black arts." She is also called a Druid and a Poetess. Another mythical woman named Gaine was said to be very learned, a seer, and a chief Druid.

We do know that some women historically held roles that were usually held by men. There were well-known and respected women leaders, warriors, and physicians. There were also famous female seers. One of the most interesting stories concerns a prophetess in Gaul called Veleda (whose name comes from a root word which means "to see"). She delivered her prophecies hidden in a tower. People who came to consult her gave their query or question to a relative of hers who then took it up into the tower. Veleda, like other oracles, often provided a response in somewhat cryptic or mysterious language.

Another famous female seer in Celtic legend is Fedelm (whose name comes from a different root word meaning "to see"). She went to Scotland to learn "verse and vision" and served as a consultant to Queen Medb.

There certainly were female magicians, both attested and legendary. An actual tablet found in Gaul talks about a group of female seers who "wove special underworld magic." Some of the Celtic goddesses—including the Mórrigan, her sister Macha, and the Goddess Bridget—performed magic and prophecy.

In later times, the British legendary figure of Morgan le Fey performed similar magical practices. Women also served as Witches or sorceresses, and their earliest incarnations as Witches were portrayed positively. Two Witches assist the Tuatha Dé

Danann in an important battle, turning trees, sod, and stones into warriors. These women are called by a different name than the Druids or male Sorcerers who also helped. Neither the Witches nor the sorcerers appeared to be maleficent. Even the god Lug describes himself as a sorcerer in the same story—as well as a harper, warrior, poet, historian, and physician.

One of the most important Druidic teachings was provided by the Druids of ancient Gaul, who bid the people to "show reverence to the gods, do no ill deed, and practice valor." These are words that many of us, including modern Druids, can still live by today.

Mystical Archetypes of the Past

by Michelle Santos

In ancient times, when the world was a simpler and more brutal place, people knew their paths in life. If born a peasant, a person would live and die on the family plot of land, never venturing farther than a few miles from home. A king was born to rule, a fisherman to fish, a woman to bear children, and a monk to pray.

However, when following a spiritual path, there were several options from which to choose. The four spiritual professions that were most common and most relevant to the present are: priest/priestess, healer, warrior, and mystic. In today's hectic, multi-tasking world, these professions have become archetypes for specific ways of thinking.

They represent attitudes, ideals, and thoughts that are hidden from our everyday lives. They are part of the mystical universe and, as Jung would say, the collective unconscious. They are the essence of our dreams, myths, and fairy tales; they are the center of our hopes and desires.

Knowing what ancient profession to which you are most connected will help you grasp the innate skills inside you, bringing them into the light of day to help you venture further on your journey of self-discovery.

Priest/Priestess

Priests or priestesses in ancient times held positions of power. They were leaders of the tribe or clan and often held a position equal to the ruling chieftain, king, or queen. They were very much at the forefront of all decisions, whether they agreed or disagreed with the governing body.

Due to their positions of power, priests and priestesses were not rebels, preferring to work within existing governmental and spiritual structures. This means that they did not choose to make drastic changes. Priests and priestesses were learned and scholarly. They often had to study for many years in order to gain the knowledge necessary to achieve their position of power.

Priests and priestesses were concerned with groups of people. As they were responsible for the welfare of entire tribes, clans, cities, or towns, they were forced to look at the big picture. Unfortunately, this means that individual needs were not often considered when making decisions for the good of all. Responsibility was a major trait belonging to the priest or priestess. As with all leadership roles, this path can be lonely but filled with satisfaction, as plans put in motion come to fruition.

In today's world, priests or priestesses are goal-oriented individuals. They are rarely seen without a list or a plan of action. Priests or priestesses are strong-willed and know exactly what they want out of any specific situation and out of life. They are great organizers and talented, compassionate leaders. Feeling more comfortable in group situations, priests and priestesses love working with others, as long as their ideas are listened to with due attention. As they possess natural leadership qualities, usually their ideas are put into motion. Since they exude confidence, priests and priestesses will often attract less secure individuals, who are drawn to their charisma, charm, and grounded nature. Some jobs that priests or priestesses might hold are: managers, college professors, politicians, school superintendents or principals, sales people, or entrepreneurs.

Healer

Healers in the ancient past were considered important assets to the community. They had knowledge of herbs, medicinal chants, teas, and potions. They understood the relationship between the physical, emotional, and mental bodies, and practiced the doctrine of the four humors, which could be regulated with food and drink.

Healers were called to attend births and deaths, to set the bones of the young, and to ease the suffering of the old. They treated general malaise (what we now call depression), cuts, gashes, broken bones, internal pain, gas, and even issues related to conception and contraception. In short, the healers cared for everyone and worked hard to create a healthy atmosphere.

Healers worked with people on an individual basis, learning from past experiences but seeing each patient as a separate entity. Although they were considered important, they were not called upon to give their opinion on government matters. Healers focused on the humanity in people, helping others to live healthier, more fulfilling lives. Compassion was a major trait belonging to the healer. As with all caring roles, this path can be draining—as the healer is constantly giving to others. However, it is also a very satisfying path, as the healer sees all the good he or she accomplishes.

In today's world, healers are very caring individuals. They listen sympathetically to the woes of others without passing judgment or offering unsolicited advice. They work to make others feel better, either physically or emotionally, never asking for anything in return. Healers can be shy, preferring one-on-one conversations to large public speaking engagements. They will often state that they feel more relaxed around animals or plants than humans.

Healers long for the simple life and exude a quiet confidence and serenity that often attracts less stable individuals. This can lead to the "stray dog" syndrome, where healers take in and nurture those who need help of some kind. Some jobs for healers include: therapists, elementary school teachers, doctors, nurses, floral shop and garden store owners or employees.

Warrior

In ancient society, there was no more valuable person than the warrior. Warriors protected the community from outside attack and expanded the lands of the chieftain, king, or queen. Clad in leather tunics, swinging metal swords or axes, the warriors kept the community secure and safe.

Although not adept at book knowledge, warriors trained for years with skilled masters in order to hone their craft. They learned the intricacies of each weapon—sword, axe, bow, spear—and usually chose one that they preferred. (Some warriors would say that the weapon actually chose them.) They trained their muscles to perform, but they also trained their minds. Good warriors needed to be able to think on their feet, react quickly, and formulate plans within seconds. Mind and body reacting as one was the ultimate goal of every warrior.

It could take years for the warrior to teach his mind to relax and allow instinct to kick in. Thus, the warriors moved as one, not thinking but doing in long arcs of agile and swift, fierce and strong movements. Loyalty was a major trait belonging to a warrior. As with all those who pledge their allegiance to another, there is the possibility of trusting the wrong person. Warriors do not usually waver from a selected path, so it is imperative that they know their loyalty is well-founded.

In today's world, warriors are doers not thinkers. They are not interested in discussing the philosophical ramifications of anything. When others bog down in details and particulars, the warriors rise up with the question, "Are we going to do this or not?" Without the warriors, the world would move much more slowly, and projects would take much more time to get done.

Warriors are not only concerned with moving forward, they also seek out and search for the weak and unprotected in order to afford them security and safety. Despite their gruff demeanor, warriors are every bit as caring as healers; they just show it in different ways. This is not to say that warriors don't enjoy a good fight every once in a while. Barroom brawls, arguments with loved ones, and on-field football fights are part of the warrior's existence, especially when young. (Age tends to mellow even the most ferocious warrior.)

Our world would not be the same without the existence of the brave warrior, firing us up and getting us moving. Some jobs that warriors might hold are: construction workers, police or military officers, professional or amateur athletes, bartenders, and bouncers.

Mystic

Mystics in the ancient world were shrouded in mystery. They were looked upon with skepticism and awe by the other members of the community. Here was a person who saw the future and talked to the dead. Mystics often lived apart from the rest of the community, as not many people felt comfortable around them.

Mystics tapped into great power, thus commanding respect and awe. Chieftains and kings would consult the mystic on affairs of state, on the success of an invasion, on the best time to conceive a son, on the outlook for next season's crops. Without the mystic, a chieftain's direct link to the divine was severed and he or she would not know the best way to appease or approach a god or goddess.

The mystic was forced to see the world on both an individualistic and a holistic level, understanding the connection between the actions of individuals and the structure of the cosmos. Weavers of fate and manipulators of fortune, mystics tapped into the universal force of the godhood, of the earth and sky, and of the elements—and they translated these for humanity. Illusion was a major trait belonging to the mystic. As with all metaphysical roles, this path can be lonely as the mystic's powers are misunderstood and feared. However, it is also a very satisfying path as the mystic is allowed access to the secrets of the universe.

In today's world, mystics often quietly go about their own business, never sharing their skills or gifts with strangers. The person in the cubicle next to you could be a mystic—you never know. Mystics tend to enjoy time by themselves communing with nature. Unlike the healer, a mystic prefers the wildness of nature rather than the order of a garden. Woods and forests are sanctuaries for the mystic, as are ocean shorelines and mountain tops. Mystics will gravitate to "between-time places," where opposites meet, order meets chaos, civilization meets wilderness, and earth meets sky.

Elementals, fairies, and spirits of the dead will often be attracted to the energy of the mystic. Mystics tend to keep to themselves and do not share their ideas freely. When drawn into conversation, their comments are insightful, as they have the ability to look at a situation from many different viewpoints. Unlike the priest or priestess, the mystic does not have a stake in any organizational structure. Therefore, the mystic tends to support new ideas and new ways of doing things, while cherishing the ways of times past. Some jobs that mystics might hold are: philosophers, scientists, owners of New Age shops, tarot card readers, park rangers, preservationists, and museum curators.

Every One of Us

Every one of us has a little bit of each archetype inside us. It is human nature, however, to display the qualities and characteristics of one archetype more than another. Remember, no archetype is better than any other archetype. All played a necessary and vital role in the society of the ancient world.

Now that you know which archetype you most strongly relate to, you can take that information and use it in expanding and deepening your spirituality. Knowledge of self is key in spiritual work. Perhaps, after taking the quiz and finding your mystical archetype, you are thinking that your archetype doesn't appear to relate to your life path. Wait and see. As your path unfolds before you, you may be surprised by the changes in yourself and in your outlook. The gods and goddesses work quietly in our lives, subtly changing our thoughts and dreams, our goals and desires.

Your journey through the mystical arts is a lifelong endeavor that you can enjoy and savor for as long (or as little) as you would like. Revel in the present and look forward to what lies ahead.

Mystical Archetype Quiz

by Michelle Santos

We all have innate skills that are a part of our genetic make-up. We are born with them; they are as much a part of us as our hair and eye color. Remember those lazy summer days when you were a kid in elementary school with no responsibilities, appointments, or schedules? Empty afternoons stretched before you, and you had all the time you needed to explore your likes and dislikes, your wishes and desires. How did you fill your days? What did you do with your time? What are your innate skills and interests?

The Mystical Archetype Quiz is designed to align you, once again, with your innate skills. Before you take the quiz, find a time and place where you can sit undisturbed for a half hour. Erase all your worries and anxieties from your mind. (I know, I know—this is easier said than done!) Have your significant other, a friend, or neighbor watch your children. Forget about dinner, the project due tomorrow, and the nasty way your boss said "good-night" to you this afternoon. Take a few deep breaths and think back to those summer days of frolic and fun. Feel the Sun warm your body. Breathe in the sweet smell of newly mown grass. Hear the crickets chirping and the birds singing. When you are feeling relaxed, list two things that you used to enjoy doing during your carefree childhood days.

1._____

_____

2._____

_____

Now, with those childhood memories in your mind, answer the following questions.

1. You and your friends plan a party. You are in change of:
   a. food and drink
   b. over-all theme and coordination
   c. parking and crowd control
   d. decorations and entertainment

2. While at a summer party, you are most likely to be found:
   a. Outside, enjoying the night and looking for a shooting star
   b. Outside, scoping out the garden
   c. Inside, dancing and talking to all the "right" people
   d. Inside, leading a discussion on medieval weaponry

3. Which elective college course are you most interested in?
   a. Midwifery Through the Ages
   b. Roman Gladiators
   c. Nostradamus: Seer or Faker?
   d. The Role of Religion in Egyptian Society

4. You are picking out dishes with your fiancé, so you:
   a. Choose the set that "feels" right to you at the time
   b. Choose the set with the best Consumer Reports rating
   c. Choose the set you fell in love with at age fifteen
   d. Choose the set that is the strongest and most durable

5. Which book would you choose off the library's shelf:
   a. Get off your Duff: Motivation for Everyone
   b. Tips and Recipes for Herbal Healing
   c. Color Guide to Your Personality
   d. Teaching Karate for Fun and Profit

6. Which person from myth and legend would you most like to visit?
   a. Calypso, Greek queen and nymph
   b. Odin, god from the Norse lands
   c. Merlin, sorcerer from ancient Britain
   d. Isis, goddess from Egypt

7. You just won $100 on a scratch ticket: what will you spend it on?
   a. A historical/fantasy knife from the Noble Collection
   b. A new deck of tarot cards/healing cards and a Renaissance shirt
   c. A garden gnome from a local artisan
   d. Software with Celtic fonts and artwork

8. While at your local Renaissance Faire, you decide to have your photo taken dressed in which historical costume?

a. King or queen, complete with jeweled crown and fur collar

b. Knight or warrior maiden, with sword, chain mail, tunic, and helm

c. Necromancer, with black hooded cloak and skull

d. Apothecary, with long, frayed robe and vials of potions and herbs

9. While on a trip to Jamaica, you stumble upon a voudoun ceremony. After watching, you:

a. Talk to the priestess about her possession experiences

b. Admire the hand-made drums

c. Sniff the glass vials and bottles left on the altar

d. View the "dynamics" between the congregation and the priest or priestess

10. If you could meet a mystical creature, it would be:

a. A unicorn

b. A genie

c. A mermaid

d. A dragon

11. If you could have one magical power, it would be:

a. Invisibility

b. Prophesy

c. Dowsing

d. Throwing fireballs

12. If there were one person you could have dinner with, it would be:

a. Napoleon

b. Florence Nightingale

c. Madonna

d. Leonardo da Vinci

13. If you could achieve one stupendous thing in your life, it would be:

a. Ridding the world of crime

b. Protecting the world's environment

c. Putting responsible, intelligent leaders into power

d. Finding a cure for all deadly diseases

14. If you lived in Colonial America, what part of your life would you most enjoy?
    a. Communing with nature on a daily basis
    b. Governing yourself
    c. Handling weapons every day
    d. Fostering a close-knit community

15. If you were involved in a religious ceremony, you would:
    a. Cook the bread for the offering
    b. Lead the people in chant and song
    c. Assess the crowd to make sure nothing negative occurred
    d. Call down the power of spirit to affect change

16. Choose the fruit that most appeals to you:
    a. Apple
    b. Banana
    c. Orange
    d. Pomegranate

17. Choose the tree that most appeals to you:
    a. Birch
    b. Dogwood
    c. Maple
    d. Rowan

18. Choose the crystal that most appeals to you:
    a. Citrine
    b. Rose quartz
    c. Onyx
    d. Amethyst

19. Choose the animal that most appeals to you:
    a. Eagle
    b. Owl
    c. Cougar
    d. Deer

20. Choose the element that most appeals to you:
    a. fire
    b. water

c. air
d. earth

Using the chart below, match your answer (a., b., c., or d.) to a corresponding letter that stands for the four archetypes. (P is Priest/Priestess; H is Healer; W is Warrior; M is Mystic).

Write the letter next to the question above. For instance, if you answered "a." to question 1, you would write an "H" next to question 1. If you answered "c" to question 2, you would write a "P" next to question 2. Do this for all your questions.

Number	Answer "a."	Answer "b."	Answer "c."	Answer "d."
1	H	P	W	M
2	M	H	P	W
3	H	W	M	P
4	M	P	H	W
5	P	H	M	W
6	M	W	P	H
7	W	M	H	P
8	P	W	M	H
9	M	W	H	P
10	H	P	M	W
11	P	M	H	W
12	W	H	P	M
13	W	M	P	H
14	M	P	W	H
15	H	P	W	M
16	P	W	H	M
17	H	P	M	W
18	P	H	W	M
19	P	M	W	H
20	W	H	P	M

When you have marked every question with your matching archetype letter, add up the total number of each letter and write down the totals below.

P=_____   H=_____   W=_____   M=_____

The archetype with the highest score is most likely your archetype. Now turn back to the article on page 255 to find more about your personality.

Guardian Animal Archetypes

by Sedwyn

Since ancient times, people have recognized the power of certain animals and invoked their spirits during ritual. Many deities, both male and female, are associated with particular animals, which also act as their earthly representatives. From prehistoric times through classical Greece, people have revered and feared certain animals. In cases such as the snake, an animal honored by one culture was deliberately made evil by another to subvert and control people's belief systems.

In modern Pagan practice it is not unusual to look to an animal for guidance and protection because of its association with a particular tradition or deity. Guardian animals serve to protect the turnings of the cycle of the year as well as one's life. There are four in particular whose history and association with ritual date back to prehistoric times.

Animal	Attributes	Archetypes	Function	Direction
Bear	Sustainer, nurturer	Life giver, mother	Life	North
Owl	Seer, wisdom	Death wielder, crone	Death	East
Snake	Mover, changer	Transformer, maiden	Rebirth	West
Bull	Vitality, life	Male, the God	Spark of life	South

The Bear: Mother Goddess

The mother aspect of the Goddess not only encompassed giving birth but also provided sustenance and protection. For ancient as well as modern people, the bear is a symbol of power. Less today than in earlier times, the bear's power was perceived as the she-bear protective mother.

The bear was one of the animals that symbolized the Goddess's various functions. Bear-shaped pottery was produced continuously from 7,000 to 3,000 BC in a wide area from Western Ukraine, throughout the Balkan Peninsula, Greece, and the Lipari Islands north of Sicily. Both the shape and function of these vessels served as symbols. The bear is one of the symbolic animals of Artemis/Diana and is also linked to childbirth.

Just as the bear hibernates, winter is a time for us to slow down and turn inward to do our self-work. We then emerge in the spring with renewed spirit. As the guardian of the north, Bear helps us nurture ourselves and find the strength of the protective mother within no matter what our gender.

The Owl: Death Wielder

One aspect of the ancient bird goddess hybrid was that of death wielder. She was portrayed as a bird of prey: owl, vulture, crow, or raven. She was the one with wisdom who prepared people for death and eventual rebirth. In later mythology, this aspect was turned into the hag—a fearful being who brought about a horrid death. But to the owl goddess and those who believed in her, death was not seen as a mournful end of life, but rather a passage in the cycle of life, death, and rebirth.

Representations of owls and owl goddesses have been found on pottery in tombs marked with symbols of life and regeneration. These have been found in a wide area and timeframe: Syria (8,000–7,000 BC), Lithuania (4,000 BC), New Grange, Ireland (3,200 BC) and Folkton, England (2,000 BC).

The owl's association with the Goddess survived into Greek culture in representations of Athena. Homer even referred to her as the owl-eyed goddess. In our present-day culture, the owl symbolizes knowledge and is frequently depicted wearing a graduate's mortarboard, although it is no longer connected with the Goddess or her wisdom.

For Pagans, the owl that glides silently through the air is a reminder of the dark power of the Goddess. Although a creature of the night, Owl as guardian of the east will carry us from darkness (of the womb and tomb) into the light of a new day (rebirth).

The Snake: Transformer

Since the Paleolithic period, wavy meandering lines represented water, snakes, and the life-force combined into one. This symbol of fecundity was often linked to Tiamat, Babylonian goddess of salt water, and Mesopotamian Inanna/Ishtar and Ua Zit who was the patron deity of pre-dynastic Lower Egypt. The snake goddess of Crete (2,000–1,700 BC) nurtured the world with life-giving moisture. Various versions of the snake goddess continued to appear well into the time of historical Greece.

The snake goes through obvious cyclical changes, as do women, the Moon, and the seasons. The snake is symbolic of the Goddess as maiden. Maidenhood is a time of transformation, when a child becomes a woman whose moisture is capable of bringing forth new life. Likewise, boys experience powerful transformations as they enter manhood.

In spite of being turned into a symbol of creeping evil thought to be responsible for the downfall of humankind in the Garden of Eden, the positive power of the snake has managed to survive. In ancient Greece, Asklepios and his daughter Hygeia were healers who were depicted with a staff around which snakes coiled. This has been carried over into our modern medical symbol, the caduceus.

Powerful transformation takes place in the form of spiritual awakening, as well as the change of maiden into woman, and boy into man. Growth of body and spirit are integral parts of the life cycle. As guardian of the west, Snake helps us navigate the transformative stages that occur at puberty and throughout our lives.

The Bull: The God

Horned gods Cernunnos, Herne, and Pan represent powerful male qualities that run deeper than the stereo-typical idea of brute strength. Along with a depiction of the Full Moon (the Goddess in her full mother aspect), a set of horns represents the Moon's waxing and waning phases. Together, this male and female energy repre-sents completeness.

In the depths of the cave at Lascaux, France, (15,000–10,000 BC) bulls depict vital life energy. In many ancient cultures, fast-growing horns were symbolic of regeneration.

Stylized horns of consecration have been found in the Temple of Knossos on Crete (2,000–1,600 BC) and at Vinca and Karanova on the Balkan Peninsula (5,000–4,000 BC). In later Greek mythology and European folk-lore, Zeus and river gods were portrayed as bulls.

While the Goddess is life giver and death wielder, the God represents the essence of what is born and destroyed. He is the cycle. The Sun King born at Winter Solstice begins to decline at Summer Solstice. He is cut down with the harvest to sleep in the Goddess's womb until he is reborn. As guardian of the south, Bull (the God) carries the fiery spark that keeps the cycle of life turning.

In Ritual

The power of these guardian animals can be evoked in ritual and around your home as ongoing reminders of the cycles you live. The owl (death wielder) in the east, combined with the snake (transformer) in the west, symbolize the passing of days and lifetimes—dark to light and light into darkness. It is an endless circle of time and timelessness. The bear (mother Goddess) in the north and the bull (father God) in the south provide an axis on which female and male energies are balanced.

The flow of life spirals forever in past and future.

Sacred Tamarisk: Egyptian Tree of Life

by Elizabeth Hazel

The tamarisk tree is a hardy shrub-like tree important to the mythology of ancient Egypt. It is associated with Osiris, and his legend makes specific references to the role of the tamarisk in the world-view of Egyptian mysticism.

The legend of the death and resurrection of Osiris has been preserved in the writings of Plutarch, a Greek diplomat, traveler, and teacher who died around 140 AD. According to Plutarch's recounting of the tale, Set plotted with conspirators to kill his brother Osiris and secretly obtained the measurements of his body. Osiris was invited to dine at a great banquet on the seventeenth day of the month Hathor, an unlucky day. Osiris also was in his twenty-eighth year and under the grim auspices of his Saturn return period. After dinner, Set offered a challenge for the guests—to fit into a small wooden cask. The other guests were too large, but Osiris, being lithe and fine-boned, was able to curl into the box.

Set slammed down the lid and trapped his brother in the box. He launched the box into the mouth of the Nile, and the river's current carried it far away.

Isis discovered Set's wicked trick, and searched far and wide for Osiris. The cask had floated across the Mediterranean Sea to a distant coast, landing at the base of a tamarisk tree.

The rapidly growing tree soon enclosed the box containing Osiris within its trunk. When the tree reached a great size, it was used as a pillar in the palace of the king of Byblos. The fragrance of this pillar was related far and wide, and finally the story came to Isis. Knowing what it meant, she traveled to Byblos.

There, Isis begged the king to allow her to take the pillar, and he agreed. She opened the pillar and found the cask, containing the dead body of Osiris. Isis's lamentations were great. The pillar was returned to the king and queen of Byblos wrapped in linen and anointed with oil. The pillar was carefully preserved and was still worshiped in a Temple of Isis during Plutarch's lifetime.

Isis returned to Egypt with the casket. She hid the box and sought the assistance of their son, Horus. Set found the box and tore the body of Osiris into fourteen pieces, which he scattered throughout the land. Again, Isis undertook a journey to reclaim these parts. When he was finally assembled, she restored Osiris to life with powerful magic.

The Tree of Life

In Egyptian cosmology, Osiris was the creative male principle, and the tamarisk was the tree of life. This tree was rooted in the ocean and reached upward to the stars in the sky, thus linking the underworld, the earth's surface, and the sky.

The tamarisk pillar was the world axis around which the constellations revolved. The wrappings placed around a corpse in the process of mummification were symbolic of the body of Osiris encased within the tamarisk.

Eventually this god-within-a-tree idea evolved into the djed pillar. The *djed* was a composite symbol of the male creative principle encased and sometimes rising through the world axis. It represented a source of stability and continuity in a changing world.

The djed is not a static concept, but an axis that can be awakened whenever specific constellational and planetary alignments occur over time through the procession of the equinoxes.

The tamarisk was a superb choice for this legend because of its botanical qualities. It grows swiftly and thrives on the banks of rivers and lakes. One of the common names for this tree is "salt cedar," because of its fragrance and ability to absorb large quantities of water. It is also a prolific self-seeding tree, which is consistent with the phallic nature of the djed pillar.

In modern magical practice, the tamarisk is considered a sovereign balm for purification and protection. Burning the crushed foliage of a tamarisk drives away evil spirits. Further magical uses of this plant include rites for regeneration, gathering creative power, and creating a conduit for accessing the energy of the tree of life. As Osiris is the oldest father god of the Egyptian pantheon, he corresponds to the planet Saturn, as well as the constellation Orion and the fixed star Sirius. The long, straight branches of a tamarisk can be used for divination much in the same way as yarrow stalks are used by the Chinese to perform I-Ching divination.

Older branches, usually long and straight and with bark of a deep maroon red, are a wonderful source of wand wood. Wands made of tamarisk are perfect for practitioners who focus on creativity and regenerative magic. The deep red of the bark conveys the idea of powerful potency. The dried foliage of this plant can be used in creating loose incenses.

The great thirst of this tree confirms its association with the element of water. As a result of this quality, a tamarisk wand can be used in rain-making ceremonies.

Any ritual that includes the use of tamarisk—as a wand, as incense, or as a fresh-cut branch for asperging—will be particularly powerful when Orion and Sirius are visible in the night sky or when the Moon is full in the watery signs of Cancer, Pisces, or Scorpio.

A tamarisk wand can be used to create a powerful circle of protection.

Tamarisk Afterthoughts

Osiris became, in the later years of the Egyptian dynasties, the ruler of the underworld. Thus Osiris and, by association, the tamarisk have a relationship with the underworld gods of Hades, Pluto, Dis-Pater, Hecate, and Persephone.

Transformation, rebirth, and regeneration are magical properties of this plant. It represents the hidden potential of a seed, a germ of life contained within a hard shell (much like Osiris was contained in the tamarisk) that may rise from beneath the surface to reach the light of the Sun.

A seed encases its latent potential for growth in a protective cocoon, much like a mummy's wrappings. In sympathetic magic, the tamarisk represents the potential to break through this protective shell. It may be used in rituals or spells that assist in breaking through fears, especially fears that have resulted in a hardening of the heart—cynicism, distrust, isolation, and resistance to love.

The tamarisk tree can be grown in many environments as it is a hardy species particularly resistant to drought. *Tamarix gallica* is a variety that flowers in mid-summer. Some varieties have pink or white flowers. It is a hardy, swift-growing tree, but rarely reaches heights over twenty feet. It is fragrant and tolerates some shade. It is a vigorous and unusual plant to include in a garden; it is especially desirable for small gardens because of its relatively small size.

The tamarisk has been imported to North America, where it thrives in almost every region. Unfortunately, it has become something of a problem in the American southwest, as its rampant growth and invasive self-seeding are creating groves of tamarisks that consume large quantities of Colorado River water. Conservationists are working to thin these groves in order to preserve the precious and diminishing water supply of this region.

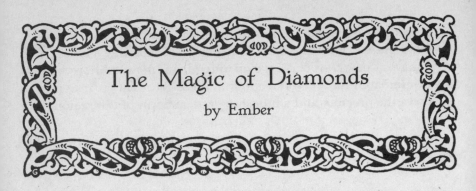

The Magic of Diamonds

by Ember

There is a good reason for our love affair with diamonds, the most highly prized of stones. They are truly ancient. We learn from a young age that diamonds are special, the world's hardest substance, and we are mesmerized by their sparkle. But beyond that, most people don't consider what diamonds actually are, and how they can be used in magic.

Diamonds are formed deep in the Earth, as much as four hundred miles beneath the surface, and are pushed upward in molten rock during volcanic eruptions. In order for a diamond to become a diamond, rather than graphite or carbon dioxide, the crystals must cool quickly and be near the surface. The process of extreme heat and pressure that formed the diamonds usually occurred over three billion years ago. Even the youngest diamonds are still one hundred million years old.

The formation of diamonds makes them significant to anyone interested in working with stones for magical properties. The diamond is composed of one of the most vital elements: carbon. Carbon forms a variety of necessary compounds and is fundamental to all biological systems, providing the basis for all life. It's contained in all organic matter and fossil fuels. So a diamond represents crystallized life.

The first diamonds were found in a river-bed in India around 800 BC. The deposits found there supplied the world with diamonds until the eighteenth century, but more deposits have been discovered in other parts of the world including Brazil, South Africa, and most recently, Canada. Arkansas is the only state in the U.S. where diamonds are mined.

The name diamond comes from the Greek *adamas*, the name for a legendary, indestructible metal. The Sanskrit word for diamond is *vajra,* which means "thunderbolt." To these people the diamond was a fitting symbol for this celestial weapon.

The Romans wore diamonds as talismans to ward off evil, dispel nightmares, calm the mentally ill, promote courage in battle, and offer protection from storms and ill fortune. The ancient Indians believed the soul could animate gemstones as it passed through various incarnations. Plato believed gems to be living beings, and people of the Middle Ages believed diamonds could heal the sick; they would keep them in their beds, breathe on them, or wear them next to the skin. They were used as talismans against poisoning and also as poison itself—diamond powder, when ingested, could be fatal. On the other hand, Europeans in the Middle Ages believed diamonds held in the mouth would correct lying. The ancient Egyptians considered diamonds a symbol of eternity and used them in jewelry to adorn corpses.

The cutting of diamonds is fairly recent. For centuries they were only carried or worn in rough form as talismans. Sometimes natural eight-sided stones were set into jewelry. The earliest known diamond was found in the crown of a Hungarian queen dated to about 1074 AD. During the reign of Louis XI in thirteenth-century France, the art of cutting and faceting stones was practiced, and wearing diamonds in jewelry became popular, even though the law stated only the king could wear diamonds. However, by the next century diamonds were becoming popular in the jewelry of both royal men and women. Diamond cutting was first started as an industry in Venice sometime around 1330 and arrived in Paris soon after. By the seventeenth century, the merchant class was wearing diamond jewelry as well. The first diamond engagement ring was given in 1477 by Archduke Maximillian of Austria to Mary of Burgundy.

There is much folklore surrounding the idea of rings, especially wedding rings. The beginning of this tradition comes from ancient Egypt. The ring, a circle, has long been a symbol of eternity to many cultures, so the connection between the circle and the ring is understandable. There was a belief that there was a vein in the heart than ran directly to the third finger of the left hand; this is the origin of the custom of wearing a wedding ring on that finger. Of course, those ancient rings were woven, most likely from reeds and hemp, and wore out quickly. Eventually, the art of metallurgy became known. But early metal rings were not the finely crafted items we know today. They were uneven and large but were made more attractive by placing precious stones in them. Evidence of this can be seen in hieroglyphs of Egyptian tombs. Jewelry was used more as currency and an expression of wealth than an expression of love. Eventually, other metals were used. The early Romans used iron or copper for rings. It took time to perfect this art. Rings were originally given in marriage as a legally binding contract. Gold won out over time as the best and favorite metal to fashion rings, and eventually a tradition of giving rings in marriage was born. Interestingly, early Protestant puritans claimed that "wedding rings were Pagan" and not to be used.

Some of the metaphysical properties attributed to diamonds include chakra cleansing, increasing energy, energizing the eyes, heart, brain, and sexual organs, purity, abundance, inspiration, and perfection. Buddhism adopted many Hindu symbols, and the diamond came to be considered a symbol of religious virtue.

Since diamonds are so expensive, it may not be practical to buy them just for gem magic. But if you own any kind of diamond jewelry, you can find ways to incorporate the jewelry into a ritual or spell. The most obvious way is to use wedding rings or other symbolic jewelry in spells and rituals to strengthen bonds of fidelity, friendship, marriage, and romance. Beyond that, you may have diamonds that are unassociated with a bond that you could use for other types of spells. For example, if you have a pair of diamond earrings, you could use one or both of them in a spell for purity or inspiration. If you own diamond jewelry that is set with other stones, you could form a unique spell combining the metaphysical properties of the other stones. Rubies, sapphires, emeralds, and opals are just a few of the stones often found set with diamonds. If you have the luxury of obtaining an uncut or loose diamond, have it cut or mounted in a way that is special to you. Diamonds of any kind make a lovely symbol for the divine power, in whatever form you identify with.

No matter how you enjoy the beauty and magic of diamonds, you'll never be able to look at your diamond jewelry in the same way again.

Mystical Spider Deities

by Nancy Bennett

Long before recorded time, the spider had a place in our beliefs. Mohammed was saved by one. Robert the Bruce was inspired by one. Many cultures celebrate spiders in their legends and history. It's hard not to be caught up in the magic of the spider.

In the beginning, say the Kiowa Plains people, there was no fire. The animals suffered. One day they noticed smoke coming from the center of a dead tree on an island. They decided to try and steal the fire from the tree. But no one could swim the waters until a water spider, Kanane'ski Amai'yehi, agreed to try. She was ingenious, bringing along a pot. When she reached the top of the dead tree, she used her web to lower the pot down and pluck out a few coals. To this day, it is she who keeps the world warm.

In Southwestern Native traditions, it is Spider Woman who is responsible for the creation of woman and man. Spider Woman used the clays of the earth to form the people. To each, she attached a thread of her web from the top of her head. This thread was the gift of creative wisdom she bestowed upon all.

Some people forgot her gift, and as a punishment, she sent a great flood to destroy them. Three times she covered the world with water. Those who had forgotten her gift were drowned. Those who remembered floated to the new world and climbed to safety through the Sipapu Pole to the womb of Mother Earth.

Spider's scientific name is *arachne*. Arachne was a Lydian girl who was very skilled as a weaver. She challenged the goddess Athena to a contest to see who could weave the most beautiful tapestry. Arachne's tapestry was a fine one, but the goddess's work was better. Athena changed Arachne into a spider, condemning her to weave forever as a warning to other mortals who would dare to challenge a goddess.

In Teutonic myths, three sisters, the Norns, spun secret meanings into life by way of the web. The Norns, also known as the Wyrd sisters, would spin, measure, and cut the thread of life. To them alone was known the precise moments of each person's birth and death. They lived in the deep roots of the Yggdrasil; they made sure the tree was kept healthy and well fed. Odin hung on this tree for nine days, and he received the knowledge of the runes from the sisters.

In the northern Vanuatu Islands in the southwest Pacific, spiders appear in paintings and tattoos as well as in spider cloth. This cloth is supple, but tough. It is also fairly waterproof and resistant to rot.

In the southern island of Malakula, spider web cloth is used as a base for artwork, ritual head dresses, and sacred clothing. When men wear these coverings they are said to be consumed by the "spider spirit." Men perform complex male funerary rituals in these costumes. The rituals emphasize the important role spider spirits play in life after death.

In West Africa, there is a spider god named Anansi who is both spider and man. He is a trickster, a provider of wisdom, and a keeper of stories, and he often serves as a link between people and the supreme being. Anansi put all the wisdom of the world in a pot to keep it safe, but the pot was so big he couldn't carry it. His son suggested that he put the pot on his back, as it seemed the wise thing to do. Anansi grew angry, as he now realized that all the wisdom wasn't in the pot. In a fit of temper, he tipped over the pot and now the wisdom is available to all people.

There was a time when the gods first visited earth. They used the tall trees to climb down from above and were saddened by how the people were abusing the land. They wanted to return to heaven, but the men had cut down all the trees. So they turned to the spider and asked him to weave a ladder to the sky so they might return home. For this action, spider was blessed by the gods, who now use the webs of spiders to visit the earth at night. In Africa, they believe that the remnants of those ladders can be seen in the morning, snagged in the branches of trees.

At Yule, we observe our own spider myth. Long ago, a poor but faithful woman set up a tree for her children. She cried because she had no gifts to give them and went to sleep with a heavy heart. During the night, spiders spun delicate webs among the branches. The gods were so touched by her faith that the webs turned into silver. Tinsel on the tree is our way of remembering this myth.

Of all the species of spiders known to man, only about twenty are dangerous. Among those is the black widow, found in North America. She is armed with a poison which can be lethal or unpleasant depending on the age, health, and size of the person she bites.

Normally very shy, black widow likes to hide in dark corners or in woodpiles. There is an antivenom available to treat black widow bites, but it is effective only once in your lifetime. The antivenom is milked from black widows, much as snakes are milked to provide an antivenom for snakebites. It takes the venom from 28,000 spiders to make a single dose of antivenom, making this medicine very costly.

In the 1700s, spiders were thought to be a cure-all for diseases. Enclosed in a necklace, they were worn live round the neck as a lucky charm to ward off illness.

In 1760, a Dr. Watson advised that a fever could be cured by "swallowing a spider, gently bruised and wrapped up in a raisin or spread upon bread and butter." Luckily for the spider, such treatments are no longer in use!

Many spider superstitions have remained with us. "Step on a spider, and it will rain." "Webs on a railing cause owners' ailing." "If you are lucky enough to have a spider land on you, it means that you will receive a gift in the form of gold or new clothes."

In movies, in myth, or even in our woodpiles, spiders continue to amaze us. They are extremely helpful, killing many harmful insects, protecting crops, and keeping the natural balance in the world. Spiders, the eternal weavers, enter every corner of our homes while we continue to spin tales about them and envy their handiwork.

Dragon and Phoenix:
Mythical Creatures of Fire

by Ellen Dugan

So when the new-born Phoenix first is seen
Her feathered subjects all adore their queen . . .
            —*John Milton*, Paradise Lost

The phoenix is a mythical bird associated with immortality, renewal, and life after death. Traditionally, this fire bird was only supposed to appear in times of peace and prosperity. It is associated with the Sun, the element of fire, and the southern quarter. The phoenix has connections to many mythologies and cultures, such as ancient Egypt, ancient Greece and Rome, China,

Japan, Russia, and Native American. The Egyptians called the phoenix Bennu, and it had links to the heron that was sacred to Osiris. The Greeks called the bird Kerkes. The Chinese called the phoenix Feng-Huang, and the Japanese knew the phoenix as Ho-oo. To the Russians it was simply the Firebird, a bird imbued with magical powers and the wisdom to fight off evil. Finally, the Native Americans of the Southwest called it the Thunderbird. The Thunderbird commanded the powers of the Sun, sky, and lightning and could bless the land with life-giving rain.

In Chinese mythology, the phoenix is a symbol of high virtue, grace, power, and prosperity. Feng-Huang was thought to be a gentle creature that only dined on dewdrops. Its icon was so highly regarded that only the Empress of China could wear it. The Chinese version of the phoenix had five colors of feathers: black, white, red, green, and yellow. The Chinese description of the Feng-Huang was a wonderful combination of many magical animals. Feng-Huang had a long, swan-like neck, the stripes of a dragon, powerful multi-colored wings, and luxuriously long and cascading tail feathers like a pheasant or a peacock.

According to Greek mythology, the phoenix was similar in appearance to a large eagle with gold and crimson plumage. This phoenix lives in Arabia, close to a well. Every morning the phoenix takes a dip in the well, and sings a song so beautiful that the Sun god Helios stops his chariot just to listen.

The Death and Rebirth of the Phoenix

Every five hundred or a thousand years, when the phoenix feels that its time has come to an end, it builds a nest of aromatic wood and sets the nest on fire with a burning twig. It then allows itself to be consumed in the flames. Or, according to some different versions of the myth, the phoenix carefully chooses a tree and build a nest out of oak and other fragrant woods. When the moment of rebirth comes, the phoenix flares out its wings, gives a triumphant cry, and spontaneously bursts into flames. The nest contains the fire and holds the ashes of the bird.

From out of the ashes of the fire a new phoenix eventually emerges. After gaining strength and growing a bit, the newly born phoenix takes the ashes of its predecessor in an egg of myrrh. Or, according to some accounts, the phoenix scoops up its entire nest and flies to Heliopolis where it leaves the egg and nest on the altar of the Sun god Helios as an offering.

The phoenix is a powerful magical symbol. If the phoenix has appeared in your life, through dreams or in meditation work, this is a symbol that is time for you to reinvent yourself. Take a look around you now and gather up only what is most important. Rebuild your life and move forward with strength, wisdom, and conviction.

The Dragon: European Bad Guy and Beloved Asian Guardian

Dragons are the main elemental spirits associated with the physical element of fire. For many Asian cultures, dragons have been popular symbols of power and wisdom. Dragons represent vitality, energy, magic, enthusiasm, and courage. Asian dragons were considered beautiful, friendly, and wise. They were worshiped and considered a little bit vain from all the adoration. These dragons lived in the sea, flew through the air, and slept protectively coiled within the earth. Asian dragons warded off evil spirits, protected the innocent, and bestowed good fortune.

Overall, Eastern dragons enjoyed more positive P.R. than European dragons. The legendary mischief of Celtic dragons is intertwined with much of Britain's folklore. There are many tales of wizards enlisting the help of dragons or defeating them when they were causing trouble.

Unfortunately, European dragons were usually considered ill-tempered and thoroughly evil. This is probably due in part to the stories of Saint George and Saint Martha, both dragon slayers. While technically Martha didn't kill the dragon herself, she did stroll barefoot into the forest, clothed in a spotless white dress and carrying a jar of holy water. Martha worked her mo-jo, hypnotized the dragon, and led it docilely back to the village so the villagers could hack the poor beast to pieces. According to legend, those naughty European dragons were thought to enjoy snacks of young virgins and to cause the destruction of village crops. They were also rumored to create all sorts of natural disasters. What amazingly bad publicity!

I wonder if dragons got their bad reputation since they were always having to fight to stay alive? I'd be testy too, if every local-yokel and wanna-be macho knight was out trying to prove their prowess by putting a skewer between my breastplates.

The Asian Dragon

On a more positive note, there are five types of dragons in Chinese mythology: the Celestial dragon, who guarded the homes of the gods; the dragon spirits, who ruled over the wind and rain and who, if they were feeling peckish could cause a flood; the earth dragons who kept the rivers clean and deepened the oceans (there is a link between what are known as the paths of the earth dragons, or *lung mei*, and what today is known as ley lines); the treasure-guarding dragons; and the Imperial dragons, whose main job was defending the Imperial ruler and his family and court (the Imperial dragons had five claws instead of the usual four).

The coloration of Asian dragons ranged from red to green and gold to black, and any combination thereof. Some were described as having wings, while some had horse-like manes. Other dragons were described as having irregular—long and short alternating—spines down the back. And some dragons could walk on water.

There is also the idea of five separate elemental dragons in the Chinese tradition. These different types correspond to the five elements of feng shui: wood, earth, metal, water, and, last but not least, fire.

If you feel drawn to dragons or they have made an appearance in your dreams and meditations, then take this opportunity to work with them. When dragons make their presence known, it signals a time that you will be able to overcome any obstacles that may be in your path. Dragons are symbols of leadership and charisma. They bring transformation, change, and movement into your life. The dragon ushers in a time of energy, passion, and courage. If you'd like to call on the creatures of fire for protection, renewal, and courage, try the following ritual.

Directions: Light a small red candle for the element of fire. Visualize the phoenix and the dragon in the room with you. Con-

centrate on both creatures of fire, seeing them watching over you
and lending their powerful support. Then repeat the following
invocation.

> *I call upon the dragons, symbols of power and might;*
> *I invoke the magic of the phoenix, attend me tonight.*
> *Courage and passion are your bright gifts; grant me these, I pray.*
> *Renewal, protection, and wisdom will bless me all my days.*

Wedding Superstitions

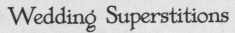

by Sheri Richerson

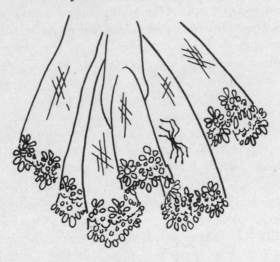

Superstitions abound and affect every part of our lives. Many people believe that superstitions are based on truth; others simply regard them as old wives' tales. When it comes to weddings, there are just as many superstitions as you would expect. These include not letting the groom see the bride in the wedding dress before she walks down the aisle, and the idea that wedding day rain means a life full of tears.

Superstitions are often contradictory. For example, another superstition says that if it is raining on the morning of your wedding day, the bride should hang rosary beads on the clothesline. This is said to stop the rain, dry the ground, and bring the Sun back out.

Other wedding superstitions are well known and some are not. Some superstitions are passed down among family members. In olden days, prospective grooms would send certain members of his family to express his interest in the bride. What they saw along the way foretold the future of the marriage. Seeing blind men, monks, or pregnant women were a sure sign that the marriage would be doomed. On the other hand, seeing nanny goats, pigeons, or wolves foretold a marriage full of good fortune.

Here are some other interesting superstitions. During a bridal shower, the bride should make a wrist ribbon and tie into it all of her bows and ribbons received that day. She should keep these in a safe place until the day of the rehearsal. The ribbons and bows should then be shaped into flowers and attached to a paper plate for use during the rehearsal. This will bring good luck. Meanwhile, the bride should not practice walking down the aisle during rehearsal. She should ask a close friend who is not in the wedding party to stand in her place and walk for her. The number of ribbons broken by the bride-to-be during the shower is said to represent the number of children she will have.

It is also considered good luck to save the ribbons and bows from the gifts received the day of the wedding, then hang them over the front door for the first year of the marriage. A bride should not remove her engagement ring once the prospective groom has placed it on her finger until after the wedding or bad luck is sure to follow. Allowing another woman to try on your engagement ring is also considered bad luck. The woman who tries on the ring will steal the groom.

In order for the prospective groom to guarantee a lifetime of good relations with his in-laws, it is said that the groom should present the bride's mother with a diamond ring on the day he presents the engagement ring to his future bride.

As the bride and the groom leave after the wedding, the groom's mother should toss a shoe over the new bride to ensure that a lasting friendship develop between her and the bride. A week to the day before the wedding, a bride should place a bit of food in her left bridal shoe and allow a cat to eat it. She should then place a penny in the shoe and leave it there to ensure wealth in the marriage. She should also have all the bridesmaids sign the bottom of the right shoe. The bridesmaid whose name is most worn on the shoe after the wedding is said to be the next in line to marry.

When choosing the veil, a bride should make sure that it is long enough. A veil was traditionally used to disguise the bride and hide her from evil spirits. A white wedding dress is said to cover the bride in joy and to ensure that she has made the right choice. A red wedding dress, according to Chinese beliefs, is said to bring good luck. A grey wedding dress means you will go far away. A black wedding dress means you will wish you were back where you were before the wedding. A green wedding dress means you are ashamed to be seen, and a blue dress means you will be true.

A bride should not make or help make her wedding dress or bad luck is sure to follow. For each stitch the bride herself sows, she will shed a tear. Should the wedding dress rip or tear before, during, or after the ceremony, the marriage will end in death. The woman who loans out a wedding dress will be plagued by bad luck and evil spirits. A bride who finds a spider in her wedding dress will have good luck. It is also said that encountering a chimney sweep, black cat, lamb, or dove on the way to the church is good luck.

The marriage will be filled with good bounty if the wedding falls within two days after a Full Moon. For a winter wedding, it is good luck to get married when the second hand of the clock is facing upward. If a bride elects to carry an umbrella before, during, or after the wedding ceremony, she should make sure it is red. This will protect her from evil spirits.

Rice-throwing at weddings began as a way to distract evil spirits so that the marriage would remain secure. The rice is also a way of wishing the bride and groom fertility and prosperity. Pearls are a popular item of wedding jewelry, but in Mexico a bride's pearls represent the number of tears she will cry in marriage. Instead of pearls, the bride should wear diamonds for good luck. It is said if a bride cries on her wedding day they are the last tears she will shed over her marriage.

Everyone knows that the groom should carry the bride over the threshold upon entering the home for the first time; however, if he stumbles it is considered a bad omen. According to Jewish superstition, knives should not be given as wedding gifts. They will bring bad luck to the marriage. Should knives be received, the bride must transform the gift into a financial transaction by paying for the knives.

Young Woman's Coming of Age Ritual

by Boudica

A growing number of Pagan families are celebrating rites of passage in recognition of a young woman's coming of age. This practice is not unusual. In Jewish tradition there is the *bat mitzvah*, celebrated on a girl's thirteenth birthday and signifying the beginning of religious responsibility. In the Pagan community, the celebration is usually held in conjunction with the young lady's first menstruation cycle, or Moon cycle, signaling her passing to womanhood, or on her sixteenth as celebration of the "half-way" mark in her teen years, or on her eighteenth birthday to mark her high school graduation.

Many times the young lady will want to choose a particular guardian deity to work with at this time. Brigit is popular. I would like to offer this very simple Maidening Ritual. It is designed for a young woman aged approximately thirteen and can be performed by the family or with a priestess officiating. It can be adapted to most circumstance.

Maidening Ritual

Before the ritual, the mother and daughter should discuss the coming changes in the daughter's life. This might be a good time to have that "mother/daughter" that you've put off. This is a good time to discuss the young woman's future plans, what she wants to accomplish, what school and career she wants to pursue.

As symbol of the passage into womanhood, the young woman may wish to sort through and get rid of some childhood toys. She may also want to choose a new name—one that she will be called and recognized by in her new circle of peers. This could be a magical name or just a secret name for her family and circle. The mother or grandmother may want to choose a personal gift for the young woman, perhaps a piece of jewelry or other keepsake to be given to her on her day of ritual.

The traditional dress for this ritual is red. The family can either make the dress, or purchase a pretty red dress, a white dress with red trim, or a black dress with red trim.

On the day of the ritual, follow the usual preparation you would follow for a ritual. Bathe with herb soaps as incense burns. Make her the center of attention and have fun. Make sure the focus is on the young woman.

When the young woman is ready, the circle is formed. A gate or a bridge can be made as an entry for the young lady to signify her crossing over into maidenhood. How this is set up depends on the young lady, the location, and how elaborate the family wants to get. It could be as simple as having the women making an arch with their arms so she can pass underneath.

Quarters are called. The mother, aunts, grandmothers, and best friends can be chosen to call the quarters. Below are some sample words you can use.

Facing east: *We call upon the element of air to bring wisdom to our ritual of womanhood. Hail and welcome.*

Facing south: *We call upon the element of fire to bring passion to our ritual of womanhood. Hail and welcome.*

Facing west: *We call upon the element of water to wash us in the emotions of womanhood. Hail and welcome.*

Facing north: *We call upon the element of earth to bring stability to us in our ritual of womanhood. Hail and welcome.*

The young lady calls the Goddess: *I (name) do ask the Goddess (name) to stand with me this day as we celebrate my coming of age. Please walk with me on this path of life and guide me through the trials I may face, then celebrate with me the happiness I will enjoy.*

All: *So mote it be.*

The mother or Priestess picks up the gift chosen to symbolize the Maidening and blesses it. Then she gives it to the young lady who walks around the circle, having each well-wisher bless her and the gift. The ritual finishes with the grandmother, who also gives the young lady the blessing of all her ancestors who have gone before her.

The young lady thanks all for the gift and blessings.

At this point, the young woman serves cakes and drink. Or if there is a party afterward, this step can be bypassed for a circle closing.

The guests congratulate the young woman and welcome her to the community.

The young lady then thanks the Goddess for joining the circle.

I would like to thank the Goddess (name) for witnessing this ritual and blessing us with her presence. Thank you, Mother.

The quarters are then dismissed in reverse order from which they were invoked.

Facing north: *We thank the element of earth for joining our circle. Hail and farewell!*
Facing west: *We thank the element of water for joining our circle. Hail and farewell!*
Facing south: *We thank the element of fire for joining our circle. Hail and farewell!*
Facing east: *We thank the element of air for joining our circle. Hail and farewell!*

The event can then be followed with a party for the young woman's friends or just with family.

Any way you do it, the focus of the day should be on this young woman, who is starting on a new path in her life and will need to be assured that she will have the support of her family of women as she proceeds.

Young Man's Coming of Age Ritual

by Boudica

Men enjoy a lot of action in their rituals, and the following Coming of Age Ritual incorporates many active events for a young man's coming of age. It is one that should probably be held in the warmth of summer as an outdoor event. The day's events should be laid out well in advance. A barbeque with lots of tasty meats, grilled vegetables, and breads should be prepared in advance.

The day should begin with a "man-to-man" talk about personal responsibilities. This talk should probably have already taken place, but if not, this is a good time to discuss the move from boy to man. It affords the time for father/guardian and son to sit and talk about the young man's plans for his life, where he would like to go, and what he wants to make his life calling.

The evening can begin with body painting. The young man can make himself look fierce or crazy. The paint will set the mood of the ritual. Tattoos are not uncommon, and this can be an opportunity for the young man's first venture into permanent body art if the family and the young man are of a mind to do so. During the evening, there should be drumming, eating, lots of talking and boasting, fisherman's tales, tall tales, stories about the family, and lively conversation.

The planned ritual should have drumming as the main pastime. You can add anything you want to bang on. If the group is musically inclined, there could be a band-like atmosphere with lots of singing along or just plain howling.

If there is a circle, suggested animal guides include: bear for north, fish for west, dragon for south, and eagle for east. The young man may invoke a special spirit guide. The ritual can be lead by either a priest, the father, or grandfather. Once the ritual has begun, the young man should invoke the god using his new magical name.

I (magical name) do invoke the god (name) to witness my passing into manhood this night.

All present should bestow blessings on the young man. A gift from the family can be given at this time as well. The grandfather should be last, and he should bestow the blessing of the family and the ancestors. Food and drink should passed around. The choice of drink would be dependent on the family traditions and the age of the young man.

When everyone has finished eating, they should acknowledge the passing of the young man into manhood with cheers for good health, prosperity, and great things to come.

When the revelry is done, the young man should thank the god for his presence that evening:

I thank (god's name) for joining our celebration and for witnessing my coming of age.

The quarters or animal guides are then thanked and dismissed. The festivities can go on all night. Everyone can either sleep in tents or on the ground if the weather and conditions permit. The focus should remain on the young man for the entire evening. He will need the wisdom and guidance of the males in his community as he starts out on his new path of manhood. Make it a night he will remember fondly for many years.

Sphinx Work

by Cerridwen Iris Shea

Mention "sphinx" and the image that comes to mind is the Great Sphinx near Giza, but sphinxes differ in type and in country of origin. The Great Sphinx near Giza, for example, is an *androsphinx,* who has a human head on a lion's body. There are also sphinxes with a lion's body and a ram's head (*crisosphinx*) and a lion's body with a hawk's head (*hierocosphinx*).

The word sphinx itself is thought to have derived from the Greek *sphingo* ("to strangle") or *sphingein* ("to bind tight"), which is the way the Greek creatures of this description dispatched their victims. The Great Sphinx of Egypt predates the Greek stories of these creatures, and it is not known what the race of creatures was originally called by the Egyptians. It is known, however, that around 1500 BC, one of its several names was Ho-em-akht ("Horus on the Horizon").

One of the uses for sphinx statues was as temple guardians. Some pharaohs had their likenesses cut into androsphinx statues. Hathshepsut, one of the female Pharaohs of Egypt, had many sphinx statues carved in her likeness. Most of them had their faces hacked off in the years after her death, when attempts were made to wipe her existence as pharaoh from the historical record. Some of the remains of her sphinxes can be found at the Metropolitan Museum of Art in New York City.

To stand in the room with these beautiful stone sculptures and stare at what is left of the faces is to feel the power when myth meets humanity. Power, knowledge, and sadness roll off the pieces in waves. The Riddle of the Sphinx that Oedipus so famously answered is miniscule compared to the power and knowledge stored by this stunning race of creatures.

Working with the Sphinx

Several questions have to be answered in order to work with the race of the Sphinx. The first is why do you want to work with them? What do you think you can gain from sphinx work? Power? Knowledge? Strength? And what will you do with what you receive from them?

If your answer to these questions is something as simple and thoughtless as "I thought it would be cool to see what it felt like to work with a sphinx," or "I want the power of the Pharaohs" you will be greeted only with silence.

In other words, don't waste their time. Ask yourself the important questions about your life's path, your life's work, and your life's desire before you start your magical workings. You can't approach the Sphinx with any sort of wavering. The Sphinx does not guide or encourage but works in absolutes. Before going to the Sphinx with desires, you have to know exactly what they are and why you want them.

Sphinx work is about soul-purpose rather than the daily details of life. Once you've chosen a path and presented it to the Sphinx, the Sphinx won't tell you if it's the right or wrong path. It's the path you've chosen. It will tell you how you now have to earn it. You may be given riddles. You may be sent on a quest. You may be refused. Refusal doesn't mean returning to ask for the same thing over and over again. A human is not going to wear down a Sphinx. It means going back and re-examining your goals, your desires, and your reasons for them. It means dissecting the innermost parts of yourself, facing parts you may not want to see, and using them to create a whole spirit.

When working with the Sphinx, you have to earn respect on Sphinx terms, not human terms. Yelling, screaming, and waving swords or muttering spells will not impress a Sphinx. The Sphinx demands more. It demands to know your soul. You must approach the Sphinx with an open heart, a solid understanding of what you seek and why you seek it, and honesty. Don't try to hide or pretend that what you seek is for the good of all if it's merely for the good of you. The Sphinx can always smell a lie.

Once you have truly determined your desires and fully acknowledged your intentions, the question is how do you work with the Sphinx? Answer: Slowly, carefully, and mindfully. It's not work for someone just starting on a spiritual path. Working with Sphinx energy is something a soul needs to grow into. It comes out of emotional maturity, a sense of being grounded and centered, a wholeness, a sense of accomplishment in life, and a happiness in the things of the world. The Sphinx will not offer options when you're at a crossroads in your life. The Sphinx will wait and let you make the decision and then force you to earn passage down that path.

That doesn't mean that you can't honor and enjoy the Sphinx before you do the actual work. Keep a statue or photo of a sphinx where you can see it often, or keep it within your sacred space. Read as much history, archaeological description, and mythology about the Sphinx as you can. Visit museums, read books, and watch documentaries. Listen to all points of view. See what resonates with you and what doesn't. If you get a chance to visit The Great Sphinx or any other such statue, do so. Feel the calm, contained, knowing energy of the centuries emanating from the statues.

While feeding your interest in the Sphinx, work on your own life. Deal with the past, create a beautiful present, and visualize a positive future. Take active steps to become the most positive, whole spirit that you can be. Take responsibility for your thoughts and actions. Treat others well. Protect, serve, and stand up for what you believe. Stop berating yourself for not being perfect; enjoy being human. Walk lightly on the planet and make a positive difference.

When you've accomplished what you can on this plane and are ready to explore more, then go to Sphinx. This means your soul, while still living in a human body, is ready for more exploration. You continue to contribute on the human plane, but you have specific goals and desires beyond the immediately tangible.

When you are ready, cast a circle and go into a meditative state. Approach the Sphinx, and give enough time for the Sphinx to acknowledge you. Then explain what you've accomplished—how it sets the foundation for where you want to go and what you want to do. Wait for an answer. You might have more work to do before you're ready to pass the guardian's gate, or you may be allowed to take the first step.

As with any entity, be polite, gracious, and thankful. When finished, close the circle and write about your experience.

It might not make sense at first, but write down every detail that you can remember. The Sphinx sets up puzzles, riddles, and quests—expecting you to perform the discovery. Give yourself time and open your awareness so that you can find the answers. Patience and an open heart are the keys to working with the Sphinx.

Star Power

by James Kambos

Stars have been used as religious and spiritual symbols for at least 5,000 years. Many of the great religions of the world can be identified by certain star shapes. The six-pointed star of David is one of the religious symbols of the Jewish faith, and the star of Bethlehem is revered by Christians, especially at Christmas. Islamic art has frequently used the mystical shape of the eight-pointed star in decorative items. And for Pagans, the five-pointed star, or pentagram, which is among the oldest shapes in the world, has deep spiritual significance.

Stars, which are actually distant suns, are universal symbols of hope, beauty, and inspiration. Before the divine power created our planet, the stars were already in place. They were glowing in the night sky before ancient hunters and sailors used them for guidance in their travels. The Star card in the major arcana of the tarot is a good example of how the star shape has been used in a magical context for centuries.

To the naked eye, stars seem to have rays and appear to glitter. Actually, stars are round and glow with a steady light. The illusion of twinkling starlight is caused as the light breaks up while passing though layers of the Earth's atmosphere. This illusion of glimmering light impressed early magicians, who looked upon stars as mysterious heavenly symbols. Soon, stars were incorporated into many magical systems, where their shapes were usually used as signs of protection, success and good fortune. Most likely, it was the magical practitioners of ancient Babylonia who gave stars the artistic shapes we still use today, by adding points or rays. These shapes became potent magical symbols that have been used ever since to decorate seals, talismans, amulets, and hex signs.

Star Shapes and Their Use in Magic

It is known that King Solomon used both five- and six-pointed stars for magical purposes. Most authorities believe, however, that the magical use of star designs my actually pre-date Solomon, perhaps to as far back as the ancient city of Ur. Magical star designs are still very much used today around the world. You may find star patterns being used by a hexenmeister in Pennsylvania as they craft a hex sign, or by a Moroccan artisan embellishing a brass tray.

Here is a list of basic star shapes and their magical meanings.

The Four-Pointed Star: A star consisting of four rays symbolizes the Sun and the four seasons. It is a masculine sign of vitality, growth, warmth, and abundance. It may also serve as a symbol of the wheel of the year.

The Five-Pointed Star: Also known as the pentagram, this is one of the oldest magical designs. It should always be used with the single point facing upwards. It represents the four elements of nature. The single point facing upward may symbolize the mind or spirit and its relation to the forces of nature. If you stand feet apart, arms outstretched and head up, you'll see that the body forms a pentagram.

The Six-Pointed Star: This is the star of David, a sign of the Jewish faith. It is formed by two interlocking triangles—one facing upwards, which represents divinity, the second pointing downward, representing strength. The six-pointed star is a holy star.

The Seven-Pointed Star: Seven is the number of the mystic. As such, any seven-rayed star represents powerful magic. It stands for the four directions, plus heaven and earth. In the center exists the human spirit, adding up to seven. It may also be used to symbolize the seven days of the week or as a sign of completion.

The Eight-Pointed Star: When the number eight is written in numerical form, you'll notice that it is continuous. It has no beginning or end. Hence, the eight-pointed star tends to symbolize eternity and continuity. It can also be used to represent the eight sabbats or eight days of power.

How to Create a Star Design

To use star designs for magical purposes, you may keep it simple, or get as complex as you wish. First, select a design which fits your magical need. Practice sketching this shape on paper or other material. The size may vary from a small design drawn on paper that can be carried with you to a larger piece of wood suitable for attaching to a building (similar to a Pennsylvania Dutch hex sign).

As you create your star, focus on your magical intent. Once the design is completed, color may be added. You may use ink, pencils, art markers, or paint. Use colors appropriate to your desire. To make the star more personal, make a circle in the center and leave it empty. In this space, you may write a name, charm, or mystical symbol.

Your magical star may be used temporarily until your goal has manifested, or your design might be a piece of art to be displayed permanently. If the design is to be used outdoors, exterior paint should be used. A paint store can advise you if a clear weatherproofing sealant should be applied.

To the casual observer your star may appear to be nothing more than a charming decorative accent. But these ancient star designs can help you create some of the most powerful and enduring magic you'll ever experience.

Comets and Meteors in Magic

by Elizabeth Barrette

Swish, sparkle! A meteor streaks across the sky to vanish in seconds. A comet hangs in the darkness, a pale scarf draped over night's black altar. Something in us responds to the marvels of firebolts in the sky. In them, we sense rare magic.

Our ancestors watched the heavens, too. Thousands of years ago, they learned the turning of the stars and the paths of the planets. They learned to predict the return of certain comets. Meteors, however, came and went without warning—except for a few reliable storms—just as they do today. You can include both in your magical practice.

What Are Comets?

Comets are balls of ice and gravel that orbit the Sun. They move slowly against the starry background, spending most of their time in the outer reaches of the solar system. Occasionally their eccentric orbits bring them close to the Sun. Some of the ice turns into gas; some of the dust also escapes. The solar winds blow these materials into a long, double tail—a straight gas tail, and a dust tail curved by orbital motion.

In their approach to the Sun, comets change from insignificant to spectacular. The tail, often visible with the naked eye, can remain in view for weeks or even months. Over many such passes they burn up and disappear.

The Oort cloud is full of comets in distant orbit around our solar system; occasionally some get dislodged by other objects or gravities to fall in towards the Sun, thus renewing the supply of visible comets.

What Are Meteors?

Meteors are pieces of cosmic debris that enter the Earth's atmosphere. Most of them are fragments of asteroids or comets; some are human-made space junk. Their speed causes them to burn up as they fall, creating the characteristic "shooting star" effect.

Most meteors disintegrate completely on the way down. However, a few survive to reach the Earth's surface. Chunks of stone or metal left in the crater are called meteorites. These hold an impressive magical charge due to their cosmic origin, distance of travel, and fiery arrival. Bits of glassy rock called tektites, created in a meteor strike, have a subtly different power.

Historical Interpretations

Ancient people looked to the world around them for hints of the future. Comets and meteors qualified as omens of great import. Meteorites, especially the magnetic lodestones, were also prized.

Comets traditionally warned of disaster. Different sources quote the possibilities as plague, war, damaging wind or flood, other fearful storms, famine, the death of a king or other changes in sovereignty, or even the destruction of the earth.

An account from 1066 notes: "In this year Harold came from York to Westminster at the Easter . . . Then all over England there was seen a sign in the skies such as had never been seen before." This was Halley's comet.

Wary of its power and threat, people avoided looking directly at a comet in the sky. They believed this might draw its doom down upon them. However, a manuscript from 1583 explains people tried "to dissuade her majesty [Queen Elizabeth] from looking on the comet which appeared last: with a courage answerable to the greatness of her state, she caused the window to be set open."

The interpretation of meteors is more diverse. Some believe they announce a birth. (Scholars still argue whether the star of Bethlehem was a meteor, comet, or supernova.) A shooting star is supposed to fall over a baby's location. One colorful explanation is that meteors are babies' souls coming down from heaven. Alternatively, meteors, like comets, can foretell catastrophe. They may fall before the death of a king, a great man, or some other person. Falling stars are also supposed to precede the end of the world itself.

Contemporary Applications

Comets and meteors occupy an unusual niche in magical practice. They were known to our ancestors, but now we can study them far more intimately than ever before. We understand their origins and their composition, if not all of their mysteries. Therefore they form a link between the past and the present.

Comets deal with long-term goals and momentous events. They can be incorporated into such ceremonies as a Wiccaning, a coming-of-age rite, or a handfasting. Choose carefully, though, for this brings the celebrants to the attention of the gods! A less risky endeavor is to hold a ritual honoring one of the many celestial deities, such as Nut or Zeus. Comets appearing in astrological charts require thoughtful interpretation. Consult an expert.

Rituals involving comets should be held outside at night. For best results, the comet must appear overhead. If it is not visible with the naked eye, put a suitable telescope inside the circle and have everyone look through it.

Meteors cover short-term desires and quick opportunities. They are famous for granting wishes. Most sources agree that you must complete the wish before the shooting star fades. Interestingly, a record from 1851 suggests that "Whatever you think of when you see a star shooting, you are sure to have." So it may not require an explicit wish. More specific options include chanting "money, money, money" for wealth, or rubbing a blemish with a cloth and dropping the cloth to make the blemish disappear.

Although single meteors may appear at any time, several showers recur at particular times every year. The most notable of these include the Quadrantids (January 1) and the Perseids

(August 12). Consider these showers of divine blessings. They make an ideal time for rituals honoring celestial deities. If you wish to request something from the gods, this is a good opportunity.

Meteorites have more staying power. They hold the cosmic energy of their birth, which can lend strength to your spells or sanctity to religious rites. Lodestones, with their power of magnetism, draw desired things to you. Stony meteorites and tektites have a mystical aura of endurance. Despite their adventures, they are still here. Use them for courage and sustenance in times of great stress.

Comets and meteors are relics from our solar system's creation. Their fiery passage across our skies is testament to transformation. We feel a resonance with them because we, too, are made of star stuff—the heavy elements in our bodies first formed in the heart of an ancient Sun. By working with these cosmic objects, we touch a rare and special magic.

Articles for Fall

Jyotish Gemstone Remedies

by S. Y. Zenith

In the ancient system of Indian jyotish astrology, nine gemstones are revered for their powers in pacifying ill-placed planets in a person's horoscope. Indians do not only wear gems as status symbols or appealing adornments, but they take the science of jyotish gemstone therapy very seriously. Gems are used for innumerable purposes such as activating inner healing, motivation, rejuvenation, protection, business success, prosperity, and all manner of mundane human aspiration.

Known for strengthening weak but beneficial planets in the birth chart and deflecting malefic planetary influences caused by naturally malevolent planets, gems are also applied as remedies for human ailments. The nine most precious and effective stones are listed below along with their governing planets.

Ruby: The Sun

White pearl: The Moon

Red coral: Mars

Emerald: Mercury

Yellow sapphire: Jupiter

White Diamond: Venus

Blue sapphire: Saturn

Hessonite: Rahu

Cat's eye: Ketu

Gem Energies

The aforementioned nine gems are mentioned in ancient Sanskrit scriptures such as the *Devi Bhagavat*, *Mahabharata*, *Vishnu Dharmotter Purana*, *Bhava-Prakash*, *Tantra Sara*, *Agasthyamat (Ratna Prakash)*, and *Agni Purana*. Most of the scriptures, with the exception of the *Tantra Sara*, noted the use of gemstones as powerful agents for absorbing and transmitting energy linked with the nine planets of the jyotish system, for counteracting negative vibrations and for producing positive effects for human. Tantric alchemists in olden times used gems as oxides and powders and introduced them to the adepts of ayurveda.

Gem work includes two types of important energies: physiochemical or "electrochemical" and *pranic* (a vital life force also referred to as *chi*). Whether orally consumed as powders or pastes, or worn against the skin as jewelry, the prescription of gems for restoring health or gaining material desires continues to be popular. Many jyotish treatises consider humankind as a microcosm. An indivisible part of the human macrocosm is thus the human body and psyche, which are influenced by celestial systems, the stars, and planets of the solar system.

Gems and Health

Each gem possesses a perennial source of one specific ray of energy. In India, it is perfectly commonplace to consult a "joystick," or Indian astrologer) regarding health matters when science and medicine have failed. Discovering which gem is auspicious for an individual at a certain time or stage in life can help solve seemingly impossible situations and dissipate psychosomatic illnesses.

The body is comprised of seven primary colors of the solar spectrum: violet, indigo, blue, green, yellow, orange, and red. Deficiency or absence of any primary color causes a disease. When lacking red rays, health problems arise in the form of anemia, fevers, inflammation, physical debility, and weakness. The wearing of gems related to "red planets" such as the Sun (ruby) and Mars (red coral), injects red rays into the body.

However, excessive red rays may cause boils, tumors, conjunctivitis, sunstroke, insanity, headache, insomnia, and carbuncles. These can be dissipated by injecting cold rays using cool stones such as moonstone, yellow sapphire, white pearl, and emerald. A balanced equilibrium of the seven rays is synonymous with good health. Below is a list of general physical issues and relevant remedial gems.

Accidents: Red coral or white pearl prevent frequent accidents or injuries. As Mars governs blood, bleeding, and cuts, red coral is recommended for healing blood disorders.

Allergies: Allergic reactions are heat-generated by Mars adversely positioned in a horoscope. Cooling gems are lime moonstone, yellow sapphire, emerald, and blue sapphire.

Arthritis: Inflammation of joints can be relieved by red coral of nine carats and yellow sapphire of five carats.

Asthma: Emerald or yellow sapphire of five carats can provide some relief. In acute cases, a six-carat moonstone can be added.

Cataracts: It is said that emerald improves eyesight and white pearl restores sight. Although ruby is the most powerful gem for eye troubles, it must be taken off upon recovery. Ruby is hot and not recommended during summer months, when it is safer to use red coral and white pearl. Emerald can be added in severe cases.

Dermatitis: White coral in seven or nine carats is recommended together with three-carat lapis lazuli.

Hernia: Red coral and yellow sapphire are recommended.

Insomnia: Emerald, moonstone, and yellow sapphire help combat sleeplessness.

Leukemia: Use red coral and hessonite, or cat's eye, yellow sapphire and hessonite.

Piles: Red or white coral with moonstone are beneficial.

Semiprecious Substitutes

If precious and jyotish-grade gems are not available or affordable, it is safe to use substitutes. Gems of jyotish quality are unheated and untreated natural specimens. Ruby can be substituted with garnet, red tourmaline, red spinel, and star ruby. In place of white pearl, moonstone, white coral, or milky quartz can be used. For red coral, red jasper and carnelian will do fine. Emerald may be substituted with green agate, jade, peridot, and green tourmaline. Yellow topaz, citrine, and yellow tourmaline are excellent alternatives to the costly yellow sapphire. Instead of an expensive diamond, the humble white sapphire or white zircon work just as well. Common substitutes for blue sapphire are amethyst, lapis lazuli, blue zircon, sodalite, and blue tourmaline. Hessonite or cinnamon stone is mostly affordable despite its rating as a "precious stone" under jyotish. Tiger's eye is a substitute for cat's eye.

Which Finger and Ring

Those fond of wearing gems on the fingers may find this paragraph of interest, as fingers are directly connected with different parts of the body via a network of nerves. The nervous system is like a vast, sophisticated telephone system. Each finger is directly connected with specific body parts. The thumb, although governed by Venus, is not accorded any importance for the wearing of gems by jyotish traditions.

The first finger, forefinger, or index finger is controlled by Jupiter, which rules the respiratory system and stomach. For remedying lung, respiratory, and stomach ailments, gems are worn on this finger. Jyotish gems are mounted with an open back so that the stone can touch the skin, allowing easy entrance of the beneficial planetary rays. Yellow sapphire, topaz, moonstone, and white pearl can be worn on the index finger.

The second or middle finger is controlled by Saturn, which rules the intestines, mind, brain, liver, and mental structure. Gems for Mercury, Rahu, and Venus can be worn on the second finger, as these three planets are friends of Saturn. Thus, blue sapphire, emerald, hessonite, moonstone, white coral, pearl, diamond, and white zircon can be used on the second finger.

The third finger is ruled by the Sun and represents the kidneys, stomach, blood circulation, and the regenerative system. The stones for Jupiter, Mars, and Ketu can be worn on this finger. This includes ruby, red coral, and cat's eye. The fourth or little finger is governed by Mercury who rules the knees, legs, feet, and private parts. Gems for remedying health matters in the lower body are often prescribed for this finger. As friends of Mercury, Saturn's and Rahu's gems of blue sapphire and hessonite or their substitutes are also worn on Mercury's finger.

Cherokee Legends of Eastern Tennessee

by Tammy Sullivan

The eastern portion of Tennessee is steeped in Cherokee legends and lore. In fact, the name Tennessee itself is a derivative of its original Cherokee name *tanasi*, which meant "meeting place." As the starting point for the Trail of Tears, the home of Chotow (the center of the Cherokee Nation), and the birthplace of Sequoyah, the land is connected to the rich Cherokee culture that once ruled supreme. While much of recent Cherokee history is sad and bloody, an overwhelming sense of pride still resonates from the people who remain.

In the Great Smoky Mountains, morning mists frequently cover the lower foothills. At the border of Tennessee and North Carolina, a young Indian brave stands in the mist. Slowly, he walks the ridge of the mountain, peering down into the valley below. Then he simply melts away.

This spirit has been reported to roam the area since before the Civil War. Cherokee legends say his name is Tsali, and he was a great hero. He helped thousands of Native people keep their homes during their struggles with the new settlers. After gold was discovered, the Trail of Tears occurred, but Tsali escaped and fought and died for the freedom of his people. Today, his spirit watches over the valley, which is known as the Land of Blue Smoke.

318

Just beyond the ridge in North Carolina, one encounters the trails that run along Brown Mountain. On the steep, darkened paths, haunting lights are known to float. According to the Cherokee, these lights are young Indian maidens seeking their mates who were killed during a great battle long ago. The lights have been documented and researched by geologists, ghost hunters, and scientists for decades.

Also along this ridge of fog-laden mountains resides the race of creatures known as the Immortals. The Immortals were a race of spirits who nurtured and guided the people. They were rarely seen, but when spotted they were said to be similar to adult Cherokees in appearance and loved singing and dancing. Their homes on the highest mountain peaks.

All across the Smoky Mountains, a race of fairy beings known as the Little People were said to thrive. These beings were small in stature—child-sized—with a zest and love for life and happiness. They blessed the people with extra helping hands during work time and were generally thought of as kind-hearted. If offended, the Little People moved on to a new place and never went back to the old. Today, they are still thought to reside on the banks of the Pigeon River near Pigeon Forge, Tennessee.

In the Cherokee Forest, there is a race of beings thought to be lost in time. Called the Shadow Dancers, they are a tribe that lives in secrecy aided by the mountain mists. The oddest thing about this tribe is that they are supposedly pale of skin and fair-haired. No one is sure if they are members of the Welsh hunters who predate the Cherokee or descendants of the White Chief that once held sway over the area.

Further inland is the Little Tennessee River. Citico Creek branches off of the Little Tennessee River and is home to a sacred cave. In a little bend just below the mouth of the creek is the Great Mythic Hawk cave. It is covered from above by a large overhanging stone and cannot be reached either by water or land.

Legends relate that two giant hawks made their nest in the cave, and indeed the white streaks that mark the rock surface from cave mouth to the water looks similar to bird droppings. The hawks were savage creatures known for carrying off children and pets. The tribe enlisted the help of the medicine man to rid themselves of the hawks. When he managed to get inside the cave and make it less hospitable, the hawks departed.

A unique event occurs along the Trail of Tears. Beneath the hundreds of feet of soil and rock, the tears of the Indian people are thought to have formed what is known as the Veil of Tears. The Veil is a stalagmite formation. In Sweetwater, Tennessee, there is an attraction known as the Lost Sea, a huge underground lake that is ensconced within Craighead Caverns. The caverns were named for the Cherokee Chief that owned them, Chief Craighead. The caverns used to be a Cherokee meeting place where powwows and council meetings were held.

Tuckaleechee Caverns is another cave system that was sacred to the Cherokee people. Nestled deep in the foothills of the Smoky Mountains, the Cherokee hid in the cave to avoid being forced to leave their beloved homeland. Everything they needed was right at their fingertips in the caverns, including a freshwater stream that ran the entire length of the caverns.

The most mystical cave system is called the Forbidden Caverns. This particular cave has evidence of a race of people who occupied the cave thousands of years ago. Later Indian legends

relate that a young Indian princess became lost as she wandered through the caverns. Later, it was considered off limits for the people and named "Forbidden." It is said that she remains there, forever crying.

The Great Smoky Mountains have a powerful magical presence, both above and below ground. The hills are populated by the echoes of a proud Indian society that watches over its sacred homeland to this day. From the majestic mountaintops to the misty foothills to the cool caverns below the earth's surface, the land is magical in this beautiful country.

Dreamweaving

by Diana Rajchel

From the age of eight to the age of twenty-four, I dreamed regularly of an "attack stairwell." In this recurring dream, I ran up a flight of stairs only to miss a step and slip. Invariably I awoke with a jerk, and upon waking felt personally persecuted by the steps. In time, this dream became a problem, regularly keeping me from restful sleep.

A solution came in time from my study with an Internet magic group. One study course examined recurring dreams. This study coincided with some heavy meditation practice. I decided to focus my skills in dream journaling and meditation to solve my dream problem. I accepted long ago that magical endeavors do not typically succeed on the first try. In my meditation, I resolved to change my approach to the stairs. Usually in my dreams I began at the bottom of the stairs and ran up. In my conjuration, I started seeing my perspective from the top of those stairs.

This simple act of dream re-envisioning has opened up a new world of magic tools for both my conscious and subconscious mind. The changes became apparent that night as I slept: I could fly in my dreams. Over the course of that first month, I flew in dreams; stopped a nightmare in the middle and decided I didn't want to have it; and upon showing up at my junior high naked, informed myself I'd better live up to my own hype about self-acceptance. I have never, ever dreamed about stairs since then.

The between-state where I accomplished my dream change is called alpha or twilight. Just as medical doctors and fashion magazines promote daily physical exercise, a determined seeker needs around thirty minutes daily to tone the mind and stretch inner vision in order to master the dream state. My maintenance takes twenty minutes twice a day; this means setting a kitchen timer and putting my mind to work on a daily basis. I focus on the idea of twilight as a brainwave pattern that posts information from the subconscious to the conscious. By entering twilight via meditation, I reverse the switch and send messages to my subterranean self. Messages are received in the form of images that affect what I manifest in real life.

One can choose from a buffet of techniques to achieve twilight state. My favorite methods include visualizing the colors of the spectrum from red to indigo, taking one hundred deep breaths, or drinking teas such as chamomile with mild sedative effects. I change techniques from time to time to avert boredom and to force myself to concentrate.

Meditative and dream techniques are not for the dilettante. It can take months or years to see results. Alas, just as diets can be ruined with a few indiscreet fudge bars and skipped workouts, meditation and concentration skills die just as easily through neglect. Once training begins, you have to stick to it; otherwise, you may frustrate yourself with how often you have to restart the dream conjuring process.

Once you have mastered slipping into altered consciousness, pick something practical to alter. For example, you could use this technique to overcome a fear of snakes. Through dream conjuring, you can confront the snake and change your reaction to its behavior. You can fly out of reach of the snake, grab it, or take a paintbrush and add to the snake's style. If you really hold a grudge, you can try my snake-phobic aunt's real-life approach and greet said snake with a garden hoe.

After you master your dream world, you can use the same techniques to manifest change in the physical world. Dream magic may be among the oldest of magical techniques—since the first recordings of magic, mystics and mages have relied on dreams for prophecy, insight, message delivery, and divine communion. The simple, natural transition from sleep to dreaming becomes its own act of magic.

I have used dream-to-reality magic as a way of communicating with my deities. Early in my practice, I suffered some doubts about the appropriateness of my workings and felt the need for some direct feedback from the objects of my worship.

I cast a circle before sleep and made a request for an audience with the Horned One. That night, I dreamed of Indiana farmland. The shadow of a stag fit perfectly within the orange disk of the setting Sun. Cernunnos told me in clear visual terms what I wanted to know, and I awoke satisfied with the communiqué.

Incubating and requesting dreams are easy ways to manifest realities through dream magic. Dreams operate in sensory symbols—in the organization of objects seen, heard, and felt—because the subconscious does not deal with abstractions. Relating the symbols of the subconscious to the abstractions of the conscious is the key to establishing magical practice while asleep. Six months of recorded dreams should provide a key to the inner-workings of a personal symbol system.

For example, people stuck on a difficult problem may dream of labyrinths and corridors. These dreams may be called upon deliberately before sleeping to work out a specific problem.

Dreams form a major part of our reality. The brain never stops working, and on some level dreams are happening in our subconscious all the time. By moving symbols into our dreams or by manipulating the symbols of our dreams, we work on our unresolved issues and manifest new realities while increasing our meditative and reflective discipline.

Dreams are an accessible path to magic, and while it takes work, dreamworking extends far more control over your own mind than you can imagine.

Mayan Sacred Structures

by Laurel Reufner

Imagine standing on a mountaintop overlooking the great Lake Attitla´n. You have climbed for a long time, nearly 10,000 feet above sea level, and spread out before you is all the majesty of the Mayan world. If you have very good eyesight, you can see the Pete´n rainforest to the northeast. If you have fantastically good eyesight, you can see the coastal lowlands beyond that. Looking upward, you can see the beautiful canopy of sky stretching as far as the eye can see. If you could reach just a little higher, maybe you could touch that sky.

With the above images in mind, it's not hard to begin grasping the Mayan worldview. The gods shared the upperworld with the Sun, stars, and sky. Ancestors and other spirits also resided there and often claimed the mountain tops, rising majestically into the air, as their place of power.

To the Maya, mountains were living entities, complete with personalities. These monster-mountains were depicted in carvings as creatures with eyes, muzzles, and ear and mouth ornaments.

These same creatures would be reflected in artwork found on pyramid temples, further connecting the artificial to the real.

Mayan mythology claimed a cosmic mountain was where life-sustaining maize originated. The gods used this maize, mixed with blood, to form the dough used to fashion man. They placed this dough into a cave-womb from which man later emerged. Caves were unique in Mayan mythology in that you entered them from the middleworld, where man resided. From there, you could access either the sacred interior of the mountains (the upper-world) or the dreary existence of the underworld.

To anchor together these three planes of existence, the Maya conceived a world tree. This was often represented by the mighty ceiba tree, whose straight trunk stretched nearly one hundred-thirty feet, while its roots extended deep into the earth.

Upperworld and underworld were divided even further. The upperworld consisted of perhaps thirteen levels, each having its own unique function. This was the final destination of warriors dying in battle, women who died in childbirth, suicides, and sacrificial victims. The underworld, known as Xibalba, was composed of nine levels and was a very dreary, dark, and watery place, reached through rivers and caves. Most Mayan went here upon death, to be tested and tormented by the gods of the underworld.

The middleworld was divided into a *quincunx* (four quadrants centered on the cardinal points) and a central axis, denoted and anchored by the world tree. Each quadrant had trees, birds, and colors associated with it based upon what was native to each region. Remember, the Mayan world covered a large area, incorporating many climate extremes from low-lying tropics to the snow-covered mountain peaks.

East, home of the rising Sun, was the primary direction. The color associated with this direction was red, a color connected to the Sun and fire. Next came north, the direction of the ancestors and death. Its color was white. West followed north appropriately enough, as the direction of the underworld. It was the direction of the setting Sun and was represented by the color black. Then came the south, the right hand of the Sun, whose color was yellow.

Each quadrant was held up by a special deity assigned to it. Who these deities were depends on where you do your research. Some archaeologists say that *chacs*, or rain deities, supported the quarters of the middleworld. Others believe these entities to be aspects of Pawahtun, who was the old god presiding over the days at the end of the year. Yet another source references sacred jaguars. At the center of it all was the world tree, whose color was green. The celestial bird, Itzam-Ye, lived within its branches.

This same celestial structure was reflected in Mayan architecture. Simple peasant structures were often one-room affairs with poles at the corners and a central pole or pillar adding additional support. If possible, the house would be aligned with the cardinal directions. The hearth in the center of each home was sacred; it was composed of three stones placed in the shape of a triangle, much like the cosmic hearth which was composed of three stars demarcating the Orion nebula.

Temples were built atop hand-constructed pyramids, which would usually align with the directions. Some temples and other special constructions would align with specific heavenly events, such as the rising and setting of Venus or the position of Orion at special times of the year. Mayan temples rose hundreds of feet over the other structures in the villages and cities, just as the mountain ranges rose thousands of feet over the rest of the Mayan lands. When possible, they incorporated the existing geography into their temple building, such as the High Priest's Temple at Chiche´n Itz´a. Rituals were performed in the cave long before the building of the temple. Temple construction utilized the sacred site by building directly above the cave and providing access via a shaft with toe-holds built into it.

The Maya continued their cosmic construction methods even in their agriculture, erecting sacred wooden poles at the corners of their maize fields. These poles were bent down along the edges of the field, enclosing the green space within and reflecting the quincunx structure of the world.

Nearly every culture has some concept of sacred geography and architecture. Even today, many peoples take comfort in these ideas by using them to understand their place within the world. The Mayan concept of the world's structure, like so many other areas of their civilization, was highly refined. Everything about the Mayan culture reflected their religious and spiritual beliefs and their need to understand and categorize the world around them.

Celtic Sacred Animals

by Sharynne NicMhacha

Many of us experience a deep connection with animals or birds in our spiritual work. These animals may appear in dreams, journeys, or meditations, and their presence is a token of the wisdom, healing, guidance and protection they have to offer. Like many ancient people, the Celts venerated birds, animals, and fish and maintained a large body of sacred lore about the symbolism and powers of each. Here are some of the most important attributes of animals in Celtic tradition:

Deer: The deer symbolizes the wild powers of nature and beauty, grace, speed, and regeneration. Deer (both stags and does) often appear to people to lure or entice them into an otherworld encounter important for their spiritual or personal growth. Finn mac Cumhaill marries a deer-woman called Sadb, and their son is Oisín, whose name means "Little Deer." A king of Ireland named Lugaid followed a beautiful deer that personified the sovereignty of Ireland into the forest. The widely venerated god Cernunnos, whose name means "Horned One," is shown in the presence of deer, bearing a set of deer's antlers.

Raven: The raven is a messenger, bringing wisdom, news, or omens into our awareness. Ravens were associated with several gods, as well as Na Mórrigna, a trio of war-goddesses that are associated with fertility, prophecy, and sovereignty. These three often appeared in the form of the hooded crow common in the British Isles.

Horse: Horses are one of the most sacred animals in Celtic tradition. They symbolize strength, courage, and power and are often associated with the land. One of the most important goddess archetypes in Celtic religion was the goddess of sovereignty. Without her blessing, the king could not rule successfully, and the people and the land could not prosper. Her primary symbol was the horse (and in many cases, the white mare). Horse goddesses included Rhiannon in Wales, Macha in Ireland, and Epona in Britain and Gaul.

Salmon: The salmon is a symbol of divine wisdom. The Well of Wisdom is described in one early Irish story as being surrounded by hazel trees (which symbolized wisdom). The trees dropped their nuts into the well, and the salmon who lived there "cracked open the nuts" to obtain the wisdom that was inside. This archetypal being was known as the Éo Fis, which means literally "Salmon of Wisdom." Even today in Ireland, sacred fish or water animals—including salmon, trout, toads, and eels—who live in healing wells are revered and protected.

Boar: Boars symbolize strength, courage, and determination. The sacred boar hunt took place just before Samhain. After that time, the animals were left alone for their breeding season. Boars also appear to lead people into an otherworld journey or adventure. In the Welsh tale of Culwch and Olwen, King Arthur and his companions assist the young lover Culwch in a series of difficult tests and adventures so that he could win the hand of Olwen. One of these tests was obtaining a comb and shears from the top of the head of a huge, supernatural boar called Twrch Trwyth.

Swan: Swans mate for life, and in Celtic mythological symbolism they represent love, partnership, and harmony in long-lasting relationships. The god Oengus mac Óg dreamed of a beautiful woman named Caer Ibormeith, and he searched for her for a long time. When he found her, he asked her father for her hand. Her father (also a fairy) said that Oengus had to ask the girl himself, for her powers were greater than his own. She had the ability to exist in the form of a swan one year and a woman the next. Oengus approached her at Samhain when she was in human form, and they flew off together in the form of swans linked by gold and silver chains.

Hound: The hound symbolizes loyalty, dedication, protection, and healing. Well-loved hunting dogs were prized by the Celts, as they were a great help in providing nourishment for their humans. Dogs appear in the symbolism of certain gods and goddesses in both statues and temples. Many of these deities were associated with protection and healing. The dogs are associated with these concepts due to the healing properties of their saliva (when they licked their own wounds).

Crane: In earliest times, the crane was venerated for its connection with water, healing, and magical power. For these reasons, the crane was viewed with fear or suspicion in later times. Women were associated with cranes, and in various stories and myths women turn into cranes. One of the most famous was Aífe, who was transformed into a crane by a woman who was her jealous rival for the love of a man. When Aífe died, the god Manannán mac Lir used her skin to make a sacred bag or pouch, called the Crane Bag, into which he placed sacred weapons and talismans.

Cattle: Bulls and cows are associated with fertility, wealth, and abundance. The bull also symbolizes strength, ferocity, and virility; the cow symbolizes gentleness, nourishment, and nurturing. In the Irish saga Táin Bó Cuailgne, or "The Cattle Raid of Cooley," the warrior-queen Medb is jealous of the wealth represented by a special bull belonging to her husband. This jealousy turns into an epic adventure. The most famous cow goddess was Boand. She approached a sacred well of wisdom that was guarded by the god Nechtan and walked around it three times widdershins in defiance. The well was offended and rose up, drowning her in its waters; she was ever afterwards the goddess of the River Boyne in Ireland.

Serpent: The snake or serpent symbolizes healing, transformation, and renewal, as it possessed the remarkable ability to shed its skin. Since it appears from under the ground, it is also connected with the powers of the underworld. On Imbolc, a certain charm was recited while watching for the hibernating adder to appear from its lair, a sign of the approach of the new season of spring.

Spend time learning about sacred animals in books, videos, and real life. Every sacred creature possesses immense wisdom and guidance; showing honor to them is a potent way to connect with the natural world.

Equine Enchantments
by Elizabeth Barrette

Humans and horses have been allies for thousands of years. Horses appear in some of the oldest artwork on Earth, in cave paintings and pictographs. Domesticated horses allowed people to carry heavier loads, pull conveyances or other objects, and ride swiftly over the landscape. Our ancestors perceived these animals as powerful, both in spirit and flesh. Thus, horses appear in religious and magical traditions around the world.

Whereas some historic tribes relied on horses for food, fuel, and an entire way of life, contemporary Pagans view these animals differently. Horses are more often kept today for pleasure riding or racing than for serious work or transport. Yet they still play an important role in our magical and spiritual practices, because they touch something primal in all of us. To see a wild horse running over the land is to see the very spirit of freedom.

Associated Horse Deities

Many gods and goddesses are connected with horses around the world. Historic tribes often used these animals as sacrifices. The body parts of sacrificed horses then became holy relics or magical artifacts, such as the horsetail banners carried in war. Deities, shamans, wizards, and other mystical folk often ride especially fine horses, often white in color. Artemis drove a chariot drawn by white horses.

Horses are associated with the Moon because their hooves leave crescent-shaped prints. Because of the correspondence to fertility and the land, Demeter is sometimes depicted with the head of a mare, and Ishtar relates to the same powers in the Middle East. The Celtic horse goddess Epona may appear as a horse, riding a horse, or in the company of two foals. She is a favorite among people who ride, raise, or otherwise work with these marvelous animals. The fairy queen Rhiannon rides a white mare between the mortal and magical realms, but at other times she is shown as a white horse rising from the sea. The legend of Macha tells how she won a footrace against a horse while pregnant, then gave birth to twins on the finish line. She then cursed the Ulster warriors to suffer birthing pangs in times of battle. Macha may appear as a swift red mare or a red-haired woman, and nothing can catch her when she runs.

In Norse mythology, Odin rides the magical stallion Sleipnir. This eight-legged gray can run across land, water, or air. Sleipnir is the son of Loki, who shapeshifted into a mare to distract the stallion Svadilfari from completing the wall of Asgard. The Greeks credit Poseidon with creating the horse and the custom of horse racing. Horses are sacred to this god and his followers. The Hindu god Vishnu is associated with horses. In his last incarnation, he appears as a white stallion, the Kalki Avatara.

Working with Horses

Legend links horses with frogs and toads. Some of the terminology reflects this, as with the "frog" of a hoof. One odd belief is that a bone taken from a toad and prepared with the correct rites can grant power over horses. Unfortunately, the exact details of such preparation have been lost.

The bit and bridle that give a rider control of the horse also have magical significance. They represent temperance, and sometimes appear in that guise in Christian art. Afro-Caribbean practitioners may place a bit on their altar to honor Oya or an iron horseshoe for Ogun. In Hindu symbolism, the reins stand for intelligence and will. Pagan riders may bless their tack to improve communication between horse and rider.

One way to greet new horses, soothe nervous ones, or reward them for performing well is to give them treats. A small piece of

apple or carrot is always appreciated. Tidbits from your magical garden work especially well for strengthening the bond between you and your horse.

Horse Charms

A pendant or other piece of jewelry in the shape of a horse can invoke the power of horse magic, especially if made of silver or gold. If made of colored stone or enamel, the horse's color indicates the meaning. Black is for mystery and magic, white for luck, gray for wisdom, red for courage or protection in battle, and yellow for enlightenment. A rearing horse stands for protection or freedom; a mare with foal represents love and family loyalty.

The most famous piece of equine magic is the horseshoe. Its crescent shape collects power and luck. Traditionally, people hang the horseshoe with points up to keep "the luck from running out." A blacksmith, however, may hang the shoe points-down over his anvil or forge, so that the magic will pour over his place of power. Horseshoes are more potent if found and not bought.

Closely related to the horseshoe is the horseshoe nail. Bent into a ring and worn on the hand, it attracts luck and protects the wearer from harm. A bent nail tossed under the bed brings nightmares to the hapless sleeper. Horseshoe nails yield more power than ordinary ones in any spell or charm that calls for nails, as many "witch bottle" protection spells do.

Chinese lore places great stock in a horse's hoof, which may be kept in the house for good fortune. In Eastern mythology, the horse represents happiness, high status, and a successful career.

A shaman's drum makes a rhythmic sound like a horse's hoofbeats. For this reason, it is often called a "shaman's horse" or "skin horse." Many drums are decorated with paintings or carvings of horses or with tassels of horsehair. In visions, the shaman may ride a spirit horse to other realms.

Horse Conclusions

Although we live in a technological society today, we must not forget our roots; much of human civilization was built with horsepower. Horses are one of the few large power animals who remain accessible to us. It's not hard to find a horse show or a riding stable in most parts of North America, and horse charms are ubiquitous. Take the time to study these amazing creatures as you incorporate them into your magical and spiritual life.

A Healing Ritual for One

by Nina Lee Braden

To construct a healing ritual for yourself, assemble the following materials: candles (white for purification, red for hurt, green and blue for healing); something to light the candles with (do not light the candles ahead of time); and essential oils of lemon, lavender, sandalwood, and melaleuca, each diluted with a carrier oil.

If you have a normal procedure for casting a circle, please follow it. If you do not, try this.

Face east, saying: "I salute the element of air and all of the creatures of air. I ask that the beings of air lend me their wisdom today."

Face south, saying: "I salute the element of fire and all of the creatures of fire. I ask that the beings of fire lend me their courage today."

Face west, saying: "I salute the element of water and all of the creatures of water. I ask that the beings of water lend me their compassion today."

Face north, saying: "I salute the element of earth and all of the creatures of earth. I ask that the beings of earth lend me their patience today."

Facing back east, say: "Begone, begone, all negative spirits!" (At this point, feel free to invite any special spirits or deities into your circle.)

Say: "I declare this circle cast. Let only creatures and energies of healing remain or enter. I am here today with a heavy burden."

Visualize your back and shoulder heavily weighted down with a bag of stones. Bend over, as if under the weight of a burden.

Say: "I come today with eyes filled with tears." Visualize your eyes weeping. Weep if you are so moved.

"I come today with a wounded heart." Visualize your heart, bleeding. Clutch your heart with your hand.

"I come today with a tumultuous stomach." Visualize your stomach tossing and turning on an ocean. Use your other hand to clutch your stomach.

Now, be still with your feelings for a few moments. Experience your emotions fully. Gradually stand up straight and let your arms fall to your sides.

Bowing your head, say: "I am in pain. I hurt for myself, and I hurt for others. I have wounded myself. I have wounded others. Others have wounded me. Others have wounded themselves. I light this candle to represent the hurts of all of us."

Light the red candle representing these hurts. Place a few drops of lavender oil in your palms. Rub your hands together, and then stroke your throat, making sure to cover the throat chakra.

Say: "I let my hurts flow. I do not bottle them up. I acknowledge them. I recognize them. Some of them I am able to release. Others await future release."

Say: "I purify myself for healing." Light the white candle of purification. Place several drops of the lemon oil in your palms. Rub your hands together, and then rub your hands over your upper chest, making sure to cover the heart chakra.

Visualize yourself bathed in a white light that swirls around you in a gentle whirlwind vortex of radiance. Let small flames of white light flicker over your body, purifying you of all pain, hurt, and negativity. Stay awhile in this position. Enjoy the light bath. Feel free to take a second flame bath of purification.

Now say: "I work towards healing myself. I ask for aid in my personal healing. I ask for healing of my feelings."

Light a candle for each healing, then continue: "In addition, I seek healing for my physical complaint of (insert condition)."

Light a candle of healing. Place a few drops of the melaleuca oil in your palms. Rub your hands together, and then rub your fingertips over your forehead, making sure to cover the psychic eye—the area between your eyebrows just above your nose.

Say: "As much as is in my power, I will aid others in their healing, with their permission. I ask for healing for (list persons for whom you have healing permission)."

Light candles representing healing for each person named. Place just a few drops of the sandalwood oil on the fingertips of your dominant hand. Rub your fingertips and thumb together, and then rub your fingertips gently into the crown of your head, massaging your scalp.

Face east and say: "I ask for the healing energies of air."

Face south and say: "I ask for the healing energies of fire."

Face west and say: "I ask for the healing energies of water."

Face north and say: "I ask for the healing energies of earth."

Face back east, saying: "I ask for the healing energies of all willing spirits in this circle."

Visualize yourself surrounded by a healthy glow, a nimbus of light around you, radiating strong energy. Repeat this visualization for each person whom you have named. Breathe as deeply as is comfortable for you. Breathe slowly. Smell the lavender, the lemon, the melaleuca, and the sandalwood. Smell them individually and smell them together. If you wish, cup your hands over your nose to better smell their blended essence.

Say: "I thank all who have given healing energy today. I salute you and praise you."

Turn slowly around the circle, holding your arms upraised.

At this point, specifically thank any personal deities whom you have invited and close your circle in your normal way.

Or you may choose to close the circle in the following manner. Face north, saying: "I salute the element of earth and all of the creatures of earth. I thank the beings of earth for their gift of patience. I am honored by your gift."

Face west, saying: "I salute the element of water and all of the creatures of water. I thank the beings of water for their gift of compassion. I am graced by your gift."

Face south, saying: "I salute the element of fire and all of the creatures of fire. I thank the beings of fire for their gift of courage. I am ennobled by your gift."

Face east, saying: "I salute the element of air and all of the creatures of air. I thank the beings of air for their gift of wisdom. I am blessed by your gift. The circle is now open but never broken. I go in peace, love, joy, and thanksgiving."

Colored Rain

by Tammy Sullivan

Weather can both nurture and destroy life on this planet. A gentle rain can lull one to sleep, while a torrent can cause a destructive flood. Some of the most inspirational weather patterns are rather unknown. For instance, why doesn't mankind report such amazing happenings as red rains more frequently? The answer may have to do with red rain folklore.

It has been accepted for ages by some cultures that red rains are the result of fairy battles that take place in the skies. In 1841, field workers in Tennessee reported that a small red cloud appeared and produced a red shower. A few years later, the same thing was recorded by witnesses in the Carolinas, Virginia, and Kentucky. India and Afghanistan have reported rain showers in every color. In 2001, India had a colored rain event. A downpour began as red and blossomed into blue, green, yellow and black before the shower was finished.

When a colored rain begins, it often lasts over a period of several days. Scientists have speculated that such rains could be due to meteor explosions in the sky above cloud-level. Whatever the cause, red rains have the most eerie effect and reputation. Often called blood rain, this remarkable phenomenon occurs frequently in parts of Italy. Huge dust clouds from the Sahara desert drift underneath rain clouds so rain falls through the dust and takes on the red color. Such rain has been known to stain the ground and objects it touches.

While the science behind red rain is clear, what about the magic? How can a modern Pagan make use of a weather event that occurs thousands of miles away? The simplest way is to catch rainwater and tint it yourself. You can use natural dyes, such as morning glory blossoms or a bit of food coloring. If you place the coloring in the vessel before you allow it to catch rain, the bowl appears to be catching colored rain. You can add a few drops of colored rain to your bathwater.

Magical people use rainwater in rituals or as a special anointment. Rainwater is packed with energy, but when you add color to the mix, you have a powerful potion. For example, red is the color of strength, and red water carries that energy.

The magical correspondences are as follows:

Yellow: Mental processes, creativity, and intelligence

Red: Strength, passion, action, and goals

Orange: Courage, success, and justice

Green: Growth, money, and beauty

Blue: Healing, wisdom, and inspiration

Purple: Divination and spiritual pursuits

Brown: Grounding, gardening, and earthy pursuits

Black: Protection and repelling negative energy

Tinted rainwater may be used in potions, elixirs, baths, anointing items, or for washing amulets and icons. It can be placed on the altar as your purifying holy water when casting a circle. One particularly nice way to use your magical rainwater is to dilute your everyday fragrance with it. Or you may freeze it and use it in ice magic or to cool off drinks.

The wonder of the earth's many colors continue through the cycle of seasons. Colored rain allows us to draw inspiration from the sky. It's just another thing to remind us of the magic of nature.

A Dragon in Your Pocket

by Cerridwen Iris Shea

How do you fit a dragon in your pocket? And why would you want one there?

The answers to these questions are easy if you're familiar with dragon magic. Working magic with dragons is one of the most interesting, empowering, and rewarding types of magical work.

So how do you work with a dragon in your pocket? First of all, you need to set the groundwork over several months or years. You need to build your relationship with specific dragons and learn how your lives fit together. You need to remember that dragon thought is not the same as human thought.

You need most of all to learn how to work with dragons—how to listen to them, how to play with them, how to collaborate with them. If you think you can command and control dragons, you're going to wind up with a lot of burn marks.

Once you have a solid comfort level and understanding of working with dragons, you can invite them along with you. Chances are, as you grow in dragon magic, you'll end up working with several of them on a regular basis. You might want one of your dragons to go with you on your daily rounds to work, on errands, and so on. You might want one or more to join you on vacation.

For such travels, you will have to talk to them, let them know if you need help. Some dragons enjoy a good quest as much as any knight. You will have to let them decide which ones go with you and which stay home.

Take a dragon symbol, such as a dragon pendant, with you. It will remind you that you're safe. Call upon dragon energy when in danger. Sometimes, calling on dragon energy can cause enough of an energy shift that the threat backs off. Sometimes the energy brings someone else to your aid. And sometimes it shores up your own skills so you can fight back.

How do you call dragon energy? It's different for every situation, every person, and every dragon. Keeping a consecrated dragon totem helps. This can be a small statue or charm you carry in your pocket—anything that reminds you of your connection with your dragons. You have to be grounded to deal with dragons or they'll knock you silly, even though they're coming to help. Breathe and reach out with your energy. You'll be able to touch the dragon's energy with your own and feel the responding flow. Be specific about why you need the help. Again, remember that dragon logic is different from human logic.

Dealing with fear in a clear-headed way is an important skill to master. It's also vital if you choose to use dragon magic. Working with dragons while panicked will only cause problems. Dragon magic is not for dabblers.

When you're not in danger, don't forget to play. Dance around a campfire and let the dragons dance with you. Dance on a beach and watch them float in the moonlight. Dance in a club and feel their fiery breath. Give thanks. Keep a small treasure chest on your dragon altar, on your regular altar, or in the southernmost part of your home. Fill it with brightly colored trinkets and toys that are just for the dragons. Let them know they are appreciated. Let them know they are valued members of your life.

Dragons don't suffer fools gladly, but they enjoy working magic with people who appreciate them. They are known for their power, strength, and knowledge. Using these attributes wisely is an important skill for humans to learn. But dragons also are practical and humorous (albeit bizarrely so), two more traits that make life much more joyful.

Cash Flow Magic

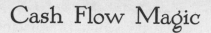

by Diana Rajchel

The second reason I took to magic was financial (the first being I was in no small amount of despair concerning my love life). I was in college (translation: broke). I worked two jobs to meet expenses, but the extra employment failed to cover the costs of all my classes. Magic became the next reasonable option. With effort and steady spellcasting, it worked: I'd suddenly have extra shifts at the radio station or a one-shot chance to earn some extra cash.

I've practiced magic for almost a decade since then, and I've developed a cautious magical relationship with money. My finances have not been perfect; I've suffered during recessions along with my fellow graduates. I am far—quite far—from my fantasies of diving through piles of money like Scrooge McDuck, but I already know that with careful management and regular ritual, I tend to find money or resources when in genuine need. When I follow a course of money magic in concert with my daily life, I live comfortably even during difficult times

Money management demands record-keeping, budget-setting, debt repayment, and saving. Pushing yourself to earn qualifications necessary for better pay also helps. These details may be boring, but they pave the way for magic to work. Any type of magic works far better when everything involved acts in accord. Any good magician working for financial health needs account ledgers and checkbooks in equal numbers to candles and incense.

Getting organized before taking up wand or athame is the best way to clear the financial slate. Take stock of what you have, and give serious consideration to what you really need. Balance your checkbook, dig in your file cabinets, and clean the change from beneath the couch cushions. Make a list of all the things you need and all the things you want. Examine the list and revise the needs list to reflect only what you need. Once you know financially where you're at, you know where you need to go.

Over time, cash flow workings become maintenance magic—workings to perform, say, once a month to maintain steady progress towards a healthy financial situation. Try scheduling these workings around the time of regular house cleansings, so all the work falls into part of a steady energy-building routine.

Regular cash flow workings can include banishing debts, counting your blessings, protecting your assets, and drawing in new resources. My most regularly practiced cash flow magic is debt exorcism (all those student loans, after all). Once a month, I collect bill receipts after their payments have cleared my checking account. I run them through my paper shredder, then gather the shreds into a bag and head out to a public park. I take a lighter, some marjoram for exorcism, and the right mood, and I set myself up at a grill and fire away. As the papers burn, I sprinkle the marjoram and chant:

> *Out and about*
> *I turn ill fortune out*
> *My debt away*
> *My earnings to stay!*

I dissolve the remaining ashes in water and clean up after myself. I see the results of this magic. My debts dwindle and fewer financial surprises jump out from the jack-in-the-box of life.

In general, I prefer not to fill the black hole of debt banishment with more debt, so I take magical endeavors to keep my finances going up, instead of down the hole. Usually this measure takes the form of a prosperity spell on my home. When I finish banishing and warding in each room of the house, I light a candle and pray to Hestia for the prosperity of my home and those who live in it. I do my best to share my prosperities in all their forms.

Keeping and tending prosperities already given also solidifies cash flow. Magic can focus on a business's overall prosperity and can enhance job security. The prosperity need not be limited to dollars. Improving morale can improve productivity. Bear in mind that office magic needs to stay under the radar, as coworkers may not be understanding. Use subtle methods, such as empowering objects already part of the office with a prosperity prayer. One technique I like is to charge a ballpoint pen and visualize it producing dollars every time it writes.

Sometimes, even with a steady job, great resources, and dwindling debts, a body just needs some extra cash. There are plenty of spells for quick money. Here is a simple money magic technique.

When I need money, I turn to the ultimate money-drawing power-house: High John the Conqueror oil. This useful root has powers of victory, prosperity, and general success. I dab on a few drops like a perfume while murmuring a spell, such as: "Glow gold and draw like a magnet, money comes, I am its magnate!" Then I give the money opportunities to come to me.

By following these tips, you should see a reduction in debt and an increase in cash over the course of two years. See financial stability. Know that it is possible.

Are You A SLIder?

Street Lamp and Other Electromagnetic Interference

by Denise Dumars

Until I started researching the subject of street lamp interference, I didn't realize I was a SLIder. SLIder is the name given to anyone who experiences the effects of street lamp interference and related phenomena.

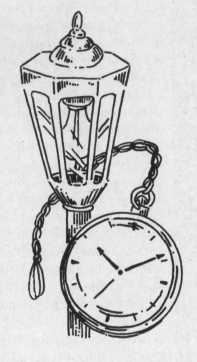

Sure, I'd driven under certain streetlights that would go out at the same time that I drove by. In fact, it happened quite frequently on a street where I used to live, but I figured it was just that I got home from work at the hour that the light was timed to switch off.

The phenomenon, which is much researched in Britain but given little attention by American parapsychologists, is not fully explained by the issue of timing. Electrical engineers, when posed the question, will agree that some streetlights switch on and off at regular intervals—especially when they're running out of energy.

Another explanation they have offered is that a car's headlights approaching a streetlight may be bright enough to "fool" the lamp's sensors into thinking it's daylight, hence shutting it off. Of course, this explanation does not hold up when compared to some accounts of lights switching off after people merely walked beneath them, or of lights spontaneously switching on for no good reason.

Some SLIders claim they can affect the phenomenon at will—extending it to the spontaneous turning on or off of televisions, radios, and computers.

Phyllis Galde, editor of FATE magazine, has mentioned that this phenomenon has happened to her, but as with many other American parapsychologists, she didn't know it had a name. The term "SLIder" was coined by British paranormal researcher Hilary Evans, founder of the Association for the Scientific Study of Anomalous Phenomena (ASSAP). He founded Project SLIDE, or the Street Lamp Interference Data Exchange. Evans has experienced the street light phenomena many times in his native London. Though he has had no "spooky" feelings while experiencing SLI, he has collected reports from many other experiencers who have. Accounts range from one man who claims the phenomenon started happening to him only after he'd had a severe injury of an electrical origin. Another experiencer states that street light interference only happens to her when she is in a highly emotional state or under extreme stress.

Most parapsychologists who have studied the phenomenon think it is related to other electromagnetic phenomena, such as the inability of some people to wear watches. The human body, , like all other objects that essentially run on electricity, has an electromagnetic field around it. Some peoples' electromagnetic fields cause traditional watches to slow down and eventually stop working over time.

My grandfather used to say he couldn't wear a watch. His watches would eventually stop if he wore them every day. I can't wear a traditional watch without it slowing down and eventually stopping, so I was delighted when the new digital watches appeared. They seem impervious to such interference, at least from me.

Then came computers, and guess what? Sometimes the mere presence of a SLIder in a room with computers is enough to interfere with their function. One of my students was the computer tech at one of the first computer labs I used in teaching. After a few weeks of using the lab, he began to swear that whenever I came into the lab, I disrupted the functions of the computers! Nowadays, more modern computers don't seem to be as affected by SLIders when they are in the room. Perhaps new advances in shielding computers from outside electromagnetic radiation explains this change.

Still, during the writing of this article, a friend told me that he has inexplicably "blown out" a brand new computer—the third one assigned to him at his workplace so far. His fellow workers are now considering him a computer jinx. After he told me that he has experienced the streetlight phenomenon as well, I dubbed him a fellow SLIder.

My research slows that SLIders often exhibit all three types of phenomena recounted here, including sometimes disrupting the magnetic strips on their credit and debit cards!

If we take these phenomena as a group, they all seem to lead us back to the idea of disruptions in electromagnetic fields. Eerie though the phenomena may seem, there is probably a scientific explanation that some day will be proven in the lab. Perhaps sometime in the future we SLIders can look forward to getting our electromagnetic fields "adjusted"—the way a chiropractor "adjusts" the spine—so that we no longer affect streetlights and other electrical and magnetic devices.

Until then, I guess we'll just keep SLIding along, and keeping the digital watch companies in business . . . When we can get our credit cards to work, that is!

The Land of the Long White Cloud

by Emely Flak

In the South Pacific, just south east of Australia, lies New Zealand. Also known as the Land of the Long White Cloud, New Zealand is where a special type of Polynesian spirituality evolved through the Maori people. It is believed that the Maoris left the Polynesian islands and headed for New Zealand approximately 1400 years ago. Exactly why or how they migrated remains a mystery.

The speculation that surrounds their perilous sea voyages also sets the scene for various myths and legends. One such story is about a Polynesian navigator called Kupe, who first sighted the Land of the Long White Cloud and returned home to share news of his discovery. The newly arrived settlers brought a culture rich in song, dance, carving, and oral history. Through isolation in a geographical landscape that is diverse, spectacular, and sometimes volatile, the Maori people developed their own distinct spiritual tradition.

Story of Creation

Like most indigenous cultures, the Maoris are deeply connected to their natural environment. With no written Maori language, the traditions are preserved orally. Their story of creation, represented through several gods, is one such myth that has been passed down through the generations. In this story, all life commenced with the Sky Father, Rangi, and the Earth Mother, Papa. From this union, many children were born who are honored as gods and remembered through song and dance. The number of children born varies with different versions of this creation myth. Some of these are Tane Mahuta, god of the forest and birds; Tangaroa, god of the sea; Kohu, god of the mist; Ika Roa, god of the shining stars; Tawhiri-matea, god of the winds and elements; and Rangomatane, god of gardening and the sweet potato.

It is said that Rangi and Papa were so close that their children were unable to move or see. The children decided that they should separate, much to their parents' sorrow. Once Rangi and Papa separated, the children started fighting. With no female children, Tane created a woman from clay and breathed life into her. This is how Hine-ahu-one was born; she became known as the Earth Maid. From these spirit ancestors came the people of New Zealand.

The Maori people link their creation myth to nature. Today, the separation of Rangi and Papa is seen in the contrast of day and night, light and dark—two distinct realms. Their sorrow is expressed through rain and mist. Rangi's tears have become streams and rivers. When Tangaroa, god of the sea, breathes twice a day, he causes the tide to rise and fall.

Sacredness

The Maoris referred to a person, place, or object that is sacred or forbidden as *tapu*. The concept of tapu underpinned their spiritual life and tribal superstitions by setting rules for most activities. Tribal chiefs and priests possessed tapu. A fire lit by a priest or chief was tapu through the passing of their sacred energies. In fact, anything touched by a priest, known as a *tohunga*, was considered tapu. As a result, a tohunga could not touch food with his hands. Instead, another person fed him. The tohunga could remove tapu from people and places to make them accessible.

After a river or stream was used for a ritual or ceremony, the water in it became tapu. Stronger tapu was associated with males who were not slaves. As soon as a man was captured as a slave, he lost his tapu. If you did not observe tapu, or the sacred laws, it was believed you would be cursed with unpleasant circumstances. Priests encouraged their clan members to observe and honor tapu in the interest of spiritual and tribal harmony.

Through their belief in tapu, the Maoris handed down sacred art and carvings. Their artifacts, such as carved walking sticks, greenstone jewelry, bone carvings, and godsticks are respected because they are believed to carry the spirit of the owners. The tohunga communed with the spirits through a godstick. Made from wood, the stick was decorated with red feathers and had a carved head on the end. Each stick represented a particular god. The tohunga placed the godstick into the ground or held it as he invoked the deity required for a ritual or blessing.

Interestingly, a dead body was regarded more tapu than any living being. Bones of the deceased were kept in a carved box, making death and burial the most significant Maori ritual. As part of this rite of passage, the body was placed on the *marae* in the meeting house. The marae is the place for indoor ceremony and community activity. In most marae, traditional Maori carvings depict ancestral history.

Funeral ceremonies would span days to ensure that the soul had completed its journey to the spirit land. There was an expectation that distant relatives and friends would gather from around the country to pay their respects. The marae was designed to be shaped like a human body, with a head, torso, and limbs. When you enter the marae, you also enter the body of the tribal ancestor. Protocol dictated how the visitors enter the marae. A visitor could not enter as soon as they arrived. Instead, they waited outside until they heard a high-pitched wail from a woman inside that signaled permission to enter.

When they entered, they lowered their heads as a sign of respect for the dead person, who represented all ancestral spirits. The ritual comprised retelling myths and legends, and singing songs to bid farewell to the person.

Maori Today

The British arrived in the early 1800s, bringing with them the usual entourage of Christian missionaries. As is typical with colonization, the Maori tribal social structures disappeared or disintegrated.

By 1840, almost all the Maori people had converted to Christianity. Today, most Maori people live in the North Island, and make up one-twelfth of the country's total population. Although they are officially Christian, two sects preserve their indigenous beliefs. The Ratana group was established in the 1920s, and the Ringatu group in the 1860s. Today, many funerals call for a Christian minister to remove a tapu or to open a meeting house. Many children attend schools that teach both English and the Maori languages. The Maori people are one of many indigenous cultures that have been exposed to white settlement and Christian missionaries in the last two-hundred-fifty years. Like most dislocated cultures, they strive to maintain elements of their spiritual traditions in the Land of the Long White Cloud.

Pashupati and Cernunnos

by Neil Campbell

The Gundestrup cauldron from Denmark and the Indus Valley seals from western India (now Pakistan) are separated by 3,000 miles and at least the same number of years, yet bear striking similarities that merit investigation into a possible connection. On the Gundestrup cauldron is probably the best known image of the Celtic stag-horned god, Cernunnos. On the Indus Valley seals are another horned deity, thought to be Pashupati, the form of the god Shiva in his aspect of lord of animals.

The Gundestrup cauldron was found by peat cutters in 1891 in an overgrown peat bog in the hamlet of Gundestrup in northern Jutland, Denmark. More than two feet in diameter, the cauldron is constructed of fourteen highly decorated silver panels. On one of the inner panels is the now classical depiction of Cernunnos, sitting in a yogic lotus posture and surrounded by animals

rich in symbolism. The cauldron has been dated to sometime between the fourth and first centuries century BC.

Thousands of years earlier, the Indus Valley seals were created from clay. The dating of the Indus Valley seals, and indeed the culture itself, is a source of continual debate. This has risen out of the prejudice of the early Christian indologists, who placed Indian history into grossly restricted timelines to fit with biblical theories. Modern indologists are now suggesting that India has had unbroken religious traditions for 12,000 years. As an advanced and widespread culture, it covered an area larger than the ancient civilizations of Egypt, China, and Mesopotamia.

In comparing the images, the meditative posture of both gods is a striking similarity. Pashupati is sitting in a pose known as *gorakshasana*, the cow herd posture. In this advanced yogic position, a *bandha*, or muscular lock, is formed, suggesting there was an established system of yoga at this time. Cernunnos also appears to be performing a bandha. If so, implications are quite profound. It would suggest that yoga, in its traditional sense, may have been practiced by various cultures throughout the world. In recent years, the emergence of such theories has stimulated research, although these theories have been met with animosity from orthodox academics.

Yet such theories regarding the widespread practice of yoga resonate with what yogic masters themselves have claimed. In his book *Ecstasy Through Tantra* (Llewellyn, 1988), Dr. Jonn Mumford (Swami Ananadakapila Saraswati) writes that his tantric guru Paramahansa Swami Satyananda Saraswati suggested that six thousand years ago, two-thirds of the human population "in Mexico, North America, France, Egypt, the Middle East, Afghanistan, India, Ceylon, Thailand, Tibet, China, Japan and other lands" practiced the science of yoga and self-realization.

Many Cernunnos images have been found in France, one of the countries the guru mentions. Trade routes running from Europe to the Middle East and India have been established for millennia, providing a door for the spread of yogic wisdom to Europe. Cultural exchange and migration of people would present a route for deities and the wisdom of yoga and meditation to have spread between societies.

In the Indus Valley seals, Pashupati's hands rest on his knees, the traditional resting position for hands during meditation. The hands of Cernunnos however hold symbolic objects. In his right hand, he holds a Celtic torque (another torque is around his neck), and in his left hand he holds a serpent with horns like a ram's. The torque is typically a symbol of power and authority in Celtic culture, identifying high status. The serpent is also a potent symbol. Serpents symbolize death, rebirth, and divine wisdom. Horns are generally a symbol of divine power and status thought to be connected with the Moon and the Goddess. If the Celts had an understanding of yoga and meditation, they may also have had an understanding of kundalini. The horned serpent may represent the goddess energy of kundalini.

As with Cernunnos, Pashupati and other forms of Shiva also have many serpent and lunar associations. Images of Shiva dating from the time of the Gundestrup cauldron show Shiva adorned with many living serpents. Around his neck hangs the *naga-kaundala*, the garland of serpents. His images typically show a cobra, with its hood expanded, sitting adjacent to Shiva's head. This symbolizes the kundalini piercing the crown chakra and the enlightened state of *shivashakti tattva*. A serpent can also be found wrapped around the main emblem of Shiva worship, the Shiva lingam, which is an icon of Shiva's formless and transcendent nature.

Shiva also has strong lunar associations. On his forehead sits a crescent Moon; one of his many names is Candrashekhara, which means "Moon-crested." The Moon rests on Shiva, symbolizing that the waxing and waning of life rests upon he who is unchanging. The Moon is also a symbol of Soma, or the bliss of Shiva's nature.

The foremost of the Shiva festivals is called Mahashivaratri, "The Great Night of Shiva." This occurs on the night before the New Moon in February or March. It is an all-night vigil involving rituals, chanting, and meditation. In Shaivism, the phases of the Moons are connected with the Sanskrit alphabet and the goddess Shakti. Each Moon phase, known as a *tithi*, is associated with different Sanskrit vowels.

With the spread of Christianity across Europe, much of the esoteric and subtle wisdom of the old Celtic traditions was lost. Horned gods become demonized, their image turned into the

Devil. Any yogic and Pagan mystery traditions that may have existed in Europe appear to have been wiped out. This was one of the greatest losses of esoteric knowledge that western civilization has experienced. The Dark Ages dawned just as we lost the last vestiges of the old Celtic religion. Any remnants of Cernunnos and the old ways slipped into folklore or hid in the rare artifacts that were not destroyed by the Church).

In the East, the imagery of Pashupati has strayed over time away from that found on the Indus Valley seals, becoming more akin to the universal image of Shiva. Yet the worship of Pashupati has continued. Written works of the Shaivite sect of the Pashupatas can be found from around 1 AD. The Pashupatas were a school of intense asceticism, through which they aimed to achieve yoga (union) with Shiva. On achieving this state of being, *siddhis,* or yogic magical abilities, became available to the successful devotee.

Hard to ignore, the Pashupatas were often publicly bizarre and offensive in their actions, which was part of their religious philosophy. A few centuries later, Shaivism reached what could be considered Tantrism's spiritual and esoteric zenith. This was when profound Tantric texts such as the *Shiva Sutras* were revealed and the school of Kashmir Shaivism, also known as Trika, became established. Today, Pashupati is still worshiped by many Shaivite groups, though very few are specifically dedicated to this form of Shiva. However, in Kathmandu, Nepal—the world's only Hindu kingdom—one group, the Pashupatinath, are still dedicated to Pashupati. The rituals that take place within their ancient temple are both vedic and tantric. Each Full Moon in the southern quarter of the temple, Pashupati is worshiped in the form of Shiva Kirtimukh Bhairava.

Perhaps modern Paganism will rediscover a sense of kinship and an enthusiastic interest in the mysteries of meditation and transcendental yoga that were taken from them during the Dark Ages and the Burning Times. In this modern era of reestablishing mystery traditions, we may find that truth and wisdom transcend the boundaries of East and West.

A Pendulum Divination

by Kristin Madden

The pendulum is one of the simplest of all divination tools. It is so easy to use that even a young child can learn. It is a simple, yet powerful method that can become as complex as you need it to be.

While beautiful pendulums may be purchased in stores, just about anything that can hang on a rope or chain may be used to make a pendulum. This eliminates the need for ornate or expensive tools. At various times, I have used a ring hung on a chain, a crystal necklace, as well as a formal, weighted pendulum.

For pendulum divination, it is a good idea at the start to limit your questions to those with "yes" or "no" answers. Be simple and specific in the wording you use. Hold the question in your mind, just as you would during a tarot spread, as you allow the pendulum to divine for you.

To begin, hold the chain and allow the pendulum to hang freely. Experiment with holding it at different lengths. A longer chain or rope will result in a slower swing than will a pendulum held closer to your hand. If you need assistance keeping your arm up or holding it steady, rest your forearm on your other arm or on a few books piled on top of each other. Be sure the pendulum is still, and take a deep breath, relaxing your body and mind. You may want to ask your spirit guides or deities for their help in this work.

Ask the pendulum to show you a "yes" answer. Take note of the motions the pendulum makes. This will usually be either a circular motion in one specific direction or a side-to-side motion. Then ask the pendulum to show you the "no" answer. This should differ from the "yes" in some obvious way. If it does not, take another deep breath and ask again. Allow enough time for your body and mind to relax so the answers can flow through you and the pendulum.

Once the responses are clear, you may ask your question. If you really want to test it, ask the same question more than once. If you cannot get a clear answer, try to rephrase the question to be more specific.

Once you have gained some success with simple yes or no responses, you might want to move up to working with pendulum charts to make the answers to additional questions even more accurate. Pendulum charts often take the form of pie charts or half circles divided into three or more pieces. You might want to create a chakra or body-mind-spirit chart to help identify the areas of your life that need attention or have some bearing on the question. The pendulum will be drawn to one area of the chart more than others. The indicating response should be determined fully before moving on to other questions.

Pendulums are also wonderful tools for diagnosing illness, injury, or energy problems. When using a pendulum for these purposes, simply hold it two to three inches over the body. Move the pendulum slowly along the body, stopping at any chakra points, joints, organs, or anywhere you believe there may be an energy imbalance. Open to your intuition and watch for any unusual pendulum motions as you move along.

Be sure to clearly identify the symbolism of the various movements a pendulum makes. This will vary with the person and the pendulum, so it is a good idea to make this clear each time you use one. A good beginning is to ask what motion will indicate a "yes" and a "no." For healing work, you may want to identify the motion for imbalance, block, injury, and other disorders.

It is important to keep it simple. A pendulum can only make so many different movements, so you may want to do a general yes/no reading first, followed by a more specific one. This way a circular, clockwise motion may mean one thing in the first reading and something else in the second reading.

These same methods can be applied to divination without the presence of the person in need of assistance or healing. As usual, use the basic yes/no response for a series of questions

related to the case at hand. Holding the pendulum over a photo, piece of hair or clothing, or even the person's name written on a piece of paper helps to focus the energy on the person in need. The use of one or more pendulum charts is very effective in clarifying issues or areas to explore, particularly when the individual in need is not present.

Carry your pendulum with you, play with it, and meditate with it. Do whatever you can to align your energies, and your pendulum will become a powerful tool, like any ritual object you use frequently. In your hands, it will become a conduit for spirit messages and your own intuition, allowing you to quickly and easily gain insight and answers for any life situation.

Simple Candle Magic to Banish Pain

by Twilight Bard

There is no doubt that while life can bring incredible joy, it can also bring incredible pain. Sometimes we suffer a personal tragedy or loss that wounds us to the core of our being. The state of the world in which we live—the daily violence and injustices we read about in the newspapers—can overwhelm us with grief and leave us in despair. In this state, it can be difficult just to function.

When you are suffering from emotional pain, sometimes the simplest rituals can be the most powerful. Although the candle magic spell below is void of grand speeches or fancy rituals and utilizes the most basic tools, I've found it a potent way to banish pain when it gets to be too much.

To perform this spell, you will need three things. The first is a black taper candle in a holder. The color black is often associated with negative energy, but in this spell works specifically because it absorbs energy.

The second component is a cup of lavender tea. Lavender has long been revered for its healing and purifying properties. To make this simple tea, add two tablespoons of dried lavender buds to a cup of boiling water. Let it steep for about fifteen minutes, then strain. You can drink it straight, or add honey and lemon.

The final tool is a service candle. The color and type does not matter. The time to light the black candle in this spell is at a highly charged, emotional moment. It is much easier to light it from a service candle than with matches or lighters.

If you are part of a group or family that is going through a rough time together, you can perform this spell as a group.

Everyone should have their own black candle and a serving of tea. The service candle can be used by all. This spell is best done during a waning Moon. However, if you find yourself at a particularly desperate time, you needn't wait ten days for the right Moon phase to come.

When you are ready to perform this spell, take your candles and your tea to a private place where you feel comfortable. Sit, stand, or kneel—whichever you prefer—and place your candles and tea before you on a table, altar, or the ground. Light the service taper.

Take a deep breath, close your eyes, and relax a moment to prepare yourself. You are going to begin raising emotional energy unlike any you have probably raised before in rituals: You are going to raise negative energy. The more negative energy you are able to raise, the more you will be able to release in this spell. The more you hold back, the more you will retain.

Go deep inside yourself and focus on the pain. Let it bubble to the surface. Think about all of the things that have caused you hurt, deep hurt. Dwell on these things as much as you can. Don't hold back one iota. Feel the pain and all of the emotions that may accompany it. Feel fury, frustration, despair, anguish. Let it grow. You may feel yourself begin to tremble or stiffen. You may begin to wail, or tears may flow freely. Go with it. It may take five minutes or thirty, but don't try to rush it. Let it build until it reaches a crescendo.

When you feel you have unleashed all of the excess, intolerable pain from within, grab the black candle. Mentally pour all of that negativity into the candle. Allow it to run through your body like a stream of water, down your arms, out of your hands, and into the wax. If you can, visualize this energy as black flak, fiery sparks, or whatever image makes sense to you. See and feel it pouring from yourself and into the candle. The black color of the candle will soak up the energy like a sponge. Empty yourself of every last vestige of it. You may feel the black candle pulsing or radiating with your pain.

Light the black candle on the service candle. Know that the flame will purify the energy as it releases it. Know that the smoke will rise, carrying the energy into the universe where it will disperse and be transformed.

Take a moment now to catch your breath. If you need to cry, feel free. Tears cleanse the spirit and have a grounding effect.

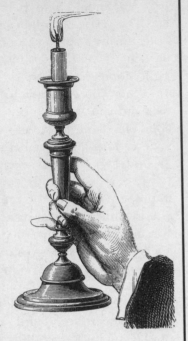

When you are ready, take the cup of lavender tea. Ask the God and Goddess to infuse it with love and healing energies. Drink it down to replace what you have purged from yourself. Feel the positive herb energy traveling down your throat and seeping through your entire body.

You may wish to meditate now, this time clearing your mind and relaxing. Deeply breathe in positive energy from the universe and let it fill you, replacing the pain you have just released. When you are done, put the black candle in a safe place and allow it to burn itself out.

It is likely that after this spell you will feel drained. You have raised some powerful energy and purged yourself of a great deal of it. Ground yourself further by eating or by taking a nap.

Later or the next day, bury the remains of the black candle and cleanse the candleholder that held it. If you performed the ritual indoors, you may wish to burn sage or sandalwood to clear out any lingering negativity.

Notice the aftereffects of the spell over the next few days and weeks. You may not feel deliriously happy immediately, but you should notice a marked improvement in your state of mind. A newfound serenity will help you cope and, slowly but surely, bring you back to your old self.

Kitchen Gods and Goddesses

by Lily Gardner

From the first days of humanity, feasting has been at the heart of every gathering—whether it was to celebrate a successful hunt or a bountiful harvest. No matter the culture or the year, one thing that hasn't changed is the importance of food in our social life and in the way we honor our gods. Today, the meal remains the centerpiece of every celebration.

Food preparation is the closest thing to alchemy that many of us experience. By grinding, mixing, and heating, we combine the energies of plants to make something that could only be guessed at the start. The first sorcerers were surely cooks and many of us are both.

For such an integral part of our existence, how do we consciously transform our modern kitchen into the sacred space that it deserves to be? One way is to transform our kitchen into a temple by using candles, crystals, and pots of herbs to adorn our space. The next step is to choose a deity to bless our endeavors.

Probably the most well-known kitchen god is Tsao Chun, most often called "Kitchen God" in China, Vietnam, and Korea. Worshippers burn incense and candles before a picture of him that is displayed in a little shrine near the stove. What is most striking about Kitchen God is that he doesn't enhance the efforts of the cook, but instead serves as protection against fire, disaster, and unwanted trouble for the household.

Out of respect for Tsao Chun, people take care not to swear, cry, or kiss in the kitchen. It is also disrespectful to cut onions on or near the stove. The week before the Chinese New Year, a feast of noodles (longevity), fish (prosperity), oranges (sweetness), mussels (luck in business), dates (fertility), and green vegetables (youth and spirituality) is eaten; a portion of the feast is offered up to him.

After the feast, Kitchen God ascends to heaven to report the family's doings to the Jade Emperor. Honey is smeared on the lips of the Kitchen God's image so that everything he says will be sweet. On New Year's Day, his image is burned and a new likeness of the Kitchen God is placed in the shrine.

The Kitchen God's wife is always pictured with him, but apparently does not report to the Jade Emperor. Why not burn incense in her honor and ask her to bless your cooking as well?

From Japan, we have the Shinto god and goddess of the kitchen, Oki-Tsu-Hiko-No-Kami and Oki-Tsu-Hime-No-Kami. They are children of the harvest god and guardians of the cauldron. The Japanese kitchen goddess worshiped by the Ainu is Kamui Fuchi, goddess of the hearth. The Ainu, recognizing the connection between the fire in the hearth and the Sun, believe that the Sun goddess visited Kamui Fuchi each morning. It was taboo to walk across the sunbeams that striped the kitchen floor in the morning as that would interrupt the visit between the two deities.

In the Indian kitchen, the family prays to Annapurna, giver of abundance. Images of Annapurna are found in kitchens, dining rooms, and restaurants throughout India. *Anna* means "food and grains," and *purna* means "complete and perfect." Annapurna is a goddess who nourishes her people both physically and spiritually. Hindu cooks know that by nourishing their guests they provide them with the energy to do life's work. Giving the very best is at the heart of Annapurna's spiritual practice.

An old Roman proverb says: "The oven is the mother." Fornax, Roman goddess of the oven, is honored during the first two weeks of February with the festival of Fornicalia. The holiday is celebrated with bread baking and corn roasting.

Chief of the Roman goddesses is gentle Vesta, the Greek equivalent of Hestia, goddess of the hearth fire. The hearth served as the center of both Roman and Greek life, not only as the cooking site for the family but also as sacrificial altar. Homer wrote this in praise of the hearth goddess:

> *Hestia, in the high dwellings of all, both deathless gods and men who walk the earth, you have gained an everlasting abode and highest honor: glorious is your portion and your right. For without you mortals hold no banquet.*

The "spin doctors" in ancient Greece explained Hestia's high standing with a story about a rivalry between Apollo and Poseidon for Hestia's hand in marriage. Hestia avoided what would have ended in celestial warfare by declaring her wish to remain a virgin forever. Out of gratitude, Zeus awarded her the first victim of every sacrifice. That's all well and good, but without her fire and the ability to cook grains, civilization would have reverted back to a life of hunting and gathering.

In the north, the Scandinavian goddess Fulla, whose name means abundance, represents the bounty of the fruitful earth. Fulla serves under the mother goddess, Frigg, and carries the coffer in which Frigg keeps her riches.

The Russian goddess Kikimora is more brownie than deity. She takes the shape of an old woman who lives behind the oven. If danger threatens, she moans and makes spooky noises to alert the family she lives with.

Like Kikimora, a Lithuanian goddess also lives behind the oven. Her name is Aspelenie, but she is sometimes known as "Hearth Snake" because she takes the form of a friendly serpent. Aspelenie is servant to the Sun goddess, so in Lithuania it is taboo to harm a snake.

Although there are several kitchen gods and goddesses to choose from, few of their stories have been recorded in the mythologies. That's where modern Pagans come in. Once you've found the god or goddess that resonates with you, record your experiences with him or her. Build a shrine, burn candles or incense, pray, and keep a special kitchen journal of recipes and successes.

May you never hunger!

Discovering Your Past Lives

by Karen Follett

To discover past lives, take a deep breath and allow your body and mind to relax. Focus on the gentle ebb and flow of your breathing. Calm yourself and center. Focus on the origin of your breath; focus on you.

In your mind's eye, trace the connection of each inhalation to the life force that is deep within you. Allow each exhalation to flow to the elements of your life. As you focus on your flow of breath—your connection with your universe—mentally finish the statement: "I am . . ."

Allow the images that finish that statement to flow. Embrace the conscious thoughts and actions that create your persona, the conscious intent and expectations that create your reality. Allow these images to flow without judgment or bias. Allow yourself to see them as they are.

Now focus your breath deeper into the life force that exits beneath the layer of persona consciousness. Focus on the subconscious. Each inhalation connects you to your conscious thoughts and actions. Each exhalation pushes the subconscious reality closer to the conscious mind. Allow the images of long-buried memories, traits, tendencies, and expectations to flow. Without prejudice or judgment, allow these images to cross the bridge from the subconscious to the conscious. Listen to each image.

Embrace the voices of life's abundance. Embrace the voices of outmoded thought or untoward action. Recognize and acknowledge the images that comprise the layers of this lifetime's "whole you."

Focus your breath beyond the conscious and subconscious layers of this lifetime.

Each inhalation draws the warm light of connection to the consciousness of your higher self. Each exhalation dissolves the linear boundaries of time and space. Focus on the ageless, timeless wisdom of your higher self. Listen to the guidance as it encourages a return to the subconsciousness or consciousness of the present life, or as it encourages you to the lives beyond present time and space.

If you are encouraged to continue, request the higher self guide you in seeking that aspect of you in a "past" life that will enhance your self understanding and provide for your greater good. Allow the images of the higher self to create a portal that leads to this life. Each breath yields a clearer picture of the tunnel, the bridge, or the doorway that your higher self has created.

A curtain of mist lies beyond the portal's threshold. Stepping over the threshold, look to the discretion of the higher self in parting this veil. Affirm that you can close the veil and return to your "present" any time you choose.

Feel your higher self connection strengthen as you inhale. See the veil part as you breathe out. With each breath, allow the scenery to unfold. The scenery may be a kind of screen projection, or it may be dimensional, an atmosphere that is seen through your participating eyes. As the images clear, allow the higher self to complete the statement, "I am . . ."

With each breath, the image of this deeper aspect of you unfolds and grows clear.

With each breath comes the clarity of who you are. With the guidance of your higher self, the reality develops, moves forward, then concludes.

As you detach from this deeper aspect of you, focus on the emotions that have become paramount now. Notice the traits and talents that have surfaced, the challenges that have been confronted, or the outcome of decisions that have been enacted. Focus on any catharsis or release that may be needed as this reality concludes. Allow the guidance of the higher self to lower the veil as you leave this reality.

Retrace your journey back to your subconscious present. Review these detached "past" images as literal reality. Complete the statement "I was . . ." View the cause and effect that occurred during the existence as an observer watching these scenes. View the cause and effect that transcends existence to effect your subconscious thoughts and conscious actions.

As you detach from the reality of the past aspect of you, focus on the meaning of this experience. Replace the "I was . . ." with the realization that this past aspect is now an aspect of your current "whole." Allow your higher self to illuminate the paths that these aspects use to influence your life. Focus on your flow of breath. Each inhalation reaches into your subconscious mind; each exhalation flows to your conscious mind. Allow your subconscious to flow with the knowledge of how these aspects create defense patterns, physical sensations, and perpetual situations recycling to your conscious mind. Allow your subconscious to flow with the knowledge of how these aspects create talents, skills, and learning to your conscious mind.

Focus your breathing to the conscious aspects of your current "I am . . ." With each breath, open your consciousness to the patterns that are interwoven from lifetime to lifetime, from the lessons and the challenges that transcend the boundaries of time and space, and from the patterns that create the reality of "what was" and continues into "what is."

With each breath, open to the illumination, integration, and balancing of these aspects that create your "whole." Open to the recognition of the timeless voices of your aspect personalities. Open to the voices that support and nourish you. Allow these voices to enrich your current life. Open to the voices that speak of unreleased wounds. Allow these voices to be calmed and acknowledged while not allowing the recycling of events that are the origins of those voices. Open to the discovery of your "past" that leads to a broader, more fulfilled self in the "present."

This meditation is one of many guides that you can use in the process of "past life" discovery. If you hear the inner voice of the higher self instruct you to stop at any time during this process, listen to it. If at any time you need the objective guidance of another person to seek release, look to the counsel of a qualified professional.

Many of the aspects of our current personalities are influenced by the polar opposite of our past personas. Lifetimes as victims can be followed by lifetimes as victimizers. Lifetimes of materialistic abundance can be followed by lifetimes of abject poverty.

Professional hypnotherapists and counselors can guide you past the bias of your current persona and into the release and integration of these past aspects of you. The value of these professionals is far greater than any amount of money paid to them. It is an investment in creating the duality and balance of a well-integrated you.

Vampire Folklore in Burial Rituals

by Laurel Reufner

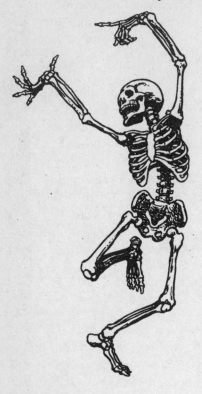

Death is an inevitable part of life, even if it hasn't always been understood. Folks had very real fears of the restless dead and the death they could bring. Eventually, cultures figured out which bodies were most likely to present a problem after death, and they developed special steps for dealing with such corpses. Measures could be messy, involving mutilation or other violent acts. People might hesitate to employ such drastic measures now, but in olden times, action could be swift when deemed necessary.

Some burial practices, usually the less drastic ones, were almost universal in their use. For instance, it's a nearly universal custom to remove a deceased body from the home head-first, the belief being that bodies need to reenter the dwelling in the same manner in which they left it.

Other procedures were reserved for the direst of situations. Beheadings, stakings, and cremation were not lightly undertaken by villagers and townsfolk, but they were employed. Most areas were under a Catholic or Orthodox influence, which placed an emphasis upon the body being whole for resurrection at judgment day. And understandably, loved ones were hesitant to see a dear one's body abused.

What drove our forebears to such extremes with respect to their dead? It was nothing short of the fear of death itself. Think of all the superstitions we have surrounding death even today. Even a hundred years ago, beliefs about death were much more intense. There were cases of "vampire slayings" even in the past century.

In old days, death could come swiftly or linger in the form of disease and plague. We didn't truly start understanding the nature of contagion and its prevention until the late 1800s. The fact that you could go to bed and not wake up, or that you could linger on painfully, frightened many otherwise rational folks. It was also widely accepted that those who died a violent death would return demanding vengeance. Others were considered doomed because of the circumstances of their conception or birth. Examples in this category include those conceived during a holy period in the church calendar, a family's seventh child, or the illegitimate child of an illegitimate child.

In addition to being treated differently at death, these people might be administered apotropaics while alive in order to prevent their return as vampiric revenants. Even then, there was no guarantee that all potential revenants would be dealt with before taking others with them. At that point bodies would be dug up, staked, dismembered, and/or burned in order to "kill" the vampire.

What measures were taken to prevent a revenant's rising from the grave? Many strictures had to do with preparing the body for burial. Combs were broken. Pots and pans were smashed or emptied out and left upside down. Cloths used to wash the body were either burned or buried with the dead. People believed that what was used by the dead should not be used by the living—certainly not a bad idea if the person died from some nasty contagion.

Some of the simplest burial practices involved inhibiting the vampire's ability to either drink blood or eat. Sometimes objects would be placed in the mouth, giving the corpse something to "chew on" should it find itself ravenous after burial. The ancient Greeks placed an *obolus*, or small coin, in the mouth of the deceased in order for them to pay Charon, the ferryman, for passage across the river Styx. In all probability, it also served as an antirevenant charm as well, since metal is often anathema to

vampires. Other objects used by various cultures included special or broken bits of pottery, cotton, dirt, wool, jade, nephrite, or coins. All of these were intended to keep the corpse's mouth busy so he couldn't chew upon other things in death—such as the villagers themselves!

Other times, the mouth would be tied shut, although some cultures would undo any bindings on a body just before burial, believing that any kind of fastening would keep the soul from leaving and the body from decaying. If the goal was to keep the mouth shut or to keep the revenant from chewing, a nail or thorn might be driven through the tongue. We do something similar today in our preparations of the dead, although for different reasons. To keep a body's mouth from gaping open, which can be rather disconcerting to the loved ones, a small device is placed on either side of the upper and lower jaws to hold the mouth shut.

If the danger was great enough, sharp objects would be used in or on the grave. A sharpened sickle might be placed over the neck of the corpse, serving to decapitate it if is should try to sit up or leave the grave. Thorns or spikes might be driven into the grave from the surface in an effort to impale a rising revenant. For those truly believed likely to return as revenants, shafts of wood might be driven through the grave's surface and into the body, pinning it in place and "killing" the corpse a second time.

As noted earlier, the eyes of a corpse were often held shut by the use of small coins. We do something similar to our deceased

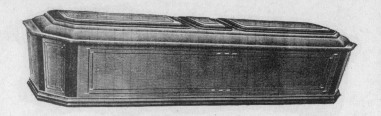

today by placing small plastic caps under the eyelids. In our case, it eases our discomfort by giving the dearly departed an appearance of peace and rest. Many find the unwavering stare of the dead to be more than a little unnerving. The question is, how much of our discomfort stems from the beliefs of centuries past and from their fear of the dead returning for the living?

Most people fear what they don't understand. While today we may scoff at what we view to be superstition, try to think what life was like before modern science exposed many of life's mysteries. Peasants of old had no concept of contagion or germs, yet they knew that when someone fell suddenly ill that there had to be a reason. Those reasons were often found in the realm of the supernatural. To expect someone who'd died by violent means to demand retribution and vengeance was also perfectly in keeping with their beliefs. Vampires were a terrifying part of their lives, demanding strong and often supernatural responses.

Going Widdershins:
Following the Moon-wise Spiral

by Gail Wood

The Pagan concept of the circle is a symbol of our union with the sacred. We are not separate from the universe and cannot be disconnected from it. The circle is an age-old symbol found in all cultures of the world. Its meanings are varied but do not stray far from the ideas of union, connection, and the eternal.

As Pagans, we move in a circle. We pass food around the table clockwise. We use the circle to contain the power we summon and to protect the work we do. We use the circle as a way to foster communion with the spirits and with each other. The circle surrounds and protects us. The circle is seen in the Moon and the Goddess and in the Sun and the God. The circle tells us of our eternity, that nothing ever ends and nothing ever dies.

We emphasize balance and harmony by moving first clockwise, or deosil, around the circle to cast it and call in the directions. When we finish our work, we then move Moon-wise or widdershins around the circle. This counter-clockwise movement dismisses all the work we have done. In my circle, we laughingly refer to it as "doing it all backwards." In most minds, the deosil is considered positive and widdershins is considered negative.

I once attended a wonderful Full Moon ritual where the energy raised was powerful. Right after a cone of power was raised to seal the magic, the priestess moved widdershins around the circle, hugging everyone, and then immediately turned deosil to continue with the ritual. The next day, several of us awoke feeling spacey and out of sorts. We realized that the counter-clockwise and then clockwise movement within the ritual the night before had given us a psychic headache by causing the powerful flow of energy within the circle to become disrupted and turbulent. It took some grounding to get back to normal.

That ritual taught me the value of balance and harmony within the circle. The widdershins movement in an opposite but balanced movement keeps the balance of light and dark, left and right, negative and positive.

As Pagans, we are taught that the widdershins movement is about unraveling and undoing. Often in our thinking, widdershins comes perilously close to negative magic. The word itself has negative connotations, with one definition saying that widdershins is "in a direction contrary to the apparent course of the Sun (considered as unlucky or causing disaster)." Another definition says that widdershins is opposite to the usual. Even the language embeds contrariness, bad luck, and negativity into the meaning of the word. No wonder we approach widdershins with caution.

Lately, I have begun to wonder if perhaps Pagans haven't overemphasized the need to keep a clockwise motion. I realized I had never examined what it meant to go widdershins. Much of my meditative work is about spiraling inward to find mystery and magic, and it was possible that widdershins energy could help bring this to completion. While Pagans refer to widdershins as Moon-wise energy, I wonder if we have really sought the wisdom of the Moon through such motion? I began to move in a contrary-wise motion to discover what moving widdershins truly meant.

Because we go against the usual or accepted practice, the first experience is disruption. Like kayaking over the rapids, we are bumped and tossed around in the energy. We can't predict where the next bump will be, and we cannot anticipate it. We cannot smooth it over, so we just have to go with the experience and enjoy it for what it is. Usually disruptions in our lives are upsetting and bewildering. We fight against them and try to get back to normal. Whether it is illness, change in routine, or a major shift, we are constantly fighting against disruption in order to get back to what is comfortable, knowable, and understandable.

Once we move into the energy of widdershins, things change and we have little control over what is happening. We have to divest ourselves of those preconceptions that continue to hold us back. This may not be easy, but we need to ask ourselves if we actually need those comforts in life that hold us back or keep us from being ourselves.

Then, just as suddenly, we find a smooth patch, and that is the third stage of going widdershins. In doing this, we have actually attuned ourselves to the rhythm of the widdershins energy. In doing so, we find grace and beauty. It may not be what others call softness or beauty, but considering what we have been through it is sweet. We have mastered disruption and change.

We begin the process of moving back into unity with the Sun-wise path. Moon-wise energy flows in and out of balance with the Sun-wise, creating twists and turns. The circle is not a good symbol for this integration; rather, the infinity symbol shows us this harmony. This symbol—a figure eight on its side—shows the ups and downs of never-ending merging, Sun to Moon to Sun to Moon, over and over in endless harmony, blending, flowing, merging, and reemerging. The infinity symbol shows one universe flowing and growing into another, then flowing back again to grow into something new.

In skating, the figure eight shows mastery of the backwards and forwards motion. It's a movement of beauty, power, and elegance. And so it is with the flowing energy of the infinity sign, Sun-wise to Moon-wise and back again. If you draw an infinity symbol in the air in front of you, your body begins to move with the flow of the energy. Your hand and arm guide your body and your entire being into the flow of energy. You feel your body ebb and flow with the movement that goes up and down, then backward and forward. You find grace in your movements, power in your thoughts, and serenity in your spirit as you give yourself over to this flow of Sun-wise to Moon-wise. Using both hands and allowing your body to follow the movement of infinity, you move into the flow of the universe. You become blessed with the unity of magic and mystery.

Wizard Marks

by Elizabeth Hazel

A wizard mark is a personal sigil or condensed magical signature. When properly designed, it unites aspects of identity and ability and functions as a representational monogram. The "chop" marks of Chinese artists and the name stamps used by people in ancient civilizations are early versions of the wizard mark. Clay stamps with the individual's monogram were worn on bracelets to mark documents printed on wax tablets. Later variations of this idea were the seal ring and the stamp with a coat-of-arms used to authenticate legal documents.

The wizard mark can be created using almost any alphabetic or glyph source. The key to creating a useful mark is selecting and combining the chosen symbols and reducing the combination to the simplest possible form. A wizard mark is not useful if it isn't easy to draw, carve, or embroider.

Alphabetic sources may include the standard Roman alphabet, Greek, Sanskrit, or a magical source like the Theban (or Witch's) alphabet. Glyphs from astrology, alchemy, Hieratic (Egyptian letters), tribal, or prehistoric art may be used. Runes can be used, as can the Ogham. Alternative sources are *kameas*, magic squares, or *gematria*. The magician should choose a symbol or letter source that is consistent with his or her practice.

Simple Glyphs

A few samples will demonstrate just how simple yet profound a wizard mark can be.

Brigit: This mark is a cauldron over a fire. The woman who uses this mark is a fiery Leo.

Heremita: An inner circle represents the protected soul, with a capacity for solitude. A line that moves from the inner to the outer circle shows her ability to reach out into the world to share and receive.

Bind Runes

Bind runes are a combination of different letters grafted into a single mark. The binding concept is certainly not limited to Nordic runes. In the binding technique, the mark can be a combination that evokes desired energies (like protection), an ideogram or condensed symbol indicating a magical name, a monogram of the magical name formed from initials or letters in the name, or any combination of these ideas.

For example, the name "Black Hawk" can be conveyed in many ways. To create an ideogram using the Futhark, the *kano* rune tilted sideways looks like a bird. The color black is conveyed by the rune of endings and death, *elhaz*. Shamanic journeys into the underworld or otherworld are indicated by the *perthro* rune on its stomach. Birds are also represented by *ansuz*.

Runes are very plastic and can be redirected, stretched, and combined in limitless ways to form an effective and powerful wizard mark. Symmetry is not a requirement, but can be deliberately used to make the mark look balanced. Asymmetrical marks are equally potent, but in a different manner.

Bind runes can combine ideograms and monograms. Runes and letters are energy patterns, and they can be added to convey or attract desirable traits. For example, the name "Mage Fire" conveys the idea of magical wisdom and illumination, and expanding light. The initials are *mannaz* and *fehu*, and the rune

that represents fire is *sowilo*. Additionally, *sowilo* conveys personal integrity and will power.

Making and Using a Wizard Mark

Developing a personal mark is a process that should not be rushed. It could take weeks, months, or even years to arrive at the perfect mark. Begin by selecting the alphabet or symbol set that feels most amicable to your personal practice. Use blank paper or your grimoire to draw your magical name. Think about whether you would prefer a monogram, an ideogram, or a combination. To create a monogram, convert your name into your chosen alphabet, then reduce it to the initials. To create an ideogram, select symbols, runes, letters, or glyphs to represent a core concept. Although creating a mark is serious business, a playful state of mind gives the best results.

Consider the meaning of your magical name and why you chose it. If you have a special totem animal or guardian entity, this might also be included in the mark. If you have a specific magical talent, you could select a symbol or glyph that represents this ability. Investigate the symbols, glyphs, and alphabets used by your magical tradition. Start with a simple combination—say, two initials and one symbol representing an idea—and play with these until you've developed something that looks good. Try using it for a while to see if it fits. If you do your homework and a sufficient amount of experimenting, you should be able to find a combination that suits you well and will not need adjustments.

There are no hard-and-fast rules for producing a mark, but if you want to use it on a variety of surfaces, try to stick to straight lines or simple curves. Elaborate curves and circles are difficult to carve and paint.

The goal is to develop a mark that is simple, elegant, and easy to use. Wizard marks should be used on talismans, boons, or written spells and can substitute for a full signature. Use it on any magical product you create—on a potion bottle, jar of incense, or clay incense burner. Embroider your mark on pouches, tarot bags, rune bags, table coverings, wrapping cloths, or ceremonial clothing. It can be carved on a wand or engraved on a custom-made metal charm worn as a necklace. Place your mark on votive candle holders with glass paint.

Wizard marks can also be carved on a candle before it is fixed. Put it on the bookmarks for use in your grimoire or important magical textbooks. If you wish, you can have a rubber stamp made with your wizard mark, and this can be used on anything you make or write. I use my mark on artwork. I also carved it into the wet cement of my new driveway (even though this irritated the cement mason).

Finally, you have the choice to keep this mark a secret or to use it openly as a part of your signature, combining it with your real name as well as your magical name.